Rod Stewart
the biography

Also by Ray Coleman

JOHN WINSTON LENNON (Volume One)
JOHN ONO LENNON (Volume Two)

CLAPTON/The Authorised Biography of Eric Clapton

BRIAN EPSTEIN
The Man Who Made The Beatles

STONE ALONE
The definitive story of the Rolling Stones
(Co-written with Bill Wyman)

I'LL NEVER WALK ALONE
(Co-written with Gerry Marsden)

THE CARPENTERS
An authorised biography of Karen and Richard Carpenter

Rod Stewart
the biography

Ray Coleman

PAVILION

First published in Great Britain in 1994 by
PAVILION BOOKS LIMITED
26 Upper Ground, London SE1 9PD
Text copyright © Ray Coleman 1994

A Conrad Goulden Book

The moral right of the author has been asserted.

A CIP catalogue record for this book
is available from the British Library.

ISBN 1 85793 5861

Set in 12/14 Stempel Garamond with Frutiger by
Dorchester Typesetting Group Ltd, Dorchester

Printed and bound in Great Britain by
Hartnolls Ltd, Bodmin

2 4 6 8 10 9 7 5 3 1

This book may be ordered by post
direct from the publisher. Please contact
the Marketing Department.
But try your bookshop first.

Contents

Introduction

Addressing his fans in the concert programme for his 1991 tour, Rod Stewart sounded worldly-wise, yet strangely uncynical, about the media focus on him in the past twenty-five years.

Wagging a finger of admonishment, he implied that many writers had been economical with the truth about him; but he conceded that facing up to exaggerations and misrepresentations was an unfortunate aspect of life as a celebrity.

He has never been diffident in his dealing with reporters and photographers. Indeed, some believe that he enjoyed the rollercoaster ride when for several years his off-stage life became an obsession to the press. His love of leggy blondes, and his enjoyment of money and the material benefits from his success, has conferred on him the role of the quintessential rock star. He chose a life in the fast lane, and a scrutiny of the interviews he has given to tabloid comics down the years demonstrates that he has often been a willing subject of the spotlight. It cut both ways: a celebrity's private life is food and drink to a tabloid newspaper reporter, while the artist, if he is as open as Rod, is happy to nourish his own myths with an endless stream of conversations with journalists.

Hypothetical though the question must now be, would Stewart have scaled the peaks he has if he had not secured acres of newspaper coverage for his romantic exploits? Did he really need the high profile of a rock 'n' roll rascal to help boost his image?

The answer is that Rod Stewart broke through, and has survived and prospered much more significantly as an artist than as a Casanova. From 'Maggie May' and *Every Picture Tells a Story*, his 1971 single and album that won world acclaim and set up extraordinary records, through to his *Unplugged* achievements more than twenty years later, he has amassed a body of work comparable to that of any of his contemporaries from the same era.

To the media, he was the North London lad who once dug graves, started singing, made a mint of money, and indulged himself with wine, women and song. Actually, there was only one thing wrong with that equation. The word 'song' came at the end. He did not need the tag of the womanizer with a slew of beautiful blondes at his side. The sideshow might have been a useful adjunct in the publicity stakes, but what has really counted has been the man's substantial musical talent. People do not go into record shops or concert halls to buy the personality of Jack the Lad; rather, they go to recognize something unique, embellished throughout a thirty-year study of his craft. From his heady, scuffling days of the 1960s, when he paid his dues in various bands, through the madcap years with the Faces, he pitchforked himself into solo stardom with steely determination.

Watching him in clubs and concerts during his formative period, and talking for this biography to many of those who saw him at various stages of his journey, I have realized how determinedly Rod Stewart has controlled his own destiny. This was never a casual stab at 'making it', but has always been a forensic study of the highways of the music industry by one who knew he had the raw material to succeed and ensure longevity. The voice, the hair, the *savoir-faire* have only been a part of it; like so many other giants from the same period (Paul McCartney, Elton John, Mick Jagger, Eric Clapton), Rod was possessed of a clear vision, a set goal, a grasp of the mechanics of the panorama of the entertainment world, and an ambition to ensure that his prodigious talent penetrated exactly how and where he intended.

Few, if any, of the great artists are dilettantes and, once embarked on his mission, Rod set about it with a precision that belies his casual air on stage. 'He has a mind like a steel trap,' says one of his former colleagues in this biography. And, alluding to a key part of Rod's make-up, he adds: 'He hates being lied to. He always wants the bottom line, even if that brings bad news. If you deceive him just once, there is no room for you in his life any more.'

In his dealings with the press – and, by extension, the mass public beyond his hard-core fans – Rod has often misleadingly appeared superficial. Stepping out with his lady, baring his soul to all manner of publications from *Penthouse* to the *Sunday Times*, from *Gay News* to the *Sun*, he has dissected the trappings of his solo stardom, the boozy facets of life in the Faces, the need to be a tax exile, the enjoyment of his money, and his lifelong, abiding passion for football. To exaggerate slightly for the sake of emphasis, the student of Stewart gets the feeling that he would pass up all his gold discs in exchange for the smile he would enjoy at having scored the winning goal for Scotland at a big match.

Rod has confronted every one of his peccadilloes head-on, many times in print and on radio and television. His willingness to be questioned has tended to result in the dramatic accent on his enjoyment of glamour and materialism, obscuring the deeper side to the man. With the fixation on his personal life, his work as an individualistic songwriter and crooner has sometimes seemed relegated to a secondary issue and, given the British disease of castigating success by its most creative artists, Stewart has been debunked as the kind of rock 'n' roll dinosaur who provides dreamy, escapist fodder for housewives.

The reverse is the reality: Stewart is, at his best, an observant, sometimes irascible and poetically romantic man whose own compositions, detailed in the discography at the back of this book, bear testimony to his soul-searching strengths. He is a remarkable musical diarist who has laid bare, in song, many parts of his eventful first fifty years. By contrast, he is a natural rock 'n' roll man who has always understood the surge of that idiom. His eclecticism as an entertainer, though, is drawn from a huge sweep of styles, from Muddy Waters, Otis Redding and Sam Cooke, through Al Jolson, Woody Guthrie, Rambling Jack Elliott, Bob Dylan and the Rolling Stones, through to pipe bands and *My Fair Lady*. Trying to pigeon-hole Stewart is a fruitless pursuit; it would be a serious mistake to file him under 'rock singer', for his musical tapestry is far wider.

● ● ●

For all these reasons and more, this biography steers clear of the well-trodden path of examining the personal life of Rod Stewart. Everybody in the Western world must know by now that he has led a helter-skelter life surrounded by beautiful women, mansions, Lamborghinis and as much hedonism as he wished to pursue. Titillation and prurience have been the benchmark of publications reporting his activities ever since Rod's star began to shine. The aim here is different. It is to explore what makes him tick, to dissect the man and his motivations, the artist and his muse, the characteristics that continue to shape him, through the eyes and words of those who have seen him undertake his glittering trajectory.

In assembling this biography, I have been fortunate in having the recollections and observations of those who for many years have observed him from various vantage points. First, my sincere thanks to John Gray, president of the official Rod Stewart fan club and editor of its quarterly magazine, *Smiler*. Consistently informative and entertaining, often critical, and a fine journal of record in tabulating Stewart's career, *Smiler* serves as the outstanding model for any publication seeking to celebrate, rather than sanctify, its artist. If a performer can be judged partly by his supporters, who combine zeal with realism, pride at his achievements with pleasure at his family's happiness, then Stewart scores very highly indeed. With his generous help and advice, plus his contribution of the newly researched, best-ever discography of Stewart's work (which begins on p. 233), John Gray has been a tower of strength.

I am grateful to Rod's brothers, Don and Bob, and to his sister Mary, for their valued interviews. Don Stewart told me, to my astonishment, that despite previous books on his brother this was the first time he had been asked by an author for an interview to verify the family's history. He kindly introduced me to Elsie, Rod's mother, who, though wheelchair-bound with multiple sclerosis, and aged eighty-eight, has an extraordinarily fertile mind and memory and was able to offer some interesting memories of 'Roddy'.

My thanks for encouragement, conversations and signposts to Peter Burton, Beverley and Martyn Burwell, Tony Calder, Jim Cregan, Dominick Conde, Lionel Conway, Lydia Criss, Michael d'Abo, Rob Dickins, Billy Gaff, Geoff Garoghan, Giorgio Gomelsky, Nicky Hopkins, Glyn Johns, Virginia Lohle, Beryl Marsden, Tony Powell, Mick Slaney, Nobby Syme, Brian Southall, Julie (Driscoll) Tippett, Mickey Waller and Martin Wyatt.

At Pavilion Books, I should like to thank my editors, Emma Lawson and Conrad Goulden, for their enthusiasm and practical help with this project, and also my copy-editor, Annie Lee.

To my wife, Pamela, and our sons Miles and Mark, my love and thanks, as ever.

Ray Coleman
Cornwall, England
Summer 1994

One   The voice The look

'IT'S LIKE A RELIGION, IT REALLY IS. IF YOU DON'T
LIKE ROD STEWART, IT'S HARD TO UNDERSTAND'
– A dedicated fan

There were Rod Stewart lookalikes, men with blond, pineapple-spiky hairstyles, looking resplendent in the snazzy kind of clothes Rod might wear well.

There was a tough Stewart 'trivia quiz', which tested the encyclopaedic knowledge of his fans. (Sample question: under what pseudonym did Rod produce his own album *Foolish Behaviour*? Answer: Harry the Hook.)

There was an auction and a raffle of Rod Stewart treasures, which, after some feverish bidding, together raised £1,440 for various charities. After his *Unplugged* tour, Rod had donated his green velvet suit, worn on stage, to the auction. The jacket fetched £200 and the trousers £150 from separate bidders. Rod's leopardskin cape from the early 1980s sold for £70, while his white waistcoat from the 1970s went for £185. A tartan waist-coat also worn by him in the 1970s was sold for £180.

This was the Rod Stewart fan club's eleventh offi-cial convention at the Forte Crest Bloomsbury Hotel, London, on 28 May, 1994. I had been steered there by a friend, the drummer Mickey Waller, veteran of the British rock scene, who proudly claims the distinction of having played on Rod's recording sessions of 'Maggie May' and 'You Wear It Well', as well as on his early solo albums.

'If you're writing a book about Rod,' Mickey said, 'this will be a perfect way to begin.' He had been before, as a celebrated guest; many of the ardent fans had been baptized into Stewart-studying around 1971 when he broke through with that anthem, 'Maggie May,' on television's *Top of the Pops*. And Waller, with his rumbustious drumming, had been an important foundation of Stewart's ascent.

'You're in for a surprise,' Waller said. 'Rod's fans are *amazing*.' And it was, indeed, a day and a night of enlightenment. For about twenty-five years, like many other admirers of Rod Stewart, I had been aware of the 'tartan hordes', as Rod himself has called them – the fervent ones among his fans who sway at his concerts with scarves above their heads and turn the shows into quasi-religious rallies. The huge list of Rod's instantly recognizable songs forms the bedrock of his appeal to these people, and to others less committed.

But what is truly astonishing is the level on which Rod touches people with the strength of his off-stage personality. He's revered for his artistry, although even his strongest fans balance their admiration with criticism. Crucially, what reaches them is Rod's accessibility. He's a touchable star, the millionaire migrant to California who has never forsaken his bloke-ish North London roots. And even now, after all these years, the line between a Rod Stewart concert and a football match remains thin at some moments. There is a tribalism about, but it's celebratory: non-threatening, non-violent. Always, Stewart's music has been exemplary. In tandem with that, he has perfected a vaudevillian act that has lifted him outside the rock 'n' roll firmament into an unassailable and unique position he alone has established.

• • •

The atmosphere at the Stewart convention is one of a carnival. Rod's sister Mary, and her brothers Don and Bob and their wives are the VIP guests, chatting amiably to fans and dancing to Stewart music. For the faithful collectors, there are Stewart-styled T-shirts, sweatshirts, calendars, tea mugs, key fobs, magazines and combs. Married couples renew friendships and swap firmly held views on Rod's latest music, his sartorial appearance, his family status. They talk of how they will wean their children on Stewart music, while watching a video of his appearance at Madison Square Garden, New York, in November 1993. For many, this is a delightful reminder of their visit to New York especially to see that show. He appeals to a new generation starved of new stars of this calibre, as much as to those in their forties and fifties. All these people are bound together by a dedication to a voice, an image, an attitude.

There is no gender or age barrier in Stewart's appeal. A striking-looking man, Stewart attracts women just by being himself, but their men do not feel overshadowed or threatened by their adoration. They consider him an ebullient showman, a 'great guy,' often even a role model. So his raunchy sex appeal for the ladies is balanced by his 'one of the lads' mateyness for the men. Neither attraction is a pose. Stewart certainly knows the show-business game, but he has always come across perfectly naturally at every stage of his career. While some artists were sucked into posing to the exclusion of their music, Rod Stewart kept an iron grip on his audience, old and new, by always delivering the vital ingredient: good music.

Stewart anointed the convention for the first time with a personal message, faxed from his home in California. After congratulating the fan club on its work in raising funds for charities, he roused a cheer from the crowd as his message was read out.

'All things are possible, and you never know, I

may one day turn up at one of the conventions unexpected. At the moment I am in L.A. working on an album for release, hopefully, at the end of the year. In the meantime, would you please convey my deep thanks to all my SMILER friends, for all their loyalty and friendship over very many years. Hope to see you all "out front" on my UK tour next year.' After signing it, Rod handwrote: DARLING OF THE MASSES.

Around the convention tables, as the music and videos continue, there is a spirit of affection laced with a cool analysis of what drives Stewart, and what brings his fans to the convention from all corners of Britain. 'It may sound a bit corny,' said a rabid Stewart supporter, Mick Slaney of Billericay, Essex, 'but when I die, I want his records played at my funeral.' He is not alone in such dedication. At their wedding in 1984, fan club members Beverley and Martyn Burwell, of Spalding, Lincolnshire, asked their organist at the church to play 'Sailing'.

Mick Slaney's mates wonder how and why he remains, at the age of thirty-six, so fanatical about Stewart. 'They can't understand it; they think there's something wrong with me. But it's like a religion, you know, it really is. If you don't like Rod Stewart, it's hard to understand. A lot of his appeal is in the atmosphere of a pint of beer, women, having a good time. A lot of blokes relate to that. Most people who don't understand him associate him with leopardskin trousers and think he's a right idiot singing "Da Ya Think I'm Sexy". That's all they know. Whereas anyone who had been to a concert and sat down and listened, especially to some of his old stuff, knows about his unbelievable lyrics. He's a songwriter supreme.'

What's impressive and refreshing about fans at the convention is that they are not enslaved hero-worshippers. To all of them, Stewart is visibly a flesh-and-blood artist who makes mistakes, personal and professional.

He's always lived the kind of life about which many might fantasize, but, to show them that the glitz might not be all it's cracked up to be, the meteor always comes back to earth. There he is, after all he has said and done, on stage, with his daughter Renée, clearly the doting father to whom family is all. There he is, wiping a tear from his eye as he sings the song 'Have I Told You Lately (That I Love You)', realizing that his wife Rachel is in the audience. Always unashamedly sentimental, while stopping short of mawkishness, Stewart has held true to the rock ethic while embracing ballads, straight love songs, and more traditional show-business values.

'My Mum adores him,' says Mick Slaney. 'I think she still sees him as a bit of a rascal ...'

'... Who wants his bum slapping,' interjects Martyn Burwell. 'Yeah,' says Slaney. 'Probably needs sorting out. A lot of older people want to mother him. He's got that little boy image, still.'

'There's that sparkle in his eyes,' says Burwell. 'I think that's because he hasn't aged as much as people around him.' There is comparison here with Mick Jagger, even Gary Glitter. 'I think he looks better in the face now he's fuller,' says Beverley Burwell. Like most students of Rod, Beverley believes that marriage to Rachel Hunter has improved him in every way. 'I think he's the happiest he's ever been, he *likes* the way he is, *likes* what he is doing.' This matters to the fans. 'She *is* good for him,' agrees Martyn. Rod's advance towards the age of fifty does not concern his followers. People do expect to go and see a 'pretty raunchy show', one said, 'and when he sat down on a stool for a large part of a show [*Unplugged ... and Seated*] some people were disappointed, even though that was an essential aspect of the programme.' 'But you've got to be realistic,' says Martyn Burwell. 'The guy is heading towards fifty; if he wants to sit down and sing a song, that's it. I imagine there would be plenty of fifty-year-olds in the country wishing they could do what he does.'

People at the level of Stewart and Jagger knew, according to these fans, that the true measure of their success did not lie in the singles charts, but in album sales, the demand for tickets for their concerts, or viewing figures for their television programmes. 'There must be literally thousands of people guaranteed to be waiting for Rod's next British tour,' one fan said. 'Whoever's trendy at any particular time, there's always a special place for Rod. We like all types of contemporary music … and then there's Rod, set apart from the rest.'

Anthony Brewer, aged twenty-eight, another supporter, said his girlfriend was 'not exactly a fan, but she likes the album *Unplugged*; it seems that every time he puts out a new record, he grabs new fans'. His own recognition of Rod had never wavered since he was a thirteen-year-old schoolboy. 'It wasn't the sort of thing you broadcast if you valued your face being the same shape as when you went in that morning,' he recalled wryly. 'You had to like the Specials and Madness, which I did, also. But I also liked Rod, which was very unfashionable in the mid 1970s and 1980s. You definitely didn't mention it to your mates.'

In that era, Rod dominated the media at least as much for his activities with women as for his music. It caused no long-term harm to people's perception of him. There is even a theory, among the thoughtful fans, that his experiences have enhanced his artistry. He now sings all those songs about relationships with a resonance born of experiences of the human condition.

• • •

When John Gray was eleven years old, BBC television's *Top of the Pops* was regularly viewed every Thursday night at his home in Sutton, Surrey. 'It was 1971. Not much impressed me. Bands like Slade and the Sweet just stood there with their instruments. But one day, Rod Stewart came on at the end with the Faces – and he was completely different. He was unshaven, threw the microphone around, and the song was somehow different from the rest of the hits of the time: "Maggie May". I didn't realize it was his first hit single, and it made me sit up.'

John Gray's schoolfriends were followers of T Rex, Slade, Gary Glitter. Gray soon discovered that Rod was a member of a band called the Faces. By 1973, aged thirteen, 'I was the youngest one in the audience at Sutton Granada for a Faces concert. I remember people giving me funny looks and saying I should have been at a Bay City Rollers concert, because I was dressed in tartan.'

Twenty years later, in 1993, thirty-three-year-old John Gray was in New York for Rod's concert at Madison Square Garden – 'and ironically I was probably one of the oldest in the audience'. He is also the president of the official Rod Stewart fan club and editor of its quarterly magazine, *Smiler*, a role he has enjoyed since 1981.

He was initially a fan of the Faces, 'heartbroken' when they split. 'I was a Faces man first, and Rod secondly, but when the split came I stuck with Rod. It was inevitable that I was going to form a fan club. I collected everything I could lay my hands on, read all the music papers for news and interviews of Rod, and taped everything off the TV and radio.'

Although it was to be some years before Rod's non-music life became the target of the newspapers and magazines, Gray detected a swashbuckling edge that set him apart. His music assumed a momentum and a creative thrust that was unstoppable. But there was also, even from Rod at twenty-six in 1971, a worldliness that outstripped so many of his contemporaries. He seemed to embody the phrase 'street credibility'.

'He had everything a young guy could hope for:

the women, the flash cars, good at football, one of the boys. He liked drinking, seemed a bit of a rogue and a tearaway. These were strong points of identification for a young guy like me. He was sometimes a little bit drunk on stage, but he always made good records. He was really one of your mates, whereas someone like David Bowie I could never relate to.' Remote, untouchable, Bowie was on another artistic planet, appealing more to the student population.

Though John Gray and many thousands of others who were converted by Stewart singing 'Maggie May' could not have realized it at that time, there was a wealth of difference between Rod and most of the other emerging acts of the early 1970s. So many had shaped themselves according to the pop star textbook ordained by Elvis Presley or the Beatles. Rod turned instead for his inspiration to artists he considered either more gritty or more demonstrative. He drew heavily from the theatricality of Al Jolson whose career in the 1920s and 1930s was glorified in two films after his death in 1950, *The Jolson Story* and *Jolson Sings Again*. From the folk music giants of the early 1960s Rod listened to the articulacy of Woody Guthrie, Rambling Jack Elliott and Bob Dylan. From the British rock 'n' roll explosion, he loved the punch of the early Rolling Stones and later the band Free. Among the 1960s acts, he identified with the individualistic vocal work of Sam Cooke.

Adding his own deft touches, physically and lyrically, Stewart coalesced into a riveting stage personality with an innate ear for delicate and original musical arrangements. And he had a natural, cheeky personality with which to sell himself.

'When I first saw him on *Top of the Pops*,' recalls John Gray, 'I'd never seen anybody use his hands like that before. He talked about the girl's face in "Maggie May" and pointed to his own. It was very unusual at that time.' The animated touch was repeated in 'You

Wear It Well'. Stewart had mastered the technique of selling a song. To a young audience not used to that level of communication in the 1970s, Stewart reached out and touched them with a brilliant fusion of old-fashioned show-business, expressive lyrics, and the irrepressible clout of rock 'n' roll.

• • •

Rod Stewart might for some years have appeared a carefree Jack the Lad, but his fierce dedication to his work across four decades may be judged by his recorded output and his extraordinary concert itineraries – and the fact that, unlike some, he has never taken a break of several years. Astutely, he has given his fans an unending stream of performance, but he has also demonstrated a vaudevillian's sense of knockabout humour. His appeal is, indeed, equal among the sexes. Women see him as hugely desirable; men see him as a macho figure who can teach them the ropes in how to net a woman.

'Whatever he's done in the past,' John Gray says, 'we as fans could identify with it as something we would have done if we'd been in his position.' In Britain, Gray reckons, about 70 per cent of the members of the fan club and Rod's following beyond it are male; in America it is the reverse. This difference can be verified at concerts if you make the Atlantic crossing: in Britain the 'singalong factor', that crucial component of any Stewart celebration, has a distinct male edge to the vocal refrains. In America, it's a higher-pitched female sound as they join in on a song such as 'I Don't Want to Talk About It'. This is mightily appropriate, since the British atmosphere evokes better the feeling of a football ground, and the vital terraces song 'Sailing' was not the hit in the USA that it was here in Rod's homeland.

'In the past couple of years, though, the male-female factor has balanced out more,' notes John Gray, whose day job is as a statistician at the Ministry of Transport.

While many thousands of Stewart activists believe he has old-fashioned oomph, Gray and some other men consider Rod's appeal in that department 'a bit of a laugh ... even "Da Ya Think I'm Sexy", which he was slated for, was intended as a knockabout, flippant record,' says Gray. 'It was Rod laughing at himself, one of his most important qualities. He's always been able to do that well, even if some of us couldn't always see the joke.'

'I get the feeling,' says Mick Slaney, 'that he's taking the piss out of himself half the time, anyway, especially these days. He wears this outrageous clothing, sets himself up to be hit by the press, but he doesn't care. All those *jackets!*' Says Beverley Burwell: 'He doesn't need to care what the press says of him, even if he ever did. He's a tough old nut.'

Besides, they chorus, showmen like Rod and Elton John, with their larger-than-life charisma, are not merely offering fine music, though their standards are infinitely higher than those of the newer rock acts. They also offer escapism, a night out via a song or a concert or a video that transports the audience to paroxysms of pleasure.

'There's a lot of Gary Glitter in him,' says John Gray of Rod's stage show. 'His performance is always meant to be fun, and that dates right back to the Faces when footballs were kicked out to the audience. The fun part of Rod is what the men love.' Yet his flamboyance may have masked, to non-believers, what a sensitive and prolific writer and performer he has been.

While his hard-core fans have stayed loyal for twenty-five years and more, Stewart has returned the gesture. He seems aware that their blind adulation would be worthless, and since he's always been a self-critical artist who wants 'the bottom line' from all those close to him, the candour of his fans must be valuable to him.

'During the 1980s, he tended to follow fashion rather than set it,' says John Gray forcefully. Albums like *Body Wishes, Camouflage* and *Every Beat of My Heart* seemed to derail him from the style that had delivered him to the summit. He seemed to get sucked into the synthesizer sound of the decade, 'And that was a mistake,' Gray agrees. 'He should have continued to use more squeaky violins and mandolins!' But when he returned with *Out of Order* in 1988, most critics considered him to have regained his status and re-scaled the heights he had achieved seventeen tumultuous years earlier with the ground-breaking *Every Picture Tells a Story*.

The Stewart fan club convention is a hothouse where fans debate, laugh, drink, share memories and, above all, demonstrate an unswerving loyalty to a star who, despite his stratospheric journey out of the orbit of their lifestyle, seems like their mate. Former Stewart musicians who have left the band voluntarily, or have been squeezed out in a natural reshuffle, continue to speak highly of him. Mickey Waller 'hasn't a bad thing to say' about Rod, though their paths have long parted since the days when the singer and drummer were shoulder to shoulder in the bands of Jeff Beck and Steam Packet. The fans are adults, some with their children. The conversation stretches from music to Rod's choice in women, his marital happiness, and his music. To some women, Rod appears vulnerable and appeals to their maternal instincts.

'Face it, people won't be sitting around tables like this in twenty-five years discussing the music and personality of Take That,' says one. John Gray says he wants to hear his man record a stunning song from a Dylan album called 'If You See Her Say Hello'. There is a strong view among fans that Rod's record company has released too many singles that have exploited hard-core supporters' wallets, by featuring old tracks as B-sides, representing terrible value.

And there's always one topic guaranteed to stir a lively debate among Rod Stewart fans. His hair.

• • •

'Rod Stewart saved my haircut,' says Rob Dickins, the chairman of his record company, Warner Music, in London. 'When I was a kid, I had hair that stuck up, while everybody else had college-boy haircuts, with partings. Then Rod Stewart came along and I thought: "Fantastic! My sticking-up hair is now OK."'

For hundreds of other men around the world, Stewart's hair is not merely OK. Emulating those trademark spikes has emerged as a badge of faith. Rod Stewart clones around the world regard his locks as a vital slice of his appeal to both women and men and go to inordinate lengths to look like him. If Rod changes his look, it is a matter for intense scrutiny and, for most, disappointment. 'There are quite a few of us who get together at the conventions and chat, compare notes,' says one Rod lookalike, Geoff Garoghan. 'He has been through a few changes and his hair is an important part of his appeal. I think for Rod Stewart, it *portrays* him. It's not a very nice thing to say but I think that they think about the hair before they think about the voice. It's perhaps more of a trademark than the voice is, though the voice is a major thing.'

For Geoff Garoghan, a thirty-six-year-old driving instructor who lives in Suffolk, serious study of Rod's hair began when he was a thirteen-year-old schoolboy watching Rod performing 'Maggie May' on *Top of the Pops*, the period that was the rallying point for thousands of young fans who would remain true to Rod right through their adult lives. 'Much to my parents' dismay, I adopted it when I was about fifteen and I have kept it all the way except when I had it cut short for a period (in 1990). Everyone was so used to seeing me with the Rod Stewart hairstyle that they told me I looked ill. So I grew it straight back again.'

When people ask Geoff Garoghan how he manages to get his hair to stand up in Stewart mode, he tells them frankly: 'The secret, which Rod has told himself, is that you literally have to hang your head upside down and dry it that way. That is the only way to do it, and I do that twice weekly … out of the shower and hang it upside down, then hit it with the hair-drier. The other secret is not to use shampoo but wash it with soap.' Of course, there is an unwritten rule of the road that so many people ignore: 'A lot of people cut their hair short on top and spike it. That's not the way to do it,' Geoff says. 'At the crown of the head the hair has to be quite long, actually, to get it right. My hair grows quite quickly; I have it cut about once a month.'

Precisely what motivates intelligent men to want to look like Rod? It is one thing to admire him and his style, quite another to studiously adopt the Stewart look, sartorially as well as in hairstyle as many do, tilting their trilby hats at exactly the same angle as Rod.

'It is a badge of support,' Geoff says. 'People do know who I model myself on. It's also something I've had for so long that I've actually grown to like. The look is not just a spiky haircut; it is a scruffy image. The hair is ruffled and looks like you've just got out of bed. And I go to great lengths to make mine that way. Actually, I don't need to, it does it by itself these days. I think Rod has always portrayed an image as being one of the lads; you get out of bed and the hair is rough and ready. And that's the way it has stayed.'

In the 1970s, he says, the reaction to people like him might have been akin to that towards a punk rocker who had dyed his or her hair green. 'I admit to sniggering at them. And that's what would happen to me, back then. But not so much now. It is certainly no embarrassment to me; it's a matter of pride and when people mention it [this includes people to whom he is giving driving instruction] I say that I admire Rod Stewart.'

Along with other devotees, Geoff Garoghan has travelled to America several times to see Stewart concerts. 'People do comment over there. I'm only five feet two inches tall so physically I look nothing like him apart from the fact that I've got a big nose and brown eyes. But when I was coming out of a concert at Madison Square Garden in January 1992, people were shouting out of their car windows at me; it was crazy!'

But he is adamant that there is no quibble in any British contest about the most natural, accurate Rod Stewart lookalike. 'Nobby Syme looks so much like Rod it's unbelievable,' says Geoff. 'When I go up to London with him, people go up to him and ask him for his autograph.' Carol Thatcher mistook him for the real man, and Rod's brother Don expressed astonishment at Nobby Syme's likeness.

Just like so many other Stewart fans who have sworn allegiance, Nobby, a thirty-eight-year-old builder, first became hooked around the time of 'Maggie May'. He was fifteen. 'I was going out with a girl and she said: "You really look like a pop star." I said, "Who?" She said, "Rod Stewart, that new man on *Top of the Pops*."' Nobby Syme can claim a unique affinity, having been born a mile or so from Rod's parental home in Highgate.

'My features are apparently the same as his exactly,' he says. 'When I go out, I get stopped all the time: clubs, pubs, petrol stations. It's autographs, the lot. I tell people I'm not Rod Stewart but they won't have it. In a club in London, an American came up to me when I was having a drink. He said: "Congratulations." I said: "What for?" He said; "'Maggie May', they're playing it on the jukebox, and it's the best record you've ever done." I said: "Well, thanks!"'

At the 1992 British fan club convention in Birmingham, 'They did have a contest,' Nobby Syme says, 'but I didn't want to get involved. By general agreement I had to enter it and I won. Some people who have the looks like this are very competitive. But I'm not, although if I didn't look like him – and I've even got his nose – I'd still admire the way he looks.'

His likeness to Rod has also landed Nobby Syme into what he describes as 'all kinds of scrapes'. Harmless enough was the approach of a couple as he got out of his car to go for a drink at a pub near Rod's home in Epping, Essex. 'How's the baby?' Nobby Syme and his girlfriend Jane were asked. 'I'm very sorry,' he told the incredulous couple, 'you've got the wrong person.'

Through the years, though, some situations have been ugly. 'I've been involved in fights with blokes because their women thought I was Rod, came after me … and their men didn't like it, you know.'

● ● ●

There's something ironic about all this. For Rod's hairstyle to be so glorified, as it has been throughout the 1980s and will continue to be in the 1990s, is uncanny, for it was in the 1960s that hair became a totem of the culture of pop music, exemplified first by the Beatles – who virtually invented long hair – and then by the Rolling Stones and thousands of musicians on both sides of the Atlantic.

Part of youth's statement, the 'Beatle haircut' became virtually a generic term. It was highly stylized. Then came the unkempt, long, straggly look. Since then, no one rock star can claim to have forcefully stamped an imprimatur on a hairstyle – until Rod Stewart arrived with his pineapple-spiky appearance. 'He has definitely dyed it,' says expert analyst Geoff Garoghan, noting that in the 1960s Rod went on stage with his normal light brown locks. 'He has lightened it up, and I must admit so do I. I followed him on that. His hairstyle has gone through a few changes. In 1991 he went through a period of combing it flat and his followers hated it. I've never heard so many complaints about a person's appearance! He explained on television along the lines that he would be fifty in a few years and he couldn't forever have a funny hairstyle. The spiky look went and he flattened it down. Sure enough, on the next tour, he bowed to pressure and the old look was back.' Any significant change of style from Rod on his hairstyle has received the thumbs-down from most girl fans.

Whether Rod Stewart devised his look scientifically or whether he happened upon it accidentally, he has always had a strong sense of style. It's not just the clothes he favours, but the way he wears them that accentuates his visual appeal. 'As he has aged,' believes Geoff Garoghan, 'he has become more gracious, definitely. Everything Rod Stewart puts on his back looks nice. I can't afford to dress like him. The man can go out in a very smart suit, collar and tie – or a bright yellow suit – and look every inch the rock star, in either. He's not a follower of fashion, but he loosely keeps up with things. I tend to dress in a style that he would, anyway, but I don't try to dress like Rod Stewart.'

Dedicated fans agree: 'The hair is very, very special. But he's also got the knack for dressing. He probably doesn't wear jumpers from Marks & Spencer, but if he were to, it would probably suit him.'

The hair. The leopardskin pants or the pink or yellow jackets. The tartan apparel. The footballs booted from the stage into a cheering crowd. The stunning lighting and sound which always had to meet Rod's own standard of perfection. Nobody ever had to explain to Stewart that to achieve success in show-business required a total package. And he could always project one item in his artillery that nobody could hope to imitate. That voice. Variously described as resembling raspy sandpaper or gravel soaked in brandy, it would wear well, maturing over four decades.

'He's got a lion's pride,' says John Gray reflectively. 'He would never end up in a Las Vegas bar doing a middle-of-the-road version of "Sailing". Or doing the holiday camps for a summer season! If he ever thought the people out there didn't want to see him or buy his records, he would disappear in a dignified way. But I can't see that happening. The audience age ranges from ten to seventy! Sitting in New York watching his concert in 1993 made me feel proud. As a kid twenty years ago, if I could have imagined where he would stand now, I couldn't have chosen or predicted a better way for him to progress. If any of the current rock lot is tomorrow's Frank Sinatra, singing well into his seventies, it's Rod Stewart.'

Two The scuffling years

'LOOKING BACK, I CAN'T THINK WHEN I EVER
PLAYED A SUBSERVIENT ROLE'
                                    – Rod on his school days

When he was seventeen, 'Roddy', as his parents and brothers and sisters called him, returned to his London home from a 'busking' trail around Europe. His dishevelled appearance appalled his mother.

'He had not changed his clothes – cord trousers, baggy sweater, grey sweatshirt and sandals – for the five weeks he had been away. I shoved them all in the dustbin and burned them,' recalls Elsie Stewart. 'He nearly cried because I burned those trousers; he said he wanted them for a concert.'

It was the kind of parental confrontation that any beatnik son might have encountered during the 1960s, that decade characterized by the assertiveness of youth. But, thirty years later, there was to be an amusing twist in the life story of 'Roddy' that recalled his mother's ceremonial burning of those smelly trousers.

Visiting his mother at the house in Muswell Hill, North London, that he had bought her, 'Roddy' was wearing a pair of denim jeans that, in designer style, featured layers of rips and holes. His greeting was as warm as ever as he approached his mother. 'Give us a big, wet kiss, then,' he said, as he often did. There was never any superstar behaviour from 'Roddy' when he was back at his parental home.

Yet as Elsie Stewart eyed her son's new trousers, she was as aghast as she had been, for different reasons, three decades earlier. 'Can't anybody *sew* those trousers for you?' she asked of the shredded, expensive denims. 'Mum, that's how they're *supposed* to look,' Rod said. The generation gap was never more simply delineated. 'I should take them back to the shop where you bought them,' Elsie said to him. 'You've been *done*.'

• • •

Even if he had wanted to, there was never any chance that Rod Stewart, the artist, would be allowed to forsake the unpretentious reality of his roots. His parents, brothers and sisters have always been immensely proud of his stardom. But his migration to California, and his millionaire status, left them totally unfazed. To Elsie and Bob Stewart and the two brothers and two sisters Rod left behind, he was still 'Roddy', the baby of the family who had, somewhat astonishingly, embarked on show-business instead of football as a profession.

'All I seem to be doing is saying goodbye to you,' Rod said to his mother just before he left Britain to become exiled in the USA in 1975. Her response was typical of the lifelong directness which he had come to value: 'Well, you chose that profession. You've got to get on with it.'

The last of five children born to Elsie and Bob Stewart, Rod was born in the family home at 507 Archway Road, Highgate, North London, on the night of 10 January, 1945. Hitler's doodlebugs were still hailing down on Highgate when he arrived in the world. Elsie's pregnancy had not been expected. Mary, sixteen when Rod was born, was the eldest, born on 26 December,

1928. Don arrived on 2 March, 1930, Bob on 30 November, 1934 and Peggy in 1935.*

One at a time, the Stewart children were allowed upstairs to see their mother and new baby brother. Elsie was thirty-nine at the time, which was quite late for a woman to give birth in those days, particularly as there had been a ten-year gap since her last child was born. 'She looked very poorly,' remembers Mary, who had taken a week's holiday from her work as a tailoress to help her mother with the new baby. Bobby says: 'I was told in no uncertain terms not to let my dirty hands anywhere near that baby.' Don, fourteen at the time, remembers thinking how brave his mother had seemed to him to endure childbirth so late in life. 'Rod felt that very strongly as he got older,' Don says.

The staunchly Socialist-voting family was bent on sheer survival during these war years. Air-raid sirens sent them scurrying to brick shelters at all times of the day and night. Elsie remembers carrying the infant Roddy into them as the bombs landed, targeting a near-by railway track. The windows of their five-roomed Victorian house (three shared bedrooms upstairs, two rooms downstairs) were shattered by bomb blasts so often that Rod's father finally boarded them up with wood.

It was a house of simple moral and ethical values and discipline. Bob Stewart, born in Leith, near Edinburgh, the eldest of four brothers, had run away from home as a teenager and joined the merchant navy because he could not get on with his stepmother. But his seafaring life bored him. Arriving in London to stay with family friends, he trained to become a highly rated plumber; by the time his fifth child arrived, he ran, with one brother, a successful building firm, Stewart Brothers. He had met Elsie at a dance in Tufnell Park, not far

*A victim of multiple sclerosis, Peggy died in 1975.

from her parents' home in Holloway, North London. Raising a large family in wartime Britain was not easy, but Bob Stewart was a tenacious craftsman. 'We weren't rich, but there was always food on the table. It was a happy house,' Mary says. Their mother's father was a butcher whose gifts of free meat helped the family budget.

A wartime father's aspirations for a better life for his children came into play when Rod's name was chosen. Elsie and Bob were going to call him Rodney, but someone mooted the idea of Roderick instead. That appealed to Bob, who told his wife: 'I have a feeling he will never want for anything if we call him Roderick!' Thus the boy was named Roderick David.

With teenage brothers and sisters around him, he was a spoiled child and indulged with toys and much pampering, according to Mary. With Aunt Rose and Uncle Archie living next door at 505 Archway Road, the Stewart household bustled with life.

As the Allies converged on Berlin, the Second World War was heading for its conclusion at the time of Rod's birth. During his toddler years, London was picking up the pieces from bomb damage and his childhood memories were of a Britain victorious but desperately trying to reassert its national identity. In the Stewart household, hard work was a byword. His father never drank but smoked incessantly, rising to around forty cigarettes a day, plus cigars. Elsie never smoked but enjoyed the occasional drink. Rod's brothers and sisters applied themselves vigorously to their parents' example of conscientious work: following Mary's dedication as a talented tailoress, brother Don went into accountancy and secured a strong career; Peggy worked in the office of Marks and Spencer in London; Bob worked as a carpenter.

There was no daily emphasis on music around the house. A baby grand piano stood idle, save the occasional tinkle from Don. A wind-up gramophone was there, with 78 rpm shellac records collected casually. But there was certainly no accent on music at Archway Road during Rod's earliest years. As he approached school age, however, it would enter the family atmosphere and make an impact on his life to provide him with a crucial signpost.

In these grey post-war years, the Stewart family, like so many in Britain, sought pleasure in the music-hall and occasional visits to the nearby Rex cinema. At home, one singer dominated the house and they eagerly listened for his records to be played on radio request programmes like the BBC Light Programme's *Housewives' Choice*. Rod's parents collected the records of the American Al Jolson, who was making an enormous impact on both sides of the Atlantic with gushing ballads like 'Sonny Boy', 'California Here I Come', 'Pretty Baby' and 'Rock a Bye My Baby'. Oozing sentimentality, Jolson, the powerfully-voiced son of a cantor, used to paint his white face with black cork and wore white gloves to increase his dramatic effect.

The ingredients of Jolson's act had a profound effect on the young Rod Stewart and would shape his outlook towards his eventual career. With his expressive hands either outstretched towards his audience or in a pleading, almost prayerful position, Jolson would go down on one knee to stir the audience's emotions. After he had been singing for perhaps two hours, he would utter his famous words to his audience: 'You ain't heard nuthin' yet!'

Recalling the effect of Al Jolson on him, Rod wrote in the *Melody Maker* on 13 January, 1975: 'I was very young when Jolson died. That was in 1950. My whole family used to collect Jolson's records, they had them all on 78s, whereas I have got them on LPs. Everything I used to hear was Al Jolson or Danny Kaye. Crosby never used to get a look in.

'So it really rubbed off on me a lot. Then when I was old enough I was taken to see his films. Not Jolson's films, the ones about Jolson with Larry Parkes – *The Jolson Story* and *Jolson Sings Again*. And that's when it really hit home – that was well before I had any idea I was going to come into this business myself. I got so bowled over by him.

'The more I read about him, and I've read several books on him, I sort of flatter myself and try to compare myself to him. I've got one thing in common with him. That's that I can't bear seeing empty seats at a gig we're playing. I have terrible dramas about that. Jolson used to have that one... I don't suppose there's a comparison between me and him – it's probably just that all entertainers have got their phobias like that.'

Such brilliant communication with a crowd mesmerized the young Stewart at family singalongs and Christmas parties, where brother Don would be the star turn, copying Jolson quite accurately. 'We all said Donny should be the singer,' remembers Mary. In later years, Rod would outstrip his brothers to emulate Jolson's theatricality, and he would muse that in the years before technology, Jolson could reach an audience of 2,000 in the Palace Theatre, New York, without even the aid of a microphone.

When he was established as a successful singer, Rod continued to reflect on Jolson's impact and compare his achievements with his own. Rod said: 'When we played the Edmonton Sundown there were 3,000 in – but we also had 3,000 watts of public address system to help us out! So there's a lot to be said for those old stars. There's no one like that I admire as much as Jolson. He blots out everyone as far as I'm concerned.' His favourite Jolson song was 'There's a Rainbow Round My Shoulder'.

Al Jolson was partly responsible for Rod attempting to achieve a 'black' voice, a sound drenched with emotion on songs that called for powerful visual theatricality, too. 'I was also listening to Eddie Cochran a lot,' Rod remembered. 'And to the skiffle things of the time. It's weird, because everybody was having the same influences. You'd think you were the only person into Woody Guthrie but years later you'd find there were 3,000 others at art schools all into the same thing.'

While Jolson was his major influence in learning how to make an impact from the stage, the entertainer Danny Kaye was another. Less vocal than Jolson, Kaye had a warm way with ballads, and a smile in his voice. Rod also enjoyed the showbizzy singing Andrew Sisters. The contrast from these American entertainers helped define Rod's outlook towards entertainment.

Rod later recalled that when he was aged eleven, 'They stood me on the piano at our house [at one of the regular family singalong parties] and I sang "Underneath the Arches", and everybody applauded like mad. That's when I got the first glimmering of my idea of going into show-business.'

An undistinguished, average pupil at Highgate Primary School, Rod failed the eleven-plus exam – 'I could have sworn I'd passed' – and went to William Grimshaw, the secondary modern school near his home. His mother recalls that he took considerable sartorial pride in his school uniform of grey pullover, grey flannel trousers, and black and white tie. Academically he was fair and discipline was not a problem; Elsie says she never had a bad report from the school, although she does not recall Rod ever bringing home any homework.

His school life seemed rewarding enough. Captain of his house, and of the football and cricket teams, he also played soccer for Middlesex Schoolboys. 'I was even a dinner monitor,' Rod says. 'Looking back now, I can't think when I ever played a subservient role.'

While he enjoyed the extrovert pleasure of music at home and sport in many locations, an innate shyness lay under the surface, a characteristic that would correlate with part of his make-up for the rest of his life. He remembers his timidity at school: 'Almost cowardly … if there was a fight in the playground I'd be on the sidelines urging others on but taking no part in it. School days were, in fact, the worst days of my life. I always felt inferior, maybe because I was shy.' Nevertheless he emerged as a popular boy at William Grimshaw, where he rubbed shoulders with two brothers who would later also find fame: Ray and Dave Davies, who would lead the Kinks to success.

Rod was elected a form prefect, but lost this position through the time-honoured schoolboy prank of discharging a fire extinguisher.

His innate sporting abilities, particularly as an attacking soccer player, kept his profile high. His skill on the field was hardly surprising: it was almost mandatory for the Stewart brothers to play, at the behest of their obsessive father, who was the manager of three teams for the local club, Highgate Redwing. The teams performed well in the Finchley and District amateur league and Rod's father became fanatical in his role as a player-manager. As a Londoner he followed Arsenal, and as a Scot he championed the Scottish national team, instilling pride in his nationality into his sons. Don and Bobby played (Don remains, to this day, a referee). 'Roddy was the best of the lot,' their father pronounced once. 'I really hoped to see him playing at Wembley.'

In later years, Rod's rabid devotion to Scotland, his father's birthplace, was the basis on which he would consider himself a Scot. 'Why couldn't you have moved up there just to have me born?' he would jokingly ask his mother.

• • •

When Rod was ten, rock 'n' roll's first major statement entered Britain from America in the shape of Bill Haley and his Comets, with a record called 'Rock Around the Clock'. In one sweep it completely polarized the popular music scene, rendering such singers as Al Jolson and Bing Crosby a yawn to the younger generation. The song was an international number one, and the film in which it featured, *Blackboard Jungle*, sealed the new emergence of the teenager with an attitude of self-righteous *angst* towards authority. Within a year, Haley's smash record 'See You Later, Alligator', and the British traditional jazz boom which spawned a new music called skiffle, had completely transmogrified the old order of pop. Lonnie Donegan, who sang 'Rock Island Line' to the top of the charts, inspired thousands of British teenagers to take up the guitar for a do-it-yourself form of music-making that was primitive fun.

When Bill Haley came to Britain for his first concerts, twenty-five-year-old Don Stewart thought his ten-year-old brother Roddy would enjoy the experience of seeing the show. He took him along to the Gaumont State, Kilburn, and remembers now that the experience struck a nerve in Roddy, perhaps subconsciously igniting an interest in performing. Interestingly, Rod was never, then or in the future, completely smitten with hard-core rock 'n' roll, preferring melodiousness, thoughtful lyrics, and subtle panache in performance to the overheated pyrotechnics of the rock giants.

Neither Don nor Rod could have realized that, within nineteen years, Rod would be in that same theatre in a very different guise ... running round the stage as the singer with the Faces.

• • •

With a fascination that would stay with him throughout his life, Rod was enamoured of model railways. At birthdays and at Christmas, his parents would give him an extra piece to add to his tracks and trains. To Rod there was something quite romantic about trains: 'I remember seeing the television documentary on the Flying Scotsman and feeling really sad at the end when they played a bagpipe lament,' he said.

Gradually, he had amassed a fair set of models from his weekly pocket money and from the hand-outs from his brothers and sisters. At the age of fourteen, his father asked him what he wanted for his birthday. 'A railway station for my layout,' Rod answered. For what Rod describes as 'no apparent reason', his father came home with a Zenith acoustic guitar which had cost a fortune, nearly £9. Rod was surprised and delighted. While he enjoyed the popular music of the day, he was not passionate about it; but he decided that as he had an instrument, he might as well start teaching himself to play it to an acceptable standard. Like thousands of others, he says, he 'struggled through the three-chord thing. I used to do a very good "C'mon Everybody"'. He also hammered away at a skiffle standard called 'It Takes a Worried Man to Sing a Worried Song'.

Since the age of twelve, when his brothers and sisters had all left to marry and set up homes nearby, Rod had certainly been indulged by his parents and brothers and sisters. Leaving school at fifteen with no educational certificates, he had no firm idea about work. Brother Don recalls that their father told Rod there was no rush, he could take his time. With an interest in art, Rod initially got a job as a trainee at Shand-Kydd, the wallpaper manufacturers, in Gospel Oak. He told his family he fancied working towards being a silk screen designer, but that ambition was halted abruptly when he was discovered to be colour blind.

• • •

At the Highgate Redwing football ground, Rod's expertise as a wing-half thrilled his father. All three of his sons had helped Bob Stewart's cherished ambition to have a family of great players. Rod, though, truly shone. At fifteen, fate dealt Rod an extraordinary blow which was to become a bizarre asset. In a midfield accident, he hurt his nose badly. 'I came home and told me Dad and he said it was just bruised,' Rod said. 'So I never had it set.' It was, though, a straight break that, coupled with the natural size and shape of Rod's nose, would develop into a physical characteristic that his fans regard with affection.

Rod was such a natural player that his father said that perhaps, just perhaps, he had the ultimate ability to become a professional. Word was that Brentford, in West London, had vacancies for apprentices. For a sixteen-year-old so keen on the game, joining this professional club seemed a perfect advance.

To his dad's delight, Rod was accepted as a trainee at Brentford. But the life turned out to be much less fun than he anticipated. The long bus journey from Highgate meant he had to rise at seven o'clock, and Rod was notoriously difficult to galvanize early in the morning. His first job at the soccer club was to clean the first team's boots. The rigid training programme was punishing for him and proved tough, too: he was nine stone, five feet eleven inches tall, but he found the exercising intense. He did not feel strong enough to take it. Although he possessed all the skills needed to stay the course, Rod did not have the same fanatical enthusiasm for football that would surface later in his life.

After a couple of months playing in pre-season matches as centre-half, Rod was told by a coach that he was unlikely to achieve professional league status. He then faced a decision. He could either slog it out and wait for several months before the managers decided whether he was good enough to retain in a lesser role, such as Reserve. Or he could leave. Rod's Uncle Archie mentioned to him that a career as a musician looked easier than the route to football. This casual remark was based on Rod's tentative playing around with the guitar at home. The long journey across London to Brentford finally sealed Rod's decision. He quit Brentford. His father's disappointment was softened by Rod's continued commitment to play for the local team.

Years later, his success in music guaranteed, Rod admitted that his heart had never truly been in professional football. The Brentford experience was something he had done happily, but it was to please his father.

• • •

In the early 1960s, as the Beatles and Rolling Stones were making their first steps towards unwittingly beginning a cultural revolution, the world was gripped with the fear of nuclear war. In Britain, as in other Western countries, the cause acted as a rallying cry for the young. A Committee of 100 was formed and from it sprang the Campaign for Nuclear Disarmament, abbreviated to CND. Colloquially described as the 'Ban the Bomb' movement, its activities reached their zenith every Easter with a march from the Aldermaston base in Berkshire to a massed rally in Trafalgar Square, London.

The activists were joined by thousands of teenagers, known as beatniks, wearing an unofficial uniform of corduroy trousers, duffel coats, sweaters and sandals. They often carried guitars. Folk music, the sounds of which were wafting across from the USA in the form of Rambling Jack Elliott, and later Bob Dylan, proved a perfect vehicle for 'message' songs adopted by the beatniks. In Soho, coffee bars began to mushroom, and at places like Bunjies, leftish teenagers would congregate to exchange views and ad-lib songs with the aid of their guitars.

The freewheeling world of the beatnik attracted Rod. The marches themselves hardly touched him as a cause: he believed in the theme of it, but not fervently. 'I could never get *that* involved in it,' he said of CND. 'At the time you would never have dared to own up that you were going for a giggle. Probably, thousands of those kids went along just to get screwed!' He would later admit that the lure of girls was at least as important to him. His parents were never sure that his motives on nuclear disarmament were genuine. On three occasions Rod was among the passive protesters arrested by police and taken to Bow Street police station for causing an obstruction, refusing to budge from sit-ins at Trafalgar Square at the end of their banner-carrying marches. A small fine, imposed by the court, was paid by Rod's father, who was merely concerned that his son did not get into serious trouble. The CND crowd was not aggressive.

More worrying to Rod's parents and brothers and sisters was the teenager's aimless drifting. 'Donny and I used to put our hands in our pockets and give him a couple of bob, because he never had any money,' his sister Mary says. Roaming free was Rod's ambition as a seventeen-year-old, and he asked his father for enough cash to visit France for his first visit outside Britain. He hitch-hiked to Dover, paid his ferry fare to cross the Channel and then hitch-hiked down to Paris. In true beatnik fashion he slept rough beside the River Seine on the Left Bank. It wasn't exactly dangerous living but it was an essential statement of lifestyle. Something inside young Rod Stewart's head must have been leading him towards the life of an artist. When he returned to Highgate after only a few days, he seemed unsettled.

Visiting central London, Rod hooked up with some of the folk-singing guitar players with whom he felt an empathy; the clarion call of music, albeit some distance yet from the demonstrative art of Al Jolson, was now pulling him. He met a singer named Wizz

Jones, a respected name on the British folk music scene. Now came Rod's first public performances as a guitarist and singer as he and Jones busked on the pavements in Leicester Square. The wanderlust, the need for more life experience, tempted Rod back to Europe. With Wizz Jones and other kindred spirits he set off for a hitch-hiking trip through France, Belgium, Italy and finally Spain. Financially it was a struggle, and they hardly had enough cash to pay for food. They slept rough in Barcelona under the arches of a football stadium, where they were rounded up by the Spanish police who considered them vagrants.

Although Rod's passport was in order those of some of his friends were not, and the British Consulate was asked to repatriate Rod and the rest of the scruffy party back to their homeland.

All this might have appeared unfocused, but it was typical of the soul-searching adventures which many thousands of young people dabbled in during the 1960s. There was little fear of unemployment, and the academic aspirations of future decades did not occupy the thoughts of those who, like Rod, had drifted in and out of secondary modern schools with no qualifications. A job would appear, somehow. And so folk music's literary culture helped to provide a backdrop for those like Stewart who were attuned to its articulacy and wanted to express it themselves. 'I read the beatnik's bible,' Rod said, 'which was Jack Kerouac's *On the Road*. I had no ambition at that time, except to be famous. Even when I left school I knew I had to be famous at doing something. It didn't matter what – medicine, jumping off the Eiffel Tower, anything! I just had to be famous.'

Returning ignominiously from that European trek to the middle-class suburb of Highgate, Rod found that, in his absence, his father's building firm had been wound up because trade was poor. His dad had now opened a newsagent and confectionery shop in Archway Road, and was up before dawn to sort out the newspapers for delivery. Arriving back home jobless and penniless, Rod had assumed the unacceptable ethic of the beatnik bum, which did not sit well with his hard-working, no-nonsense family.

Rod's behaviour as an itinerant, especially by contrast with his orthodox brothers and sisters, distressed his parents. When he disappeared for some days to stay with friends, his father recalled later: 'We hadn't seen him for ages when a policeman friend of mine told me he had just seen Roddy in Highgate. "He looks bloody horrible," said my friend. So I said: "If you see him again, tell him that if he's not home in half an hour you'll arrest him." He did and Roddy came home and he did look horrible. We threw all his old clothes in the dustbin and then he had his hair cut. From then, he was different.'

• • •

From America came the sounds that would ignite still more the music in Rod's soul. Bob Dylan was making an impact, with his own songs wedded to wailing harmonica and powerful acoustic guitar backing. Songs like 'Blowing in the Wind' and 'The Times They Are A' Changing' brought a sharp new focus for the world of folk music, and suddenly Rod's interest was heightened. It was too early for the realization, but the twin influences of Al Jolson's glorious entertainment and strength of performance, plus Dylan's genius for articulacy in his writing, would eventually combine in Rod's hands to assert a uniquely strong combination.

For the moment, though, he was not popular at home. 'I didn't dislike his music,' his sister Mary says, 'but I disliked the way he was drifting, wasting time and earning no money when we all had to earn our keep. I didn't think anything would come of the music. Mum and Dad were worried. The years were going by, he had no career and not much of an ambition. He was a carefree lad, though. You couldn't get angry with him.' Her lectures to her kid brother simply reminded him that his absences for long periods abroad, or on CND marches, had worried their mother and father unduly. 'They were in their mid fifties, not ages when they should have been so concerned about their youngest son's safety,' she says now.

Brother Don, taking a tougher line, was asked by their father to give Rod 'a good talking to'. He recalls: 'I vividly remember Dad saying: "Try to get him a regular job, because he's going nowhere." Then I gave Rod a good rollicking.' Tears flowed from Rod, 'But what I said had no effect,' Don says.

Although there were the traditional parent–teenager clashes, Rod had an innate affection for his mother and father. Describing his father in later years, he said, with that touch of exaggeration that he has always possessed, that his dad 'has one tooth because he doesn't believe in going to the dentist. He's a rotund five feet ten. A lot of Scots haven't got good teeth. It's got something to do with the water, apparently.'

But he would always take note of his father's discipline, and next in Rod's life came what he called 'humiliation'. To earn his keep and a few pounds of pocket money, his father insisted he rose early in the mornings to sort out the newspapers for delivery and take some to houses nearby. Getting Rod out of bed by seven o'clock was 'horrible', his mother recalls now. At eighteen, Rod was appalled at the indignity of having to deliver papers in the company of ten-year-old boys employed by his father.

A bizarre diversion came next. Rod recalls that he was consumed by a fear of dying. Whether this was traceable to the ultimate message of the nuclear disarmament lobby is difficult to evaluate. But he took a job that would forever be aligned with his pre-show-business years – as a grave digger at Highgate cemetery.

He dug only three or four graves in total and worked only two days a week. It poured with rain most of the time, Rod remembered. When he began the job, the other men in the cemetery initiated him by putting him in a coffin and closing the lid. 'That scared the shit out of me, but I've had no fear of death since. It cured me.'

The three-week experience at the cemetery emphasized Rod's leanings towards the politics of the Left: he was able to survey the last resting place of Communist icon Karl Marx. Ruminating later on his fear of death and confrontation, he said: 'I've always believed the only way to tackle that kind of fear is to face up to it. That's why I dug graves for while.'

● ● ●

By now, Rod had bought a harmonica in order fully to adopt the fashionable sound of the era. From Earls Court to Hampstead, from Soho to Richmond, clubs and coffee bars featured the vibrant backdrop of the exciting new sound called folk music. From Liverpool, the Beatles featured John Lennon on harmonica with their début single 'Love Me Do', and their first chart-topper, 'Please Please Me', had shaken a sober pop scene in 1963. It might not have been folk music, but finally, after years of adult domination, twenty-year-olds were making a statement. In London, Brian Jones played harmonica with the Rolling Stones, whose earthy brand of rock 'n' roll, closer to rhythm-and-blues, gripped the teenagers pouring into Ken Colyer's jazz club in Great Newport Street, off Leicester Square, and the Marquee Club in Oxford Street. It was the start of a special musical thrust, and young people like Rod Stewart throughout the country were caught up in it.

In Britain in 1963, with the Beatles, the Rolling Stones and others just getting a foothold, long hair and rebelliousness by youth was not fully accepted. Rod was still a part-time beatnik, to the concern of his family, who became tired and worried by his unpredictable visits home, invariably looking shabby and saying he was hungry and broke.

After the Spanish incident, he encountered the police again during a visit with about twenty beatnik friends to Shoreham, West Sussex. They were living on a barge which they had cleaned up, but local people considered the boat and its inhabitants a hideous blot on their landscape and complained to the police. Action came quickly. Hosepipes were turned on Rod and his mates, who teemed out of the boat to safety. The police then towed away the barge as the depressed, tousled beatniks headed back to their homes.

The experience probably dampened Rod's enthusiasm for the beatnik lifestyle. It was, anyway, reaching its natural end as a movement. With the recognition of 'new' pop sounds from successful British artists such as Dusty Springfield and Cliff Richard, smartness was in. Fashions were changing in tandem with the new music.

A bright, fast-thinking young man, Rod was now developing an intuitive penchant for current trends. He also had considerable self-esteem and he tired of the casual beatnik image. Too many friends construed it as dirty, particularly his family, for whom Rod always maintained enormous love and respect despite the minor confrontations.

The timing was perfect for his next change. He latched on to the Mod look that was filtering into pop fashion. Mods spent every penny they had on clothes and their hairstyle was crucial: a sharp left parting, but slightly bounced up at the back.

Nor was it long. Rod's family were relieved to find that he had now begun to have his hair styled, borrowing his sisters' lacquer. A new pride in his appearance had been stimulated by a regular girlfriend, whom Rod had met on one of the marches. 'She came from Bristol and was very hoity-toity,' he recalled. 'That's when I started getting this hairstyle together. I remember we used to go on the tube from Highgate station, which is renowned for its draught up the escalator. When a train came in it would blow your hair all over the place, so there I was, with me hair all backcombed and lacquered, holding it in place with me hands.'

From that citadel of high fashion, John Michael in Carnaby Street, Rod bought a collarless leather Beatle-styled jacket and a polo-necked sweater. Matelot shirts and washed-out denims completed his pretty hip look in 1963.

He was still impoverished. Money came from helping his brother Bob make picture frames. To Rod, like thousands of other reprobates who had been born in the early 1940s, rock 'n' roll now seemed not just a possible career, but a vocation. There was little else on the horizon. As he began to take music more seriously, Rod told his brother Bob he needed a new guitar. At a shop off Oxford Street, Bob signed as guarantor for the hire purchase agreement as Rod happily went home with his new Gibson acoustic. As the weeks went by, Rod could not repay the instalments for the £40 owed. An irate scene with Bob followed, and Don paid the sums due. 'Roddy paid me back in the end, but it took time,' Bob says now. Observing Brian Jones in the Stones and John Lennon in the Beatles, Rod soon became adept on the harmonica, too.

• • •

London and its clubs were alive to the sounds of a new music. As hundreds of bands migrated south from Liverpool in the wake of the Beatles, the Rolling Stones fired up the southern scene. Rod began to visit Eel Pie Island at Twickenham, where the Stones had played their early apprenticeship, and he visited the Manor at Harringay, and the Marquee. On the grapevine, he heard of a Birmingham band called the Dimensions that needed a harmonica player and backing vocalist. This resulted in his baptism into the hard world of band politics. Soon after Rod joined, singer Jimmy Powell hired the band as his accompanists and any thoughts Rod had of singing went out of the door. It was, though, valuable stage experience for the eighteen-year-old Rod, 'dressed up immaculately', as he remembers, as he took the stage as harmonica player in the Powell line-up.

Rhythm-and-blues had infiltrated to the jazz clubs, and at Ken Colyer's on the edge of Soho, the Rolling Stones had made a huge impact. As the Stones took to the road, Jimmy Powell and the Five Dimensions were featured there. 'We died a slow death. It was terrible,' Rod recalled. As a semi-pro, he was not encouraged to sing with Powell initially: 'I think Powell was just a little bit jealous. He knew I could sing. But I was lucky to be in a band at all. I was pleased to be playing anything, and harmonica was definitely THE instrument to play at the time. So I settled for that.'

The showman in him began to surface even in these early days, as the Powell band played weddings and rugby club dances. 'Occasionally I joined in a few backing vocals and I tended to blow Powell off the stage because I really overdid it, you know, shouting so loud on the backing vocal whenever I got the chance.'

By now, he had improved his art as a player of the 'harp', as the harmonica was described. Rod observed that Mick Jagger 'sucked as well as blew'. This was part of Rod's important instrumental education at that stage.

Rod considers his stint with Powell to have been an amateur role. He was still doing odd jobs such as fence-building for his father, to earn money. But for three months from October 1963, his haphazard position in the band gave him useful experience and confidence on stage as they played private functions like weddings as well as prestigious clubs like Ken Colyer's and Chelsea's Six Bells.

Leather-jacketed and in tweedy trousers, Stewart was assuming the sartorial and musical style that would eventually mark him out. What he needed was a break to pitch himself into the new music of his choice: soulful rhythm-and-blues, as played by the Rolling Stones. While his love of folk music was undiminished, Rod loved the raw sounds of the early Stones. He saw them often at clubs, and on 30 December, 1963, on what would be his final show with Jimmy Powell before he drifted away, the Stones were top of the bill at Ken Colyer's. Rod hung around all the London clubs, soaking up the atmosphere and the music. By the start of 1964, by which time British rock 'n' roll was fit for export to the USA in the hands of the Beatles, the Stones, the Animals, the Searchers and the Dave Clark Five, Rod Stewart was uniquely qualified to enter the scene.

Music was by then truly in his blood. He had absorbed the unashamed showmanship of Al Jolson, the poetic power of Bob Dylan, Rambling Jack Elliott and Woody Guthrie (Dylan's inspiration), and now he tapped into the earlier sources of the Stones, the band he was growing so attached to. Great American blues singers such as Howlin' Wolf, Jimmy Reed, Chuck Berry, Bo Diddley and B.B. King were influencing Mick Jagger, Keith Richards and Brian Jones. The sound of their music had an electrifying effect on Rod. He always preferred the raw, authentic sound of the Stones to that of the Beatles.

Music was slowly proving to be his lifeline. On the route to stardom, though, the ingredient of luck is essential to kick along natural talent. Rod's moment of fortune came in the unlikely setting of Twickenham railway station late on the night of Sunday, 7 January, 1964.

Rod had been to the nearby Eel Pie Island club to see the band being led by Long John Baldry, a six-foot seven-inch tall singer who fronted the Hoochie Coochie Men. A young veteran of the British blues scene who had played with the Rolling Stones' mentor Alexis Korner and his band Blues Incorporated, Baldry was to prove a pivotal figure for Stewart and also for Elton John.

As he stood after that show on the cold and foggy Twickenham station platform awaiting a train, Baldry was astonished to hear, coming from another platform, the wailing harmonica riffs to a classic Howlin' Wolf blues song called 'Smokestack Lightning'.

'I was yodelling away waiting for the last train back to London,' Rod recalls. 'He was waiting for the same train ... He came over to me and said: "Why don't you join the band as a second singer?" I said: "What's it worth?" He said, "Thirty-five pounds a week." I said, "I'll take that job, thank you." And that's how it started.' Rod added that he was rather drunk at the time, or he might not have had the nerve to accept.

Stewart was entering a band that carried immense respect on the blues scene. Baldry told him he would be making his début the following Tuesday at Eel Pie Island. Rod was both ecstatic and nervous at the prospect.

Baldry's memory of their first classic encounter at Twickenham station is more animated and detailed than Rod's. Describing 'a perfect setting for a Gothic thriller', Baldry told the *Toronto Star* what happened after he heard the harmonica playing: 'Gingerly stepping along the platform I went to investigate the source of this stirring sound ... I realized there was a nose protruding from the swathing of a gigantic woollen scarf. "Good evening," I said to the nose. "You strike me as being a bit of a blues fan. Your harmonica playing sounds very authentic."' They got chatting about music. 'I learned that his name was Rod, and he lived in Highgate about a mile or two from where I was living at the time and that he had attended my show earlier that evening at the Eel Pie Island hotel and had enjoyed my performance ... I invited him to come along and jam with the Hoochie Coochie Men the following Tuesday.'

On the morning of Rod's return to Eel Pie Island, Rod's mother phoned Baldry. 'Have you asked my boy to play harmonica and sing with your band?' she questioned him. Baldry assured her that was so. Rod was not faking the story. 'Well, just make sure he gets home on time,' Elsie insisted.

While Rod's memory is of joining the band from the start, Baldry's recollection is that it was for a jam session that he was inviting Rod. If that were so, Rod's performance would surely never have got him the permanent job that followed. When the big night arrived he was late, as he often was. Then he told Baldry that he did not really want to sing. Truthfully, he said, he knew only three songs. The experienced Long John recognized that statement as nerves. There followed the faltering Stewart, making his début with a significant band, playing pretty primitive harmonica.

It was a sad Hoochie Coochie Men that Rod joined. Baldry had assumed the leadership from Cyril Davies, a pioneering harmonica player and singer on the blues scene. He died from leukaemia, aged thirty-two, just as Rod entered the band. Baldry and the whole British blues scene were mourning the loss of a special talent.

Rod had just passed his nineteenth birthday when he took off as a professional musician with the Hoochie Coochie Men. Four musicians augmented Baldry and Stewart, who had officially taken the spot of Davies while Rod assumed the role of vocalist. 'I remember when I first joined, nobody wanted to know,' Stewart recalled. 'John was the only one in the band who believed in me. They were a horrible lot in that band but they all changed their mind in the end. John and I used to do a few duets. The first song I ever sang professionally on stage [with Baldry's band] was "Night Time is the Right Time". And I took a leaper [a stimulant] to do it. I had to because I was so scared. I was up for about three days but I didn't 'arf sing that number. Then I started singing "Tiger in Your Tank", which was my showstopper, then "Dimples", and things like that.' Impeccable advice on stagecraft from the young trouper Baldry to the novice Stewart was succinct: 'Never keep your legs together when you're singing. It looks daft.'

Rod's voice was at the transitional stage between folk-music orientation and the identity that would later make him so instantly recognizable. Like so many British singers, he was striving for a 'black' sound, akin to that of Otis Redding, without much success. 'I wasn't very good at singing then. I was too conscious of trying to sound spadey, I suppose. I had to work to find myself, you know. Everybody's got to go through that period.' He never considered himself a blues singer: 'I'm a folk singer if I'm anything.'

Across Britain, from clubs like the Twisted Wheel in Manchester through the Bromel Club at Bromley and the national headquarters of the blues, London's Marquee, Rod's name began to be discussed by a young crowd who developed an 'ear' for fine music. 'In this band,' Baldry told the *Melody Maker* proudly of the new line-up he fronted, 'are the best blues players this side of the Atlantic. And Rod Stewart is a real find. He is one of the few teenagers who has got on to the real rhythm-and-blues scene.' This was a very busy band, appearing on bills alongside such magical American artists as Sonny Boy Williamson and Memphis Slim, who Rod knew from his days in Paris with Wizz Jones, when they had accompanied the noted singer-pianist.

After his years of wandering, Rod's parents were relieved to see the yellow-painted band truck arriving outside their Highgate home most weeks. The last to be called for *en route* to the M1 motorway, Rod clambered in among the equipment and seemed in heaven. Elsie and Bob pronounced Baldry, who was four years older than Rod, 'a very nice man', and breathed some relief that their errant son's years of uncertainty seemed to be coming to an end. In Britain in 1964, if you were in a group, then you were in good company. The Beatles and others had made pop music respectable.

Rod hoped there would be another benefit beyond the £35 a week salary: women. His scorecard was reasonable, but was slightly hampered by a hilarious suspicion among some of the audiences that his singing partner might be more than just a colleague. At Eel Pie Island, in the men's toilets, someone scrawled on the wall: 'Appearing here next week: Ada Baldry and Her Hoochie Coochie Ladies, Featuring Phyllis Stewart.'

Baldry demonstrated the lie in this rumour. When he moved from Hampstead to a new flat in South Kensington, he often made the place available to Rod for the night so that he could entertain girls. The reputation of a randy rocker was beginning to start among musicians as Rod, the brown-eyed handsome man, appeared to have a girl in most places the band revisited.

Three   Paying his dues

'ROD WAS VERY SERIOUS ABOUT HIS WORK,
ALWAYS IMMACULATELY DRESSED, NEVER TOOK
DRUGS'

      – Mickey Waller, Stewart's ex-drummer

How young, innocent, energetic and resource-
ful pop music was in the 1960s! The landscape was mas-
sively different from the decades that followed. There
were lively TV pop shows but there was no video. Even
cassettes had yet to make an impact. A buoyant club
scene throughout the land gave young bands, keen to
learn their instruments properly as well as how to please
a crowd, a wonderful circuit for their apprenticeship.

Armies of young entrepreneurial managers ran
alongside the acts, eager to get the best recording con-
tracts. Single 45 rpm records frequently sold 250,000
copies to earn a silver disc for the act. And, long before
lawyers and corporations dominated the entertainment
map, there was a chance for sheer talent to shine
through.

The biggest plus, however, for British acts was
their source of inspiration. The Beatles had drawn from
Tamla Motown and the rockabilly of such Americans as
Jerry Lee Lewis and Carl Perkins. The Yardbirds, from
which sprang Eric Clapton, Jeff Beck and Led Zeppelin
founder Jimmy Page, favoured white-sounding rhythm-
and-blues, while hot bands like the Stones and the

Animals preached their interpretations of the sounds of Chuck Berry and Bo Diddley.

Soaking up all these influences, Rod Stewart was mining gold in his musical education. Inside the Hoochie Coochie Men, he learned greatly from Baldry's flamboyant and carefully executed stagecraft, his natty dress, his mannerisms that wedded show-business the-atricality to an understanding of blues feeling. From Cyril Davies, Baldry had learned from a master of rhythm-and-blues, and it showed.

To this surfeit of great music, Stewart added a cru-cial inspiration of his own. Now an avid record collec-tor, he discovered the voice of Sam Cooke. Walking one day from Highgate to Gospel Oak, Rod heard Cooke's big 1961 hit ballad 'Cupid' on a transistor radio. Stewart was hooked.

Born on 22 January, 1931 in Clarksdale, Mississi-ppi and raised in Chicago, Cooke was the son of a Baptist minister and had sung in a choir since the age of six. For six years from 1950 he began an illustrious career with 'You Send Me', an American chart-topper in 1957. More successes, including 'Another Saturday Night', 'Twisting the Night Away' and 'Bring It On Home to Me', confirmed his exceptional talent. In December 1964, he was shot dead in Los Angeles.

Enjoying eight British top thirty hits during his life, Cooke made a big impact on Stewart, and on dozens of other singers of the era. Although Rod liked all the fine soul singers such as Ray Charles and Otis Redding, he latched on to Sam Cooke for a pragmatic reason: 'It had to do with the way I sounded. I was real-ly open-minded and would listen to anybody, but I knew I sounded a bit like Sam Cooke.'

It was the tough but tender tone of Cooke's voice, not the phrasing, that was naturally aligned to Rod's own. Recalling his earliest vocal work, Rod described his own voice as 'a very bad, mid-Atlantic cowboy voice'. But two years of playing Cooke records endless-ly, and identifying the texture of sound he sought, even-tually produced precisely what he wanted.

So far, he had not developed the gravelly, brandy-soaked timbre that he later described as 'like black vel-vet on sandpaper', which would deliver him to fame. His voice was warm and powerful. But probably he needed to do a little more living, gain more experience in other band settings, to discover what lurked beneath those vocal cords.

The catapult that would start Rod's journey to success came with a series of disappointments that might have quashed the spirit of less determined nine-teen-year-olds. Rod was now certain that a life in music awaited him; he had visual and vocal style, a strong knowledge of music, and grit. In later life, he would muse that stardom and riches are probably reserved for some people; it was not said boastfully but philosophi-cally. After the bumps of his young life, the Swinging Sixties moved successfully and swiftly for him.

• • •

By August 1964, the Rolling Stones were all over the airwaves with their single, 'It's All Over Now'. It was a significant breakthrough, proof that a blues-based band faced no barrier in reaching the summit. Talent scouts descended every night on the Marquee club, which by then had moved to Wardour Street, Soho, from its origi-nal Oxford Street home. Here, further superstars were being nursed in their first bands: Eric Clapton and the men who would form Led Zeppelin among them.

John Rowlands, a former comedian, now a fast-talking entrepreneur who went on to manage singer P.J. Proby, spotted Rod at the Marquee during a Baldry session. So did Mike Vernon, a record producer speciali-zing in the blues. Stewart, they both decided, had star quality that existed beyond the confines of the Baldry unit.

With his partner, Geoff Wright, John Rowlands offered to manage Rod personally. Realizing Rod was ambitious and having solo hopes of his own, John Baldry did not object to the idea of Rod having a career outside the Hoochie Coochie Men. Besides, rumblings of discontent from Rod had surfaced two months earlier. L.J.B. and the Hoochie Coochie Men had recorded for United Artists the single 'Up Above My Head (I Hear Music in the Air)', a gospel song written by the noted Sister Rosetta Tharpe. Rod duetted with Baldry on that track, but received no credit on the label; and Baldry had appeared alone on TV's *Ready Steady Go!* to promote the A-side, called 'You'll Be Mine'. Ambitious for recognition as he improved his act, Rod was hurt.

So when Rowlands and Wright signed Rod to management, and took him into a small studio in Soho to record some tracks with backing musicians, the writing seemed to be on the wall for his role alongside John Baldry. Soon afterwards, Rod was signed by Mike Vernon to a solo deal with Decca, the same company that released the Rolling Stones.

Rod was pulling away; this was a big break for a nineteen-year-old. In September 1964 he went to Decca's studio in Broadhurst Gardens, West Hampstead, to make his solo recording début. Sticking to the blues roots he had honed within the Hoochie Coochie Men, Rod chose two Sonny Boy Williamson songs, 'Good Morning Little Schoolgirl' and 'I'm Gonna Move to the Outskirts of Town', for his first single.

But over at the EMI label, the Yardbirds, who had a higher profile than Rod, issued the same song and scored well. The omen for Rod's début was poor. Interviewed at this time by his local newspaper, the *Hampstead and Highgate Express*, Rod sat in the Stewart family's local pub, the Wellington, at the junction of Archway Road and North Hill, sipping on a half-pint of bitter. Wearing a tartan scarf, blue and white striped 'butcher boy' trousers and high-heeled boots, he described his clothes as 'All Mod Tat'. He said he was not pinning too many hopes on his début single. 'I don't tear my hair out at nights and I'm not making too many plans.' What he really wanted was a car, an Austin Healey Sprite.

There was cautious optimism as he recalled the previous week at a Hoochie Coochie Men show. 'I was dragged off stage by a gang of girls. I just climbed back on again and carried on singing. It doesn't bother me at all. I try to forget about the audience when I'm singing. The screaming doesn't bother me too much.' Having toured the whole of Britain, he nominated Bristol and Liverpool the liveliest venues, with, ironically, Scotland 'the worst place I've been to … it's a drag'.

He spent about seven hours a day travelling, usually arriving back in London in the early hours. That meant sleeping during the day. 'It's hard work, I suppose,' he said, 'but it's the sort of life I like.' Describing the pop industry as a rat race and 'as phoney as everyone thinks it is', Rod added: 'I happen to sing rhythm-and-blues, the fashion of the moment. I'll stay on the bandwagon as long as it's there. Sure, I'm in it for the money.'

Painting a vivid picture of his ideal girl, he said she should be black-stockinged, wear white shoes, a flowered shirt, and have 'peroxided hair'.

• • •

The big debate within the pop world in 1964 was whether young white singers like Rod, with a middle-class background and no problems of survival, had any right to sing the blues, a music which had been born from the deprivation of black Americans. Entering the debate with the information sheet published by Decca to promote his single, Rod declared: 'A white person can sing the blues with just as much conviction as a Negro. All these coloured singers singing about "Walking Down the Railroad Track" ... they've never walked down the railroad track in their lives! You've got more to sing the blues about in Archway Road than on any railroad track I know.'

The British rhythm-and-blues scene was, he said, becoming polluted by 'third- and fourth-rate bands that are giving the music a bad name. Most of them would be better off at home listening to Big Bill Broonzy'. At nineteen, Rod was opinionated, thrusting, ambitious, and now, suddenly, a solo performer with a will to win. The competition was intense.

Listing the facts of his life in the Decca promotional sheet, Rod listed his proficient instruments by then as twelve- and six-string guitars, harmonica, banjo and mandolin. His favourite musicians were singers Billie Holiday, Bobby Bland, Frank Sinatra, Nancy Wilson and Sam Cooke; jazz musicians such as drummer Buddy Rich and saxophonists Ben Webster and Gerry Mulligan. From mixing with musicians, Rod's tastes in music were more eclectic, for he now veered towards jazz and stated that an ambition would be to sing with the Count Basie Orchestra.

Two asides demonstrated his droll sense of humour, which would always be a part of his personality. Under the heading: 'Not Very Fond Of ...' he wrote: 'SCOTLAND'. Under the heading 'Dislikes ...' he wrote: 'PLONKERS'.

● ● ●

'Good Morning Little Schoolgirl' was a creditable record. It caused Rod no career damage. While the Yardbirds' version was a hit and his was not, he had at least made his television début performing the song. *Ready Steady Go!* was the hottest pop programme of the early 1960s, a vital Friday evening platform for dandy Mods like Stewart. In the pub after appearing on the programme, a nervous Rod met, for the first time, a guitarist with a struggling band called the Birds from West Drayton, Middlesex. His name was Ronnie Wood. A kind of rapport was apparent but neither knew that within a few years they would be on the road to becoming virtual brothers for life.

Baldry, too, was asserting himself as a soloist at this time. A key 1960s figure, Jack Good (first producer of Cliff Richard) had been the producer of Baldry and the Hoochie Coochie Men's single, which irritated Rod. Now Good got Baldry a solo spot on a TV show called *Around the Beatles*. That was probably enough to arouse the competitive ire in Stewart. But when the TV recording caused Baldry to be late arriving for a Hoochie Coochie Men show at Portsmouth, Rod hit the roof. Awaiting Baldry, the band began its show. 'I had to hold the stage and I really couldn't,' Rod remembered, 'When he turned up, I swore at him and he sacked me. I cried … I didn't think people got sacked in show-business.'

Ten valuable months in the Hoochie Coochie Men ended with a colliding of egos. Rod's management then paired him with a Southampton band, the Soul Agents, and another group called the Ad Lib. Unhappy with both, Rod struck out alone. Although the split from Baldry and the Hoochie Coochie Men had been bad-tempered, each strongly respected the other's talent. Baldry always had a generous spirit about him. He had provided an unknown harmonica player at Twickenham railway station with a stepping stone to success, and taken him around Britain to gain vital confidence. The rest was up to Rod.

● ● ●

From beatnik to Mod was a giant step for Rod, and the transformation delighted the Stewart household. Now financially a little more stable from his earnings in music, he told his astonished parents, sisters and brothers that he spent £1 a week at the hairdresser.

Whenever possible on Saturdays he would still enjoy turning out for Highgate Redwing, to the pleasure of his father. On Saturday afternoons the four men in the family would cluster around the television set to watch the soccer results. It was the same TV set which Rod's father had bought specially to watch Arsenal play Liverpool in the 1950 Cup Final.

Stewart senior's dedication to Arsenal had little impact on Rod. Discussions about soccer teams could get 'very intense, very heated', Rod's brother Bob remembers. It was hardly a church-going household – 'that was for weddings and funerals' – but football came close to their religion: 'An epidemic, always being talked about by the men,' says Bob.

Father Stewart, perpetually smoking his cigar as he checked his pools entries, was a betting man. 'Horses, dogs, the pools. Dad always had these wonderful schemes, and had a few windfalls, but he never made any real money,' Don says.

Nor could Dad fully comprehend the ups and downs of his youngest son's pop career. It was not a 'regular job', as the four older Stewart children had pursued. He never chided Rod, but made the odd remark. 'Dad was a bit short-tempered, especially with me,' Bob Stewart says. 'I used to get clouts round the earhole. I was the rebel in the family as a kid; Roddy and Donny did OK.'

Fascinating, to father Stewart, was Rod's attachment to Glasgow Celtic and the Scotland football team. The tartan trousers that Rod wore in his next group would be a token of his unswerving devotion to everything connected with his father's homeland.

• • •

Everyone in the pop world in Britain in the 1960s either knew, or was aware, of Giorgio Gomelsky. The son of a Russian doctor and a French mother, he was an experimental film-maker who had hitch-hiked round the world to arrive in London at the start of an exceptional decade. From the club he named the Crawdaddy at the Station Hotel, Richmond, Gomelsky was to be the catalyst for stars including the Rolling Stones, the Yardbirds featuring Eric Clapton and Jeff Beck and many others. With great panache, he had even been instrumental in getting the Beatles to see the Rolling Stones perform at his club on 14 April, 1963. That was the first time the Beatles experienced the Stones and their feverish audiences and it marked the start of a friendship of Britain's two biggest groups.

Gomelsky leaned towards jazz and managed a fine pianist, Brian Auger, who led a band called Trinity. In 1964 Auger had won the Best British Pianist title in the *Melody Maker* Jazz Poll. Bands who played the Marquee were a community; everyone, especially the managers like Gomelsky, knew who was looking for a new gig. After Rod's departure from the Hoochie Coochie Men, Baldry wound up the group, saying he was losing £400 a week. He had a stab at solo work, but was now hanging loose. At Gomelsky's office, a pert and pretty eighteen-year-old, Julie Driscoll, was working as secretary to the Yardbirds; but she had also sung at the Crawdaddy.

Energy and inspirational ideas were Gomelsky's strengths. With keen ears, he envisioned a British white soul revue, on the lines of the Ike and Tina Turner show and the Tamla Motown artists' concerts, which were sweeping the States. In mid July 1964, Gomelsky walked into his office and said to Julie Driscoll: 'Come and listen to Brian Auger's Trinity; we're putting you and that band together with Rod Stewart and Long John Baldry, and we're going to put you out as Steam

Packet.' For the teenage secretary, it was great news.

Julie remembers: 'The band started that weekend. It was a brilliant concept by Giorgio.' First, he organized a rehearsal in an old school in Regent's Park. 'I told them not to take the stage together, but to walk on one after the other, to build the impact. They cracked up at that,' Giorgio says. 'It was so unusual for rock 'n' rollers like these to consider slicking themselves into a routine. They resisted at first but they knew it was right for this type of show.'

The line-up of Rod, Baldry and Auger was augmented by Rick Brown (bass), Vic Briggs (guitar) and a lively drummer named Mickey Waller. A young veteran of the scene, Waller had known Rod since his Eel Pie Island days with Baldry, and greatly respected the singer.

In tartan trousers at last on stage, Rod nearly reached his beloved Scotland as Steam Packet secured a frantically busy diary of dates across Britain. 'Rod was very serious about his work on the road,' says Mickey Waller. 'Always immaculately dressed, never took drugs. I was struck by his dedication as a singer.'

Julie Driscoll, who had been recording since the age of fifteen when she worked in her father's band, remembers Steam Packet as 'a happy union, but I don't think there was a particular musical policy. We all had alternating roles between backing and solo work. Rod and I duetted a bit. The whole idea was young, innocent, naïve. It was a nice sound and did well, but it would be laughed at today'. Frustration in the band surfaced when they 'knocked audiences for six' but gained no recognition. The major problem for the band was that nobody wrote original material for it; and they failed to secure a record contract.

Mickey Waller remembers earning £40 a week, Julie Driscoll says she was paid £20 a week. 'I'm not bitter. I was never in it for making money.' When word leaked that Baldry and Stewart were getting more, some musicians baulked. But there was unity for the sake of some good music: the three singers duetted on Martha and the Vandellas' 'Dancing in the Street'; Julie sang with the soulfulness that would bring her later success on Mary Wells' 'My Guy'; Rod offered Sam Cooke's 'Another Saturday Night'. 'Actually, they were ahead of their time,' Gomelsky says. 'They were a wailing success. It was complicated by the fact that the singers were on different record labels. Egos started to come into it because of that.'

Rod's parents, brothers and sisters turned out for Steam Packet's big night and the high spot of the nineteen-year-old's career – when he appeared at the London Palladium for two shows on the same bill as the Rolling Stones on 1 August, 1964. 'That's when I knew,' Elsie Stewart says, 'that Rod was going to be famous.'

Giorgio Gomelsky did not see Rod as particularly ambitious. 'He was young, good-looking, having a good time. He enjoyed parties and always seemed to be losing his voice. I told him that if he didn't watch it, he would lose it completely one day.'

In a short-lived romance, Rod dated Jenny Ryland, best friend of Julie Driscoll. 'She came to a gig,' Julie says, 'and they took it from there. Rod always liked leggy blondes and she was one of the first.' In every town Steam Packet played, Rod seemed to have a girl awaiting his return, according to Mickey Waller.

Though he looked dandy with his beautiful coiffed hair and immaculate Mod clothes, Rod was tough and used his tall and lithe frame forcefully when necessary. Once, returning to London in the early hours after an appearance in the North, the band stopped at the Blue Boar motorway café. In the car park, Mickey Waller recalls, 'Some horrible motor bikers were taking the piss out of us. There were three of them. We all sat in the van not wanting to know. But, surprisingly, Rod got out and walked over and gave them a right sort-out. It was quite a punch-up. He was a good fighter.' Returning to the van, Rod told Mickey he was not a natural fighter but his anger had seen him through.

The pleasing musical notion of Steam Packet seemed to be on a treadmill. With no firm identity, they could not secure a record deal. 'A big problem is that we weren't writing our own songs,' Julie Driscoll says. 'Too many covers of songs by other acts were done, because they were great for live work. So we sat in the middle between jazz and blues and rock. Everyone had stage charisma, without doubt. Giorgio would come to gigs and tell us where we were going wrong. He always tried to get artists to live his dreams. But we all had our own and needed to do our own thing.'

As the band careered across Britain, it must have dawned on Auger and Baldry that even in this curious coalition, Rod Stewart was a first among equals. Decca had not pursued an option to his next record after the flop of 'Good Morning Little Schoolgirl'. But he was now taken up by the mighty EMI's Columbia label, for which he recorded a curious song written by Barry Mason, later to find success as the writer of Engelbert Humperdinck's 'The Last Waltz'. Entitled 'The Day Will Come', the single, released in November 1965, was strangely unsuited to Rod, and died an inevitable death.

Shortly after that, the balloon went up in Steam Packet. Brian Auger always considered the band as an extension of his Trinity. Taking a vote from the band's management and themselves, Auger and Baldry decided to exclude Rod from a forthcoming date in Saint-Tropez – to save on the band salary. Julie was appalled when she was informed that Rod's exit had been agreed because 'an extra body was not needed'. She says: 'I thought it was unfair then, and still do. It was put to me that he could not be afforded any more. There was no need for this to happen. On musical merit, Rod was in the band

Rod (far right) with his
friends
(photos: Mary Stewart/Smiler)

In his cowboy outfit (Mary
Stewart/Smiler)

At the seaside, aged twelve
(Mary Stewart/Smiler)

Al Jolson, Rod Stewart's
early hero, whose theatricality
and audience communication
impressed him

Sam Cooke, the 1960s hit-
maker of such songs as
'Cupid' and 'Twistin' The
Night Away', whose vocal
style was a major influence
on Rod

As he was with the Jeff Beck
Group, 1968. At New York's
Fillmore East triumph, he
wore the trendy shades of the
period (Richard Rothmen
and Tom Lucas/Star File)

Smiling Faces, minus Kenney
Jones, arriving at New York's
JFK airport in August, 1971.
From left: Ronnie Wood, Ian
MacLagan, Ronnie Lane and
Rod (Jeffrey Mayer, Star File)

Backstage during a Faces
concert at Madison Square
Garden, New York,
26 November 1971 (Jeffrey
Mayer, Star File)

Tartan pride: declaring his heritage, 1972 (Harry Goodwin/Star File)

Legends of the future Elton John, Marc Bolan and Rod after appearing on BBC TV's Top Of The Pops in February 1972. Elton and Rod had sung back-up to their mentor Long John Baldry on his single, 'Iko Iko'. (Harry Goodwin/Star File)

Building up the stage
charisma while touring the
US with the Faces, 1972 and
1973 (Bob Gruen, Star File)

The terrible twins, Stewart
and Wood, on stage with the
Faces at Madison Square
Garden, New York, February
1975 (Chuck Pulin/Star File)

The tousled look, in the Faces
(Mick Rock/Star File)

and part of the attraction. But there it was; Rod had been given the bullet.'

The sack came as a terrible blow. Rod was now collecting too many disappointments in such a short career. He was a striking-looking young man but was being applauded for his voice. His confidence had been boosted by solo recognition, But inside groups, he seemed to be on a rollercoaster to nowhere. As with Baldry, so with Steam Packet: just as he seemed to gain momentum, he was apparently considered to be something of a threat. Rod was especially disappointed at Baldry, whom he considered a friend, for agreeing with Auger that he should get the elbow.

Just as Rod left Steam Packet, in the spring of 1966, Columbia released his third solo single. A totally redundant 'cover' of Sam Cooke's song 'Shake', this followed his first two into obscurity. It seemed, also, that Rod was always going to be the first one to leave a band that was on the road to self-destruction. Only a few months after he was the first one out of Steam Packet it disintegrated.

Reflecting on Steam Packet, Rod said of Auger: 'He gave me the sack; I think he always wanted to be on his own like he is now. I don't blame him because we overshadowed him. John overshadowed me and I overshadowed Julie. It was one of those. It's just a shame that nothing ever got down on wax.'*

Of the personality difficulties in the band, Rod said: 'Julie was always in love with somebody and Mickey Waller was in love with her and Brian Auger wanted more money. The dramas we had in that group.' Looking back, there was 'never anything really original' about its approach: 'We probably sold ourselves more on our characters than on our music. It was a good visual band with everybody trying to outdo each other with

* Although not intended for release at the time, a Steam Packet album of demonstration tapes was released in 1973.

clothes.' The important point from Stewart at that juncture was that while appearance was important, the music had to be firmly based, too. Later, he revealed his irritation that Baldry had aligned with Auger in 'giving me the elbow. They thought I was getting too much money. I was getting 10 per cent of the gross'.

Julie Driscoll and Brian Auger reverted to his Trinity, and Julie sang on the group's huge single hit with Bob Dylan's song 'This Wheel's on Fire'. Baldry joined Bluesology (where he was to nurture a pianist named Reg Dwight, later to assume the name Elton John). Mickey Waller went on to join Jeff Beck, who had succeeded Eric Clapton in the Yardbirds but was now hungry to launch his own unit.

•   •   •

Names and records that would endure for decades were making their biggest impact in 1966. Bob Dylan, by then a great favourite of Rod Stewart, appeared at London's Albert Hall in an epochal concert, with electric accompaniment for the first time. For this startling development away from his acoustic roots, Dylan was barracked with cries of 'Go home!' The Rolling Stones with 'Paint It Black', the Beatles with 'Paperback Writer', Frank Sinatra with his number one hit 'Strangers in the Night' and the Kinks with 'Sunny Afternoon' were among an avalanche of memorable sounds.

As well as an inventive record scene, Steam Packet had shown that there was a huge circuit for live shows. The band had played to audiences of up to 1,000 enthusiastic fans at clubs like the Mojo, Sheffield, the Il Rondo, Leicester, the Coatham, Redcar, Mr Smith's, Hanley, and Birmingham Town Hall. For every band, like the Hoochie Coochie Men and Steam Packet, that died, six more would be launched. Britain swarmed with managers keen to exploit the boom in groups triggered by the armies of twenty-year-old musicians from Liverpool, London, Manchester and Birmingham. So, inevitably, Rod leapfrogged from one problem into another hopeful situation.

Rik and John Gunnell, who ran the London Flamingo club in Wardour Street and also managed Georgie Fame, Chris Farlowe and Geno Washington, came up with the idea of a new supergroup and their planned line-up was formidable. Shotgun Express was a corny name but it boasted an original, lyrical guitarist, Peter Green, and a superb drummer, Mick Fleetwood. Rod joined as singer alongside an energetic Liverpool-born singer, Beryl Marsden. Pianist Peter Bardens and bassist Dave Ambrose completed an impressive band.

Posing for crass press pictures with shotguns in their hands, making a poor single called 'I Could Feel the Whole World Turn Round Underneath Me' (which featured, strangely for a soulful song, violins), the band was directionless from the start, despite the fine musicianship. That single bubbled under the British Top 50. But as they clambered into their Ford Transit to join hundreds of other bands travelling the motorways, an unspoken tension developed. Beryl Marsden, who was dating Peter Green, says: 'I liked Rod, thought he was a very talented guy and we sang well together when we did duets.' The 'needle' between them came because she felt he fancied himself too much as a solo star. 'When he was in a generous spirit, all was well. But without saying anything, I could sense his moods that said, without words: "I don't want to be in this band; I'm better than this." And I'd sense him trying to actually out-sing me. I wouldn't even take the bait.' Rod was too hungry for stardom to tolerate a band that had no clear identity.

Beryl felt the fundamental problem with the band was that 'the music hadn't happened organically, but we had been manufactured. There was a lot of money out there to be earned in the clubs we played, like the Flamingo in Soho and the Ram Jam Club in Brixton. But we didn't see big wage packets at the end of the hard week's work, and that led to discontent, too'. Lightweight soul was the loose policy; again Rod found himself doing cover versions of existing hits like Eddie Floyd's 'Knock on Wood', Wilson Pickett's 'In the Midnight Hour' and the bluesy song then being popularized by the Stones, 'Hi Heel Sneakers'.

A little-known aspect of Rod was observed by Beryl Marsden as they travelled. 'He seemed very shy with girls. Very withdrawn, I'd say, when it came to going over and pulling a bird!' As the years passed, she found it difficult to reconcile the heavily publicized 'Sex God' with the twenty-one-year-old she had known in 'that band of very strong-minded individuals'.

Shotgun Express ran for seven months before splitting at the end of 1966. Beryl Marsden returned disconsolately to Liverpool. Rod was again at sea. Peter Green and Mick Fleetwood would later form the first incarnation of the hugely successful Fleetwood Mac. Rod summed up Shotgun Express succinctly: 'A poor imitation of Steam Packet.'

• • •

Rod was again in limbo, but his list of friends and contacts in the music world was impressive. Among them was Chrissie Shrimpton, sister of top model Jean. Rod knew her as the best friend of one of his former girlfriends; Chrissie was dating Mick Jagger and she asked the Stones singer if he fancied trying his hand at record production ... and how about the singer being her friend Rod Stewart?

The result was an extraordinary session in August 1966. On a song called 'Come Home Baby', written by Carole King and recorded by Wilson Pickett, Jagger assembled superstars of the future. To duet with Rod, he brought in the singer P.P. (Pat) Arnold, Keith Richards on bass and rhythm guitars, Ronnie Wood, keyboardist Keith Emerson, who later went on to form the super-group Emerson, Lake and Palmer, top pianist Nicky Hopkins, and Jimmy Miller producing. But because of a mix-up between Jagger and Immediate Records over who was paying for the session, the recording lay dormant. (It was finally released in 1975 on the Springboard label compilation *Rod Stewart and the Faces*.)

Now Rod's band work as well as his bumpy record career were both inactive. So far, his journey across the 1960s rock 'n' roll terrain had given him valuable experience, a fine reputation as a promising, gutsy singer – and a load of frustration. Soon the band-hopping would have to stop. He needed promotion to the first division.

Something else concerned him. He would need to start writing his own songs. The artists who did so seemed in a different league. Performers who did not, in the main, compose, including the golden greats he had so admired, from Al Jolson through to Bobby Bland and Frank Sinatra, would never lose their appeal. But a hip new generation in both the USA and Britain was pointing up a new direction. From the States, with their own brilliant compositions, came Simon and Garfunkel, the Beach Boys, the Mamas and Papas and the Lovin' Spoonful, augmenting the folk music giants such as Bob Dylan and Peter, Paul and Mary. In Britain, as well as John Lennon and Paul McCartney and Mick Jagger and Keith Richards, a whole raft of self-written songs were in the charts by such acts as Ray Davies (in the Kinks), Graham Nash (in the Hollies), and Pete Townshend (in the Who).

First, though, Rod needed some heavyweight companions. Jeff Beck, the high-pedigree guitarist who had made a big impression in the Yardbirds where he

followed Eric Clapton, met Rod and asked him to join
an all-star line-up he was assembling. A dazzling guitarist, Beck chose his front-line men with skill. He
recruited Ronnie Wood, who, after his apprenticeship
with the Birds and a band called Creation, hugely popular in Europe, became Beck's second guitarist. Here was
born the lifelong kinship of Stewart and Wood. With
such substantial talent, Beck led a world-beating group
which seemed unstoppable on its way to the top.

The band got off to a poor start, however. They
were under-rehearsed for their début concert, where
they opened the show on a package tour starring Roy
Orbison and the Small Faces on 3 March, 1967. Reviewing the concert in the *Melody Maker*, Chris Welch
wrote: 'The group were obviously un-rehearsed and in
the first house on the opening night, Jeff walked off
stage when the power failed. Rod Stewart attempted to
salvage what remained of the act. In the second house
they played badly and created a very poor impression.'

That was an understatement. Rod later recalled
that he felt awful soon after taking the stage because he
had looked down to discover that, 'I hadn't done my
flies up.' The electricity had been pulled after just one
song and the curtain came down, almost knocking Ronnie Wood to the floor. 'I caught him; he knocked into
me and sort of did a dance off stage,' Rod said.

Later, he reflected that the keyboards player in the
Small Faces, Ian MacLagan, might have 'pulled the plug'
because he feared that the Beck group was going to steal
the show from them.

The band had been formed too hastily for such a
major slot on a tour. Only a week after Beck's call to
Stewart and one rehearsal, they were on that stage. As
they pulled out of the tour immediately, Rod declared:
'We shouldn't have gone on the tour without enough
rehearsal. We didn't have enough numbers. It was a
real let-down … But we will carry on and do club

appearances.' He added that a new drummer was joining them: Mickey Waller, an old friend from Steam
Packet.

Now the Beck band began how it should have
done from its inception, touring the clubs and ball-
rooms of Britain like any other new line-up. Right from
the start, there was a rivalry problem between Beck and
Stewart. Rod as the singer got the acclaim and recognition after a good show. Audiences would go up to him
and slap him on the back, saying: 'Great show, Jeff!'
Beck, whose band it was, fumed.

• • •

Over in the Rolling Stones camp, their co-manager
Andrew Loog Oldham, with his new record label, Immediate, had heard from his friend Long John Baldry, that
Stewart was free of a record label. Soon, Rod was visiting
the offices of Immediate in New Oxford Street, where
Mick Jagger often dropped in and expressed his wish to
produce records. According to one observer, an episode
followed that showed conclusively that Stewart was on a
certain path to superstardom.

Tony Calder, Andrew Oldham's partner, says: 'I
remember Rod coming into my office and feeling: This
guy's *got it!* I actually saw a star in front of me. I got
that feeling at the nape of the neck that says: "This is
going to be a big name." Andrew and I loved him. But
Mick was very jealous. He said (when Stewart had left
the room), "You like him, don't you?" And Andrew
and I replied: "Of course we do. He's going to be a
superstar." I wanted him badly on Immediate.'

According to Calder, Jagger agreed to produce
Rod's début single for Immediate. But as the time
neared, he pulled out. 'Mick threw a tantrum, said he
was not going into the studio. He was jealous. I said:
"Make your mind up." He won't admit it now but it

was obvious he could see that here was Rod, looking pretty and younger ...' Stewart was, implies Calder, a threat to Jagger. Although Rod might not have been such an acrobatic singer at that stage, he'd paid creditable dues with Long John Baldry, whom everyone respected. 'Mick went in to produce and he never finished it,' Calder states.

At the time, two ambitious young tigers like Stewart and Jagger were understandably eyeing each other. But in reality, as Rod later pointed out, there was a wealth of difference. 'I think Mick is more of a showman than I am. And I'm more of a singer than he is. That's not a put-down of either of us,' he told *Rolling Stone* magazine. 'I don't sit in front of a mirror and work anything out. [My stage show] just develops and if people like something I leave it in. Jolson, my hero, used to jump up on the piano. Everybody's been doing it, jumping up on pianos, sliding across the stage.' But, Rod said, he had never seen anybody actually slide across the stage in the style he did.

Tired of Decca, which housed the Rolling Stones, Oldham and Calder were seeking to build with Immediate a new creative environment for songwriters, record producers, and artists. Among their signings was Michael d'Abo, the ambitious young singer with the group Manfred Mann, who were on the crest of a wave with such hit singles as '5-4-3-2-1', 'Pretty Flamingo' (on which the singer was Paul Jones) and 'The Mighty Quinn'. A pensive songwriter, d'Abo also had a career outside his band and was appearing as Gulliver in *Gulliver's Travels* at London's Mermaid Theatre when Oldham and Calder advised him to stretch into record production. They said they had seen this exceptional singer with the Jeff Beck band, named Rod Stewart, and asked d'Abo to go and see him at a London club.

'They had given me the names of two other singers they wanted me to work with,' d'Abo recalls.

'One was Cat Stevens, the other Chris Farlowe. I'd never actually heard of Rod Stewart before they mentioned him to me.'

After being 'very impressed' with his club appearance, d'Abo invited Stewart to his home in Albion Street, near Marble Arch. 'He'd arrive with alarming regularity with his guitar under his arm; I had no idea that he played harmonica or that he had a love for Sam Cooke and we got on extremely well.' D'Abo, who was a notch further ahead than Stewart since his band had made hits, sensed that 'Rod was latching on to me because I had made it ... not to the degree he would later, but I was into production and played piano and he looked up to me in some way'. Musically, their rapport was strong: 'He was very into folk music, played me these Scottish folk songs and had almost a Tim Hardin quality. I thought: "This guy's great" ... but I wasn't hanging on his every word.' There was, d'Abo recollects, 'something of the troubadour about Rod; he was the sort of guy who could spend the night on anybody's couch. And he always seemed to be ringing his folks in Highgate from our house'.

A thoughtful songwriter, d'Abo had recently composed a song called 'Handbags and Gladrags', which had been earmarked for Chris Farlowe. When d'Abo played piano and sang it to Rod, he said he was 'mightily disappointed that the song was spoken for'. Frequently, when Rod arrived at the d'Abo house, he would ask Mike to sing and play it for him. 'That's the song I want,' Stewart told him, looking ahead to his début on the Immediate label.

Finally, Rod 'accepted with good grace' that Farlowe had prior claim on 'Handbags and Gladrags' as a single, and d'Abo persuaded him to record his new composition, 'Little Miss Understood'. Recording at Olympic studios in Barnes, this never completely worked, according to d'Abo. 'I liked Rod's natural voice but didn't think he necessarily made the best of the phrasing.' Two singers, Vicki Brown and Kay Garner, were used for the first session, but their sound was considered superfluous. The final version showcased 'Rod's great singing, and had the most extraordinary drum sound', says d'Abo the producer. 'But though it was a well-received record, it didn't cause too much of a stir.' A nondescript bluesy composition co-written by Stewart and d'Abo, 'So Much to Say', was put on the B-side. The record received little radio play, and, as Rod recalled eventually, it was 'back to the drawing-board' for his record career. Recalling 'Little Miss Understood', Rod said later: 'I came very near to selling out when I released that … Mike's a great guy but he would try and tell me how to sing.'

Although the single did not hit, the European picture sleeve, with Rod's name emblazoned across the top and a portrait showing him moodily catching the atmosphere of the day, increased his profile. Back at Highgate, his family eagerly awaited his breakthrough, though the early signs on the record front did not look promising.

• • •

In the 1967 flower-power 'Summer of Love', the Jeff Beck band looked a safe bet for outstanding success. The musicians were formidable and as they smoothed their act around the country Rod's guitar and Beck's guitar intertwined perfectly – 'like a glove, we really used to have it tight,' Rod said of their chemistry.

In May, just as the Beatles were releasing the milestone album *Sgt Pepper's Lonely Hearts Club Band*, Rod went into the studios with the Beck band to record the album that would become *Truth*. By the time it was released, the Beck band had begun an American tour. Jittery with nerves at the prospect of performing in the home of his beloved music, Rod later admitted losing his voice on one occasion as the band performed at major venues such as the Fillmores in New York and San Francisco and the Shrine, Los Angeles. 'I suffered from the most frightening experience ... the voice just went,' Rod admitted. 'It was stage fright, I suppose. I just went to open my mouth on "Ain't Superstitious", and nothing came out.'

By now, he and Ron Wood, who had become 'Woody' to Rod, were carrying around a small bottle of brandy in case of a crisis. He went behind the stage curtain to have a quick swig. Beck covered for him, mouthing the words to the songs. 'They must have thought I was a ventriloquist,' Beck smiled later. Mightily embarrassed, Rod reappeared 'after the brandy hit the bloodstream. Sure enough, back came the vocals'.

Writing in the *New York Times* of the band's appearance at Fillmore East on 14 June, 1967, Robert Shelton noted: 'The group's principal format is in the interaction of Mr Beck's wild and visionary guitar against the hoarse and insistent shouting of Rod Stewart. Their dialogues were lean and laconic, the verbal Ping-Pong of a musical Pinter play.' In an enthusiastic review, Shelton declared that the new British group had upstaged the Grateful Dead, an amazing achievement. Reporting to London's *New Musical Express* from Manhattan, June Harris sounded breathless, incredulous at the 'standing ovation he received in the *middle* of their performance'. America had never seen a team like Beck and Stewart. 'The only possible description of their twofold dynamite would be to suggest it's like watching the brilliance of Jim Morrison teamed with Eric Clapton.'

As a European tour was followed by another successful tour of the USA in the autumn, disenchantment with Beck set in for Rod. Despite Beck's technical ability, the two men were incompatible. Gregarious and cheery, enjoying the touring and the access to girls on the road, Rod was an upbeat personality. Beck was more introverted, often sullen and moody. For the bandleader and the singer to avoid each other off stage and barely look at each other in the dressing-room area pointed to inevitable trouble on the horizon.

● ● ●

In the mid 1960s, rock musicians with charisma and ability were beginning careers that would stretch well into three future decades. The Jeff Beck Group was managed by Peter Grant, who was also in charge of a plan by Jimmy Page to launch the band that became Led Zeppelin. Travelling around the USA, watching the Beck band, Page would occasionally jam. Observers would later allege that he orchestrated his musical policy for Zeppelin – the biggest band in the 1970s – after studying the sound and texture of the Beck band, and noting the strength of audience responses.

By the time the Jeff Beck Group began its second US tour in Chicago on 11 October, 1968, it was in an immensely powerful position. The impact of the new, thoughtful, self-composing artists had established albums as more important than transient hit singles. That was a perfect vehicle for such a musicianly band as Beck's. And the influential band called Cream was splitting up at that time. This trio of Eric Clapton, Jack Bruce and Ginger Baker had pioneered a new fusion of rock and jazz, whetting the public appetite around the world for brilliant instrumental work allied to a host of imaginative songwriting. Cream's final concert at London's Royal Albert Hall in November 1968 left a huge hole among connoisseurs of the 'new rock'. 'But Jeff Beck seemed reluctant to go for it, as he certainly should have done,' commented Nicky Hopkins, who became keyboards player in the Beck band in January 1968.*

---

* Hopkins died in Nashville on 6 September, 1994, from a stomach disorder. He was 50.

Hopkins was no stranger to Beck, who had hired him months earlier as a studio session player on the *Truth* album. This had by then sold a quarter of a million copies in the US. Beck was hot. Tiring of session work, Hopkins was looking for a band job when Beck invited him in.

Hopkins naturally believed he was going into a band on the crest of a giant wave. 'Rod was the apparent leader of the band, the guy up front swinging the microphone,' Hopkins remembered of that US tour. 'Beck was a wonderful guitar player who kept himself to himself in a strange way. But there was absolutely no hanging out together as a band.' He wasn't aloof in a supercilious way, 'but gave the impression of wanting to be back in England working on his cars, which fascinated him'.

Musically the band was unbeatable, Hopkins continued. 'Rod believed he was on a winning groove. At the Boston Tea Party [almost an American version of London's Marquee], the recording manager from Epic went straight up to Rod afterwards ...' Hopkins overheard him say: 'Nice show, Jeff.'

The seeds of Rod's discontent stretched even beyond his difficulties with Beck as a person – although he always emphasized his admiration for his guitar work. The mightily successful album *Truth* had scarcely recognized him in the credits, and since his popularity had soared in the States on their tours, Rod was miffed. There was, too, a simmering problem over money: both Stewart and Wood believed they were being under-rewarded considering their contribution. Nor did Rod like the superiority fostered by the accommodation arrangements on the road. Beck had a suite at the Hilton Hotel in New York while Rod and Woody shared a room at the less salubrious Gorham.

Members of the band, who noted Rod preening and combing his hair in any mirror he saw, in dressing-rooms and cafés, formed the view that he would not be able to stand Beck's method of downgrading him. He was going to be a star, and nobody was going to be allowed to deflate him.

'I remember how brought down Rod was that this band was going to break up,' Nicky Hopkins reflected. '*Beck Ola*, the follow-up album to *Truth*, had some great stuff on it, but there was a note of apology on the sleeve to the effect that in these days of heavy music, it was hard to come up with anything original ... "so we haven't". What a way to kill an album!' In fact, the album reached number fifteen in the US chart and thirty-nine in Britain. But by the time it did so, the musically superb Jeff Beck Group had split.

The end began when Beck fired first Ronnie Wood and then Mickey Waller. To Rod, the dismissal of his best mate Wood, who was a gifted player even then, was virtually an act of treason. Ronnie was briefly re-hired for some US dates, but the atmosphere within the band was at an all-time low, despite the arrival of a strong drummer, Tony Newman from Sounds Incorporated.

Communication problems, financial arguments and other factors finally sealed the band's fate. 'I had been the first to leave,' Nicky Hopkins said. 'Rod was sad because he seemed to realize that here was a band that really could go the distance. But it was on a path to self-destruction.'

Beck was 'very jealous of Woody and me', Stewart said later. 'We had a sense of humour unto ourselves. And we never let anybody join in with us. Especially Beck. It got to him after a while. I think that because he couldn't sing, he thought to himself: I can't do without Rod, so I'll fire Ron Wood. So he did. It was most unfortunate because Woody was a real good bass player and the mainstay of the band.'

After two years of commercial triumph but

personal unhappiness Rod quit the Beck band in July 1969. As he did so, Frank Sinatra was enjoying a hit with 'My Way', the Beatles were nearing the end of their unity and singing 'Get Back', the Who were singing about a 'Pinball Wizard' to launch their rock opera *Tommy*.

Rod looked back on the Beck experience with some affection and gratitude for how it enriched his music: 'The old ego ran away with Jeff. He was never really a bastard to me. But it was down to the pay. We never earned a great deal. But I was happy enough with the music. I learned so much with that band because it was there that my voice started to change. I learned phrasing, how to blend with three or four instruments. And that rhythm section of Ronnie Wood and Mickey Waller was just incredible.'

As a new decade loomed, Rod's bruising experiences in bands had to end. At twenty-four, he was a highly distinctive singer in need of an anchor. Though he was only an adequate guitarist, he had begun to refine something that nobody else in rock would ever be able to copy – a voice that would be instantly recognizable.

His old mate Ronnie Wood pointed the way. Licking his wounds from the Beck saga, he joined the bright and hip Mod group from the East End of London called the Small Faces. Wood succeeded Steve Marriot. This was a most peculiar gap to fill, Wood told Stewart, because he was a bass guitarist while the departing Marriott was a singer. What on earth would the Small Faces do without a vocalist?

Four   Into the Faces

'SUDDENLY, HE EMERGED AS A PERFORMER IN HIS OWN RIGHT. BEFORE HE LOOKED VERY YOUNG, A KID ON STAGE'
                    – Martin Wyatt, Rod's former record company boss

With the dawn of the 1970s came profound change in contemporary music. Pop singles by acts like Stevie Wonder and Tom Jones were still selling a quarter of a million copies in Britain alone. But gradually, a new word was born to describe the music of the growing number of album-orientated bands. It was called *rock*.

Led Zeppelin, Jethro Tull, Pink Floyd and Ten Years After were among the pathfinders. Emulating them in style were hundreds of lesser bands who took their *music* very seriously. Some made albums they claimed were significant or important. But they weren't much fun to watch.

There was a gap – a need for a lively, unpretentious, good-time rock 'n' roll band that swung without any inhibitions on to a stage and spread exuberance. The Faces were perfectly formed for their time. Rod always believed that presentation was very important in a rock 'n' roll setting. The philosophy of his next band at last placed him aboard a rocket *en route* for the stratosphere.

• • •

The Small Faces embodied psychedelia spliced with the Mod look. The band now joined by Ronnie Wood comprised Ian MacLagan on keyboards and Kenney Jones on drums. 'Everyone's frightened to sing!' Woody told Rod one night in the autumn of 1969. 'Come and have a listen!'

Rod went to the band's rehearsal, and as he stood at the top of the stairs before joining them he heard music without vocals. Descending, he said to Woody, 'This *is* a great band.' Kenney Jones asked, 'Why don't you join us?' It was an offer Rod could hardly refuse. After the débâcle of Beck, he would be realigned in a promising situation with his best mate.

'What they were looking for was a singer,' Rod noted. 'They kept thinking it would be all right. But all they had was some excellent backing tracks with no real leading force, nothing to work around. All groups need an identity and that identity usually stems from the lead singer. I'm not a great singer,' he told British music critic Penny Valentine in 1970, 'but I think I have an identity of my own, vocally. A group needs a sound that is instantly recognizable.

'Mick Jagger isn't a great singer but you know from his voice that you're listening to a Stones record. Dylan isn't great vocally but he's Dylan and you know straight away.'

Ian MacLagan explained the apprehension of the other Faces about inviting Rod and Woody in. In words that now seem totally prophetic about what actually happened, Ian said at the time: 'We didn't want to get into the situation where he would be the front man and we would just end up playing behind him. We had gone through all that with Steve Marriott.' They had tried to do vocals themselves but discovered they were 'quite pathetic ... it was a case of having to get a singer'.

In reality, Stewart's arrival clinched it for the band. They were immensely lucky to attract a singer of his calibre. From his experience, particularly in the States on tour, Rod had acquired a swagger that the girls loved and men admired. The charisma of Stewart and Woody together at centre stage was to develop into one of the most glorious partnerships of 1970s rock in Britain and the USA.

There was an early hurdle to cross. They needed a manager. And whoever was to referee this strong-minded but spiritually co-operative unit would need to be a diplomat as well as a canny businessman. All the strongest relationships between rock stars and managers that developed successfully had been intense: Brian Epstein and the Beatles, Colonel Tom Parker with Elvis, Kit Lambert with the Who, Andrew Oldham with the Rolling Stones. An ingredient beyond mere business lifted these associations into high-energy symbiosis: the best manager was literally in the wings of the act. It was fundamentally his job to take care of business. The most imaginative of them also lived through their artist's soul to some degree.

The man who would help steer Rod Stewart to the top had perfect credentials. At twenty-two, Billy Gaff had been an economics student at Woolwich Polytechnic. Actively involved in booking bands for London's powerful Robert Stigwood Organization while he was still a student, Gaff had seen Rod during his stint with Long John Baldry and the Hoochie Coochie Men. 'The first time I ever met Rod was in the dressing-room at the Cooks Ferry Inn, Edmonton. Rod had burned his face bright red from a sunlamp,' Gaff recalls. Though there was no friendship between Stewart and Gaff during that year of 1964, Gaff admired his music. One of the thousands of college *aficionados* of the British soul scene, he was a regular at the Flamingo club in Wardour Street. Meeting Rod a few times when he left the stage, Gaff registered that he had a distinctive voice.

When he left college, Gaff was asked by Robert

Stigwood if he would look after a new band he was managing called Cream. The job offered was road manager. 'I said I wouldn't know what to do,' Gaff recalls. 'Robert Stigwood said: "Have you ever looked after children?"

'I said: "Yes, my sister's got three." Robert said: "Just think of it like that and you'll be fine."'

So began Gaff's immersion into the late-1960s maelstrom of British supergroups. His road management of Cream, a trio of great musicians with different temperaments, was to equip him well for the storms ahead with the Faces.

• • •

The epicentre for London's rock 'n' roll social life was the Speakeasy club in Margaret Street. As manager of a band called the Herd, featuring guitarist Peter Frampton, Billy Gaff visited the club regularly. In 1969 two major departures from existing bands provided Gaff with his big chance. Frampton quit the Herd and joined up with singer Steve Marriott from the Small Faces. Together, they would launch Humble Pie. This was one of the earliest of the proliferating 'supergroups', so named because they united existing stars from established bands.

'That left the Faces high and dry,' Gaff says. 'That night in the Speakeasy as we all talked about it, Ronnie Wood was there, saying he wanted to quit Jeff Beck. So the plan was for him to come and replace Marriott. 'I said: "Can I manage you?"' They agreed, but shortly afterwards called Gaff to say they were without a strong singer to fill the gap left by Marriott. 'Woody called Rod, who came over and joined the band. It was as simple as that.'

Their record company wanted them to go out as the Small Faces on the crest of their strong hit single in

1968, 'Itchykoo Park'. 'To do that without Steve Marriott was not on,' Gaff observes. 'But so that we didn't lose the commercial potential of the name, we all decided we should keep some of the name.' Hence the Faces were born.

After getting the Faces free from their Immediate Records contract, the first challenge for Gaff was to get them a new record deal. Gaff faced rebuffs from several record labels, including the Beatles' Apple and the Who's company, Track. They laughed away the band without the advantage of Steve Marriott as singer. And Rod Stewart, they implied, was a has-been. He had been around, making unsuccessful singles, for nearly six years!

The bridge to their future home, and to Stewart's career, was built by Ian Samwell, who had written 'Whatcha Gonna Do About It' for the Small Faces. As a supporter of the new band, he got Gaff a meeting with Ian Ralfini, then the British chief of Warner Brothers Records. 'I don't think Ian was terribly keen,' Gaff says. But his luck was in. Joe Smith, the American chief of the label, visiting London at that time, had a feeling for the combined talents of Stewart and Wood. He said to Gaff: 'I'll make this deal.'

Good fortune had smiled on the Faces on the record front, for they were part of the birth in Britain of the company Warner Reprise, which was anxious to acquire British talent. While they went on to the Warner label, the second British act signed, Fleetwood Mac, went on to Reprise. An advance payment of £30,000 for the Faces' début album was enough to give Rod money for a new car, a sporty Marcos Volvo.

'The band hung out at the office, knew everybody, and things were casual and great fun,' recalls Martin Wyatt, Warner's head of artists and repertoire in those years. Rod was not, he felt, the star of the band from the start: 'They were all very strong characters. Rod was the new boy whereas the other guys knew each other well. Billy Gaff did make a fuss of Rod; there was considerable cossetting. They all wrote songs, but the main problem that developed was in that very area, because Rod was a dominating writer.'

Travelling with them, Wyatt reflects: 'They were a very hard drinking band. Definitely not drugs, all booze. I'd get into trouble a few times for taking their various girlfriends to gigs. The girls used to ring me up and say: "Martin, are you going to Brighton?" and I'd say yes. About three of the girls would then cadge a lift in my car. When I got to the gig, the band would say: "F—g hell, Martin, what did you bring the women for?"'

'I love feminine girls,' Rod said around this time. 'Girls with long silky hair. It helps if they are nice and slim, too. I suppose that could be 'cos I'm a bit of a skinny guy myself. I'd look silly with someone too large! I like them to look as soft and romantic as possible.' He stressed that he preferred girls with opinions. 'I like my girlfriends to wear beautiful scents. Lovely smells really turn me on. I like a girl to be nice and chatty ... but not too noisy. She has to have lots of go in her because I like to shoot off out to nightclubs halfway through the night and have a good time.'

Describing himself as 'fussy', he said his kind of girl had to be good at domesticity, 'Like cooking. Although I like going out a lot I really enjoy a tasty, home-cooked meal.'

As the Faces became established as Britain's finest rock 'n' roll fun band, Rod became a prime asset. 'I think he saw the Faces as a chance to make a big name for himself. Suddenly, he had this confidence,' says Wyatt, who had seen him perform in Baldry's band and with Shotgun Express. 'Before, he had looked very young, a kid on stage. Suddenly, he emerged as a performer in his own right.' Right back in his earliest days on stage at the Marquee, Martin Wyatt had registered that Rod was definitely going to be a star. 'But quite where, I wasn't sure. A lot of his presence that we saw later developed because he was so confident behind that Faces line-up. Although there was a group co-operation situation, he was a leader,' Wyatt says.

Under the headline: 'Rod thinks the new Faces won't be Small', Penny Valentine wrote in *Disc and Music Echo* on 21 March, 1970: 'Stewart is a tall, thin man with a shock of hair cut like a pineapple. On stage his actions are a cross between Jagger and Mike d'Abo. He minces, struts, does all the right things at the right time. His voice is one of strangled anger. No fresh-faced newcomer to the music scene, he is now twenty-five and seems to have been around for ever. Because of his apprenticeship when his music was finding its feet, he has accumulated that rare musical commodity, money ... he dresses expensively.'

• • •

Even the Warner deal was not so easily secured as it appeared, because Rod by then had a solo deal with Mercury, an imprint of the Philips (later Phonogram) company. Towards the end of his association with Jeff Beck, Rod had been courted by a producer for Mercury Records. Lou Reizner, an American living in London, was part of a new breed of record producer: he breathed rock 'n' roll and knew, from the moment he set eyes on Stewart inside the Beck band, that he was going to be a star.

Reizner was under orders from his Chicago head-quarters to muscle into the British scene. With sour memories of his series of flop singles for Decca, Columbia and Immediate, Stewart jumped at the chance of actually making solo *albums*. He mused to Reizner how Decca had told him that his voice was 'far too rough', a criticism they also made of his image. Rod had told the stuffy people at Decca: 'That's how it is.' They accepted that, and let him go. 'I was heartbroken,' he says of their decision. Reizner was more into the spirit of the age, and Stewart became friendly with him.*

An example of Stewart's resourcefulness came when he was selecting material for the album. One night he arrived at the home of Mike d'Abo and told him he had secured a solo record deal, under the production of Reizner. This impressed d'Abo, since his friend Reizner had been the one who had encouraged the Manfred Mann group to release one of their hottest records, 'The Mighty Quinn', as a single.

'So now we can record "Handbags and Glad-rags",' enthused Stewart to d'Abo. 'It doesn't matter about Chris Farlowe's version,' he added, reminding the writer of his early disappointment.

Telling d'Abo he wanted him to play piano and arrange the track and others on his album, Rod was returning to a song he had always loved, and, in a style that marked his life professionally and personally, making sure that he finally got what he wanted.

'What struck me about him,' says d'Abo now, 'was the confidence and conviction whereby he could visualize what he wanted.' A recording date for the session was set at Lansdowne Studios in Notting Hill, with Ronnie Wood on bass, Mickey Waller on drums, and Ian MacLagan on organ with d'Abo on piano. Surprisingly, since this was his first album, Rod was determined to have woodwinds featured on 'Handbags and Gladrags'. 'At very short notice,' d'Abo recalls, 'Rod said: "Let's have some guys in with oboes and flutes."' As the song's arranger, d'Abo was also confronted with a key change: 'Rod had this very high voice; I was used to doing this song in the key of G and he wanted it raised to B flat.'

*Lou Reizner, a well-respected, inspirational producer for Rod, died in 1977, aged forty-four.

Energized by the idea of recording the song he must have considered predestined for him to sing, Rod asked for the session to take place quickly. D'Abo says: 'I had twenty-four hours in which to get an arrangement together and I booked three oboists, a couple of bassoon players and four flautists. I then had to work literally through the night with the arranger/copyist who was from classical music and had not worked in pop before. The big innovation was that in addition to my piano playing part – and Rod quite enjoyed my Floyd Cramerish country feel – there was a counter-melody going over it on woodwind.'

D'Abo finished scoring the arrangement with the copyist at four in the morning. Next morning, the classical musicians walked in to record the song ... and everyone was surprised at Stewart's physical technique of recording. Instead of sitting or standing in a booth, he walked around among the musicians with a hand-held microphone, virtually acting out the song to them. This idea was usually the preserve of artists far older, more experienced, than Rod, who was only twenty-five at the time. Rather than being cocooned in a corner booth, 'Rod liked to be part of the action, coercing the musicians, saying more of this and less of that,' Mike d'Abo says.

As much as he was slowly but surely taking that level of grip on his recording habits, immersing himself in the sound, Rod also stamped his own interpretations on the lyrics which had so attracted him. To the mild irritation of d'Abo, who as the song's writer was something of a purist, Rod changed around some of the words to suit his own nuances.

Instead of what d'Abo had written – 'Once I was a young man and I thought all I had to do was smile' – Rod decided to sing: 'Once I was a young man and all I thought I had to do was smile.'

And he changed 'The handbags and the gladrags

that your grandad had to sweat so you could buy' to 'The handbags and the gladrags that your poor old grandad had to sweat to buy'.

These small, subtle changes were of a kind which artists of the stature of Frank Sinatra might advance, but in the case of a young singer like Rod, it was quite adventurous, even daring.

In the hands of Rod Stewart, Mike d'Abo's song would go on to become one of the singer's most cherished stage performances in the 1990s, as well as one of his best-loved recordings. As well as the haunting melody, it was the potent message of the lyric that struck a chord with Rod.

'We were talking about a girl of about fifteen or sixteen who had got her eye on the main chance and was staying out late and missing school, and Rod loved singing songs about schoolgirls,' says Mike d'Abo. 'I was trying to say: you think you've got it all made, you're looking good, but I tell you, there's more to it than that and if you could only be aware of more lasting family values, or of your family, or of the values of generations before, well, don't lose touch with those, because they are really what will get you through life.' It was a writer's challenge to materialism early in life, and an appeal to a young girl to listen to 'inner voices'.

As a piece of rhyming poetry portraying real life, it was perfectly tailored for the essence of Rod, the emerging storyteller. It wrenched from him the trademark quality of passion that would make him stand out as a singer who always converted other people's quality work to his own heart.

In January 1970, a month before the release of his début solo album, Rod visited the US on a promotional tour for Mercury Records. Rod told the trade magazine *Billboard* that he was pleased Mercury allowed him to record with the Small Faces; his solo effort would, in turn, promote the band. It sounded charitable and idealistic at the time, but the reality was to be problematic.

Rod had been working in London studios to produce his first LP. Naïve though he was when he went into Morgan Studios at Willesden to cut it, he decided on a formula that worked well for him. The musicians, who included Mickey Waller, Ronnie Wood and Ian MacLagan, would arrive at a series of riffs to form the backing track of a song. Then, getting into the feel of the rhythm, Rod would write lyrics around their sounds. Many songwriters worked the opposite method, presenting lyrics to musicians, but Rod preferred the sound to generate a mood first. This unorthodox approach worked. With some self-written songs about his beatnik years, and featuring songs of romantic *angst* like 'Cindy's Lament' and 'I Wouldn't Ever Change a Thing', the album was a début of astonishing strength.

Including also the Jagger–Richards song 'Street Fighting Man' and the folky 'Dirty Old Town' from his earliest musical inspiration, Rod's début collection was eclectically powerful. Called *The Rod Stewart Album* in America, *Old Raincoat* failed to chart in Britain but sold respectably in the USA, where Rod's name was strong from his Beck days. He was on his way.

While Rod made an impact with two aces – introspective, plaintive songs which were perfect for his highly personal voice – the Faces began their recording career ignominiously. *First Step* was an album that lacked any identity; it sounded as if they were in rehearsal at the South London warehouse where they got together to plan their concerts. A single, 'Flying', backed by 'Three Button Hand Me Down' (another Stewart evergreen of the future) got them on to *Top of the Pops*. But it did not reach the chart. For a band of this status to get the break of appearing on *Top of the Pops* (which then attracted around 17 million viewers every Thursday) and not chart was a flop indeed. Even an average single should have hit the lower reaches with that level of exposure.

• • •

University campuses were the lifeblood of rock in the early 1970s. Bands that would prosper into the 1990s enjoyed a vibrant university circuit that offered little money but a valuable training ground.

In the Midlands, at such gigs as Leicester University or Trent Polytechnic, or Nottingham's Boat Club, the local sales representative for Mercury was Tony Powell. He was at the centre of an extraordinary record company ping-pong game: his job was to promote Stewart albums, which in turn generated free promotion for the Faces records on the rival Warner Brothers label. Based in Nottingham, Powell was an early supporter of both Rod and the Faces, but his job as the man from Mercury was firmly to promote sales of Rod's albums: his requests to his London HQ for promotional material for Stewart albums were considered bizarre. They were more used to sales representatives wanting back-up to promote 'safe' middle-ground singers like Nana Mouskouri.

'It was the joviality factor that endeared the Faces to the student crowds,' Powell recalls. But something fascinating was happening: Rod, with his more personalized work on his solo records, seemed to pull in a slightly more thoughtful music fan. So the act had a two-pronged hold over audiences at a time of considerable rock development. And Rod was actually promoting the Faces 'by the back door'.

The situation brought mirth from Stewart towards the Faces in their dressing-room. 'Oh well, *my* record man's here tonight ... where's yours?' he would tease the band. As his friendship developed with the enthusiastic

Tony Powell, Rod also enjoyed the record man's expense account. 'Rod always seemed to think that people from record companies had a bottomless pit of money. Rod always had that reputation of not putting his hand in his pocket! So it was always: "Oh, OK, somebody from the record company's here tonight ... good, we can go down the pub (or the restaurant); he's buying!"' Powell's listed expenses seemed to be dominated by the name Rod Stewart. 'He'd really latched on to something very interesting ... that this man from the record company, who was desperately trying to keep everything smooth, could pay for everything.'

Although Stewart was to develop into a tremendous catch for the Mercury label, the label's strategy with his first two albums seems, in retrospect, strangely sluggish. *The Rod Stewart Album* (as it was called in America – it was later *An Old Raincoat Will Never Let You Down* in Britain) and its follow-up, *Gasoline Alley*, were impressive débuts. But they were released initially only in the USA.

At first, Rod was not concerned about this. But gradually, as fans told him they had been buying import copies, he began to wonder. He and Billy Gaff applied pressure on Philips, who had assigned him to Mercury, to present his records to the British public. To placate him they established a new label, Vertigo, to launch Rod. With the Warner situation Stewart found himself embroiled in record company politics, but it worked beautifully to his advantage. 'Billy Gaff traded Warner off against Mercury and that was good business,' Tony Powell says. 'Rod quite rightly went along with Billy's game.'

Striking a rapport with Stewart, Powell was moved from Nottingham to work in the London office as artists' liaison manager. He recalls visiting Rod at a recording studio to tell him the news of his arrival south. Rod's reaction was: 'Good, you can buy the drinks, then.'

Rod's partnership with the Faces was to prove an enjoyable romp for all five of them, and would thrill millions in the five years ahead. But the utterly different flavours of his solo outing and the Faces on record pointed up entirely different outlooks towards making music.

Rod was from the beginning a thoughtful singer-songwriter and, evidently, an able producer of his own work. The Faces, from the moment they took the stage on their first American tour in the spring of 1970, were an exciting live band, darlings of the critics who were anxious to debunk pomposity in rock.

American audiences reserved a special affection in 1970 for British rock, and the Faces were in a position to exploit this. The stamp of Stewart's name gave them an enormous advantage as they traversed the States from San Francisco to New York. For four months on two tours that year, the Faces blitzed the biggest cities in the USA with their joyful rock 'n' roll.

Always a confident performer, Rod developed his unique, acrobatic microphone technique during these arduous tours. His height and athleticism meant he always looked striking – but the clincher came from his aggressive stomping around the stage, mike diagonal across his body, often amusingly like a whirling dervish. Clothes always hung well on him, even casually. Some singers pouted – Rod never did, but he oozed raunchy sex appeal to the girls who formed his core audience. Importantly, men didn't feel excluded, for this was a tough-sounding band intent on generating a smiling night out for its crowds. The key to it all was simple: Stewart, Wood, Jones, Lane and MacLagan had been around the track several times and, faced with a golden chance, they were simply not going to blow it.

By the time they had begun their second trek around the States, Rod had released his second solo album. One album in February and another in September would leave rock artists of the future stunned by such speed, but the 1970s were like that. And Rod seemed in a hurry. *Gasoline Alley*, a title drawn from a conversation with an American girl who named it as a location to be avoided, was a lament about going home, an experience Rod had keenly felt when he returned from the 'vagrancy' charge in Spain in his teens.

Again, the album contrasted handsomely with the punch of the Faces' work. Mixing his own compositions (Woody wrote the melody and Rod the lyric for the title song) with old favourites like Eddie Cochran's 'Cut Across Shorty' and Dylan's 'Only a Hobo', Rod again exhibited a mature taste in selecting good compositions. Highlights of *Gasoline Alley* were Bobby and Shirley Womack's 'It's All Over Now'; 'Lady Day', about a girl I fell in love with a long time ago and she didn't want to know me'; and 'Jo's Lament', 'about a girl I put in a family way'.

'Once I know how the vocals are going to go, I have a good idea of how all the instruments should be played,' Rod said when he tried to explain his record production technique. 'I have an idea for the sound and the lilt of the song. There's no hidden mystery in it. It's just feel. I was gifted with the feel of music. I've got no knowledge of music, or studios, whatsoever. I can just about tune a guitar. I can feel it here [pointing to his head] and I can sing the song as it should sound.'

And so were born the two aspects of Rod's extra-ordinary appeal. While the Faces was a band that pulled in young women as well as men, his albums had a firm masculine tinge. Often emphasizing his working-class ethic and his years as a drifter, they were often full of self-examining remorse about his relationships with women. Even at twenty-five, still playing the field – particularly on the road on the American tours – Rod seemed to be forecasting in song the magic carpet ride of the love life that awaited him. His lyrics were easily identified by any man who knew about turbulent romances.

His most soul-searching songs about women and love were yet to come, of course. As the Faces sped around the States, Stewart was the intense womanizer he had always been, but now with greater opportunities as they swarmed at his feet and in the hotel lobbies after the shows.

Touring the States at that time were dozens of British bands who developed a fearsome reputation for wrecking hotel rooms. Born of boredom and the need for bogus 'excitement' after the 'high' of a performance, the hotel-trashing syndrome was at its worst in the hands of some of the 'heavy metal' bands of the period. The Faces were not exempt from trouble-making, stampeding into the rooms of their management and crew to cause havoc.

And they drank. Before, during and after a show. Rod recalls that the 'tanking up' for which the Faces became famous had begun quite innocently. It calmed their intense nervousness, their fear, because so much had seemed at stake in their earliest days. They seemed to drink more in Britain than in the States. A bottle of beer in hand, the Faces created the atmosphere of 'football terrace rock 'n' roll'. Many who saw them in those years testify that they would be drinking hard in the pub before the concert began. It could have been because the contrast from playing to crowds of nearly 20,000 at the giant arenas like the Spectrum, Philadelphia, followed by venues such as the Greyhound, Croydon, was difficult to come to terms with. Strangely, the image of good-natured boozers on a great night out served the Faces beautifully. It was a trademark no other band could copy successfully, for a very good reason. Drunk or not, the music stayed intact.

• • •

'There was never any chance of Rod getting into debt,' says the Faces' manager Billy Gaff. 'He spent what he earned and was always interested in acquiring assets, particularly property.' Rod's enthusiasm for money was always remarked on by his colleagues: Mickey Waller remembered that in the Steam Packet days, wherever in Britain the band was, Rod insisted on the Friday pay packet being sent up from the management in London. 'And he'd go to the nearest bank and pay it in straight away,' Waller says.

Appropriately, Rod stayed in North London when he bought his first home of his own with the advance money for his record royalties for his solo albums. This Colonial-style house was in Ellington Road, Muswell Hill, near his family. The Faces used it as a rendezvous and were sometimes to be seen and heard strumming their guitars on the balcony.

With a musician's respect for the way Rod had marshalled his career since the demise of Steam Packet and the departure from Jeff Beck, Mickey Waller always stayed in touch with him. Waller was now playing with a blues band called Steamhammer, but was not surprised to hear that with the combination of sex appeal and stagecraft, Rod and the Faces had taken America by storm. Rod always rated Waller's work as a drummer and kept him for his studio work.

In one phone conversation, Stewart asked Waller if he knew of any good musicians who might give a kick to the third solo album he was making. Waller promptly suggested that Rod should see Steamhammer at the 100 Club, Oxford Street, London. The night Rod walked with Waller down the steps of that famous former jazz club provided the axis from which his lively career would take off.

Playing in Steamhammer were two guitarists who caught Rod's attention. Martin Pugh was the lead player whose lyrical edge intrigued Rod. The classically trained

Martin Quittenton, together with Pugh, played acoustic
guitar on Rod's first two albums and was to figure on all
Rod's solo outings on the Mercury label. His contribution to Rod's career would, however, stand with the
evolution of Rod's third solo collection.

When Rod invited Quittenton to his new home
for a working trip, to stay overnight, they pursued
Rod's established formula of looking for melodies to
which he would later add lyrics. Quittenton did not
think in terms of huge popular hits, but he unwittingly
stumbled on an excellent tune. Later, when he had left,
Rod phoned him, saying he believed he had written
some good words for it. But it was just another song to
them both. It was called 'Maggie May'. (Later Rod
revealed that his lyrics were about an experience he had
had with a woman when he was eighteen and she was
thirty-eight. Hence the line in the song about the morning sun catching her face and showing her age.)

Even after it had been recorded, for the album that
was to become *Every Picture Tells a Story*, nobody registered that it would be a smash. Rod and Quittenton
had constructed it with their subconscious musical
thoughts reflecting on Bob Dylan's hallmark album,
Blonde on Blonde. It was a song they virtually 'knocked
off' in workmanlike fashion; neither thought much
about it as the sessions for the album proceeded. 'When
you're involved in something,' Quittenton points out,
'it's hard to stand back from it.'

At the time, it might have seemed average. With
hindsight, it was a spectacular breakthrough for a career
that was now steaming ahead. Rod had imaginatively
planted a mandolin solo into the arrangement, and to a
simple but insistent melody written by Martin Quittenton he gave yet another story of a tortuous entangle-
ment, his distinct vocal full of despairing melancholy.
On the album, it jostled with Rod's perfect choice of
other people's songs to augment his own: Dylan's

poignant and little-known 'Tomorrow is a Long Time', Rod's own beautifully haunting 'Mandolin Wind', and the majestic Tim Hardin composition 'Reason to Believe', which so many artists were 'covering' at that time.

This last track was coupled with 'Maggie May' as the single from the album. 'Reason to Believe' was chosen as the A-side, particularly by the record company, who said they knew a potential hit when they heard one. And nobody thought any more about it.

'We recorded it in two takes at Morgan Studios, in Willesden,' remembers drummer Mickey Waller. 'Just the three of us, Martin, Rod, me. We used to record very quickly. Rod wrote the lyrics to Martin's chord sequence overnight. He used to sing along with us on the backing track and then go in at a later date to put his vocals down. And he didn't like anybody in the studio when he was doing his final vocals.'

When the single arrived at the radio stations, disc jockeys took an immediate shine to 'Maggie May'. They had, after all, been playing the definitive version of 'Reason to Believe' by Hardin, the song's creator. Here was Rod Stewart on his most commercial single to date … and someone had blundered by consigning it to the B-side. 'It wasn't even going to go on the album,' Rod said later. 'Everybody said to me: "It hasn't got a chorus, it hasn't got a hook line." I told them: "Don't worry about things like that. It's a nice song. It tells a nice story."

'Some enterprising disc jockey in Milwaukee or Chicago turned it over when it went out as the B-side of 'Reason to Believe' – and there lay the fate of it. If he hadn't done that, it would have gone down the toilet even further.' That disc jockey was followed by radio people all round the world, and Rod was launched.

By 9 October, 1971, Rod had secured his place in the history of pop music. The single and album occupied the top position in both the British and American singles and albums chart the same week. In the albums chart, he held off such multi-million-selling classics as Simon and Garfunkel's *Bridge Over Troubled Water*, Carole King's *Tapestry*, and the Moody Blues' *Every Good Boy Deserves Favour*.

In Britain, the single and album held the top position in their respective chart sections for six weeks. 'Maggie May' was finally deposed by Slade's 'Coz I Love You'. 'The single is a freak,' said Rod, delighted but rather perplexed by its runaway performance. 'It must have been a one-in-a-million chance. I still cannot see how it is such a big hit. It has no melody! It has plenty of character and some nice chords, but there's no melody to it.' The album, however, was described by him as 'having a permanence, lasting value', because the songs would bear examination.

In both Britain and America, the album was finally shifted from the top slot by John Lennon's *Imagine* album (which ironically, featured an old colleague of Rod's, Nicky Hopkins, on keyboards). But *Every Picture Tells A Story* had an extraordinary run at the top of the albums chart, not relinquishing its dominance until 11 December.

That would have been a stunning achievement enough, but Rod's awards were piling in as gold discs were being pressed for him and all the musicians who played on his records. That month, Rod won the Top British Male Singer section in the *Melody Maker* Readers' Poll. Robert Plant was in second place, followed by Roger Chapman and Elton John; Mick Jagger was sixth. Describing Rod's win as 'a just reward after so many years slogging in the business', the paper noted that Rod had also secured fourth place in the international division, which was topped by Neil Young.

Interviewed about his winning groove, Rod struck a note of modesty and loyalty to the Faces. 'In the past year and a half I've started doing things off my own bat instead of relying on other people to tell me what to sing. It's worked out OK and I've got a lot more confidence. But doing that first album was a big plunge.' He said that Stewart the Album Maker was no less important than being in the Faces. The Faces were immensely popular as a live act, from working hard across America. But somehow, that had yet to be converted to record.

'The Faces' two first albums, *First Step* and *Long Player*, haven't been wild sellers, particularly in Britain. So they've got Glyn Johns to produce the next one,' he said. His use of the word 'they', unconsciously distancing himself from his mates, was interesting. 'Mac, Ronnie and Kenney respect Glyn from the days when he cut *Ogden's Nut Gone Flake* album, artistically the best thing that the band did.'

Of Faces concerts, Rod said they had not set out to create a football atmosphere at their concerts. 'The audience created that. We didn't start it, honest. It was just a good-time band and there was no barrier between the stage and the crowd. They joined in with what we were doing from the first shows, which was having a good time.'

Modesty was one thing, reality another. Rod was fiercely disciplined, while the Faces, for all their bonhomie, were a ramshackle band that looked set to burn out. And he had contributed to that effect. The line had been drawn. It could not have been more sharply focused. Rod was an unstoppable solo star – and a millionaire with the album *Every Picture* – inside a band that still hadn't passed the ultimate test of making a good record.

Five   Fame and style

'PEOPLE SAY: ARE YOU WORTH ALL THAT
MONEY? I OFTEN ASK MYSELF. I TELL MYSELF
THAT NOBODY IS FORCED TO BUY MY RECORDS
OR SEE MY CONCERTS'

– Rod Stewart

Ronnie Wood addressed the situation perfectly:
'We never foresaw the Rod thing as being quite so big.
Everything was getting along great and then – bang! So
many people in the business can dangle carrots under
your nose but what they can't guarantee is who you're
going to live with, spend months on end with. Rod was
incredibly good about the whole thing. He swore blind
that the band is still his cup of tea.'

Others had visions of an inevitable rock 'n' roll
Armageddon. How could Stewart reconcile his clarity
of thought, his straight shoot for the top, with a band
that was now virtually consigned to being his backing
group, while its members had delusions to the contrary?
However superb they were on stage, the singer was a
shooting star. 'The Faces stifled Rod,' declares their
manager, Billy Gaff. 'He always wanted to be in show-
business. He wasn't able to do it because they would
say to him [when he displayed heavy theatricality]:
"Hey, man, that's poofter stuff!" He used to wear
ladies' knickers on stage. Rod was totally theatrical, a
showman. And a great one.' (He sometimes wore the
knickers, claimed an ex-girlfriend, to avoid a seam being

visible through his stage trousers.)

Rooted in rock 'n' roll lifestyle as well as music, Jones, MacLagan, Lane, and to a lesser degree Wood, must have believed the effect of Rod's success would lift the band along with it. But Gaff detected an atmosphere that would eventually make his job untenable.

Like many other bands of the period, the Faces sometimes lapsed into thinking they were providing high art rather than sheer pleasure. On the opening night of one tour of the USA, they informed Gaff they had decided not to perform any of their best-loved songs. In his words, they were 'seeking to prove something to the world, forgetting they were entertainers. I told them the kids would not know anything they were singing and would feel cheated. They would not listen. The show and audience response was appalling'. He lost his argument with them but next night they sang their hits. Rod had not been a party to the decision to ditch their hits. 'He never mixed politics with his art,' Gaff says. 'He loved his music and knew it had to *entertain* people.'

The Faces was therefore a highly political band to manage, says Gaff. 'Ronnie Wood was a pussycat, a nicer person you will not meet. Kenney Jones was nice too.' Less glowing in his observations of Ian MacLagan and Ronnie Lane, the band's ex-manager adds: 'I think they were terribly jealous of Rod's success with his solo records. He was huge in America when the Faces had hardly made a dent on the chart.'

Jealous is an understatement. Lane, Jones, MacLagan and, to a lesser degree, Wood, gave their manager 'strict instructions', as he describes them, not to allow Rod's name to be promoted over the name of the Faces in any advertising material or at the front of the concert halls. 'ROD STEWART AND THE FACES' was totally forbidden, and woe betide any promoter or agent (and Billy Gaff) who did not follow this Faces demand.

This led to amusing covert operations by everyone connected with Faces tours. Promoters and agents, knowing Rod's name on advance advertising would sell tickets, 'gave me hell', Gaff says. 'I knew perfectly well that behind the scenes they were advertising Rod Stewart and the Faces. But when the band hit town, they tried to camouflage that fact by changing the signs at the front of the theatre, to make sure Rod's name had been taken down. That was the length we had to go to keep everybody happy for all those Faces years.' Describing it as 'a horrible period', he cites one night at the Cobalt Hall, Detroit, when Rod's name had not been eliminated from the front-of-house. 'There it was, Rod's name in big print underneath the name of the Faces.' One of the band 'hit me over the head with a bottle'.

'The game was up early, as soon as Rod had those hits,' says the group's tour publicist, Peter Burton. 'When we arrived at a town to those marquee signs that said: ROD STEWART AND THE FACES, the band deeply resented it. They were relegated to being a backing band. Ronnie Wood was a charismatic performer and an awfully nice man, but there was at least somewhere for him to go. Ronnie Lane felt marginalized as a writer as much as anything else.' Wives and girlfriends added to the tension: 'There was a lot of power play and whispering jealousy around.'

Rod, too, remembered gliding into cities in limousines and seeing his name over the Faces. Checking into his hotel, he felt bound to call the promoter's office to ensure that his name was removed. This was an amazing gesture for any artist. Throughout the world, entertainers did precisely the reverse, complaining that their name either was not prominent or was too small. And here was Rod Stewart, superstar, loyally insisting on the opposite.

• • •

As the European awards poured in for Rod, to join the gold and platinum trophies from Britain and the USA, he had been in the Olympic Studios, Barnes, under the production baton of Glyn Johns. This would yield the third Faces album, *A Nod's as Good as a Wink to a Blind Horse*. Johns had an unbeatable pedigree as a rock producer. He had produced part of the Beatles' final album, *Let It Be*, before moving on to work with the Rolling Stones, the Who, Led Zeppelin and Eric Clapton. A former musician who had begun on the ground floor as a studio engineer in the early 1960s, he inherited the Faces' production role at a difficult time; when Marriott had quit for Humble Pie, he had produced for that new band. But he always respected the original Faces and wanted to see if the live appeal of the new line-up could be captured in the studio at last.

He walked into a unique situation, with the lead singer tearing away with a winning solo career. 'They were a fantastically exciting live band. But it became abundantly clear very early on that his solo success was where his real interests lay,' Johns says. The exhilaration and spontaneity of live performance was recaptured in the studio 'by the rhythm section, but as far as Rod Stewart was concerned, interestingly enough, not at all. Of all the vocalists I've ever worked with, he is the most calculating. He would record one line of a song at a time, and then re-do one word, if necessary. I know that's more common now but it was certainly not then, in my experience. I never heard him sing a song all the way through.'

It didn't take long for an unspoken tension to develop between Rod Stewart and Glyn Johns, who never considered Rod to be anything other than the band's vocalist. Technically, Rod was not the boss of the Faces, but by virtue of his towering popularity there simply had to be a chasm. 'I resented enormously his very cocky and egotistical attitude,' Johns says. 'Particularly in seeing himself as leader of the band. He was in a band of unbelievably fine musicians who had all had great success before they were involved with him. But he was constantly referring to how wonderful he was as a solo artist. Good luck to him with that; it was quite valid and I don't blame him. But the solo success didn't necessarily make him any more important in the band, as I saw it. I am pretty certain he did not care for my attitude and I made it very plain that I did not see him as as important as he believed.'

Nor did Rod commit the same amount of time to recording as the others, in Johns' view. 'I thought he was the singer in the band and he did an OK job. In my involvement with the Who, Roger Daltrey never adopted the attitude that he was more important than anybody else in the making of records. I thought the lyrics Rod Stewart wrote and the lyrics we recorded were abysmal on the whole. He was blessed with an extraordinary-sounding voice and used it pretty well. I don't think he contributed anything more or less than anyone else in the band. The combination of them all together was really good. I think Rod tended to forget who he was on stage with. I know Woody hadn't much to his credit until then, but the other lads had all been in enormously successful bands for years and were serious stars in their own right, much more so than Rod at the time, I believed.'

Whatever the friction between Stewart and Johns, the singer acknowledged that production flair was needed to give the Faces a blood transfusion in the studio. *A Nod's as Good as a Wink to a Blind Horse* had done the trick, tearing to number two in the British charts and to seventeen in America.

The clincher for the record was a hit single written by Rod with Ronnie Wood. 'Stay with Me' had a memorable hook which was a blatant message to groupies as well as an affirmation of Rod's sexual image as the singer. In the morning, he told the girl by his side, don't say you love me, because you know I'll only kick you out the door. Later in the song, he tells her that yes, he will pay her cab fare home and she can even use his cologne. He wanted her there to 'stay with me' for the night ... but he didn't want her there in the morning.

In the decade that shaped women's liberation, Stewart was at least facing up to his own peccadilloes. A curious mixture of chauvinism, frailty, and sensitivity in his approach to women, he had been across America as a member of the Faces at the time of the boom in the groupie industry. And here he was, in song, facing up to it with lyrics of disturbing honesty. Hitherto, his song-writing had tended towards introspection. Now came full frontal confrontation with relationships. In 1972, it was surprising – because despite his swashbuckling image as a womanizer, in his approach to women Rod was always coquettish.

Rod's relationship with the press has been bitter-sweet. According to Billy Gaff, his manager from 1970 to 1982, Rod 'loved the image' that the newspapers fostered, that of a playboy. 'Tony Toon [Rod's personal publicist] built that side of Rod up, and knew what the press wanted,' Gaff states. 'It was all done with Rod's OK. Tony wouldn't have lasted that long if Rod had not approved it all. I think he liked to see the women upset, crying over him!'

But a different view of Rod's relationship with the media comes from his former press aide, Peter Burton. 'Essentially, Rod is a very private and reticent man. What he has to express, as with many creative people, went into the songs, so doing press interviews was a crashing bore for him. Writers, painters and songwriters know that part of their creativity is doing publicity. Americans are ready with sound-bites. Ask one question and they are *away*! British performers seem to resent the intrusion on their privacy. Rod was one of those people who did not feel he had anything in particular to say beyond those songs.

'It was always difficult to get him to do much media work. I said at the start of one tour, by which time he was big: "What press are you going to be willing to do?" He replied, "Nothing, Pete. Unless you can get me the front cover of *Time* magazine." When *Time* magazine duly arrived at the Beverly Wilshire Hotel in Los Angeles to interview him, I was in New York. I got a call from a colleague saying Rod would not go downstairs. We had to tell *Time* magazine: "Awfully sorry, the artist is being temperamental." The magazine went away. He did eventually get *Time*, but a long time later. The press always wanted *Rod* during the Faces years but I tried to fend them off, saying he was tied up. I'd say: "Ronnie Wood would be happy to talk to you. Or Kenney Jones." But that was rather like the Beatles situation, where reporters were told Lennon and McCartney were unavailable, but George Harrison or Ringo Starr would be prepared to sit for an interview. It was not quite the same.'

While his reputation was for hell-raising, Rod stayed true to his North London values – or, as he preferred to interpret his origins, his Scottish ancestry. His father disliked the image of the boozing side of the Faces and told Rod he was embarrassed to see them on television 'looking like a bunch of layabouts'. Rock stars the world over have had to tolerate criticism from parents, 'but Rod really did always listen to his Dad', his brother Don affirms. 'Once Rod wore a shirt on stage with something obscene printed across it. Dad gave him a hell of a roasting. He dealt with him directly: "You can cut that lark out." Rod never wore it, or anything like it, again.' Whatever the size of his bank balance or his fame, Rod always showed humility towards his parents.

His father was a heavy smoker (which Rod detested), and Rod was a heavy drinker (which his father abhorred), but, as one family friend says: 'Rod adored him. He liked him because whatever happened to Rod, his father never changed his attitude to him. He was the young son, whether he was the beatnik bum or the millionaire singer.'*

Despite his well-known frugality – and Rod never made any bones about his enjoyment of money – he never had any problems about lashing out. When his money rolled in he wisely stashed it away in the Jersey bank accounts he had opened in the late 1960s. 'I know exactly how much money I have got and I'm not going to divulge it to anybody,' he declared at this time. Of the accounts in Jersey, a tax haven, he smiled. 'It just goes to show that I knew years ago that I would make some money one day.'

Before, during and after the Faces years, Rod had a reputation for parsimony. But the general view is of caution. 'I think he liked to play along with the mean image,' Billy Gaff says. 'I never thought he was that way. He wasn't mean, in my company, by any stretch of the imagination. Rod finds it difficult to buy you a drink, but he had no difficulty in paying royalties or commission.'

As the money came in, he bought his parents a new house in Woodley Road, Muswell Hill. He drove a Rolls-Royce. And his first serious girlfriend entered his life just as he switched homes from Muswell Hill to Winchmore Hill.

Her name was Dee Harrington. The twenty-one-year-old daughter of a squadron leader in the RAF, she had been in Los Angeles for four months on holiday when her friends took her along to a Faces promotional party at the expensive Hollywood club, Bumbles. Pert,

*A photograph signed by Rod occupies the prime spot on the mantelpiece at his mother's home in North London to this day. Rod has signed it, touchingly: 'All my love Mum and Dad from Rod (the youngest).'

leggy, blonde, a former model then working in London as assistant to a record boss, Dee was surprised to experience Rod being pawed by a load of girls at the party. She held back, and, towards the end of the evening, Rod somewhat shyly asked if she would like to dance.

She said yes. It was 29 July, 1971. Next night, she saw Rod with the Faces for the first time at Long Beach Arena, the first time she had encountered stadium rock. She found Rod witty and polite, full of jokes, and, perhaps surprisingly, quite serious when he was away from the rest of the band.

They were perfectly matched from the start, and Dee seemed precisely what Rod sought from his woman: striking, wholly feminine, with long flowing blonde hair, intelligently single-minded. Though she liked rock, her tastes in music were varied. On the afternoon before the first Faces show she attended, a limousine took her cruising with Rod along Sunset Boulevard, where they shopped. 'We got stuck at traffic lights and all these people were shouting: "See you tonight, Rod."' Stewart lapped it all up. 'That's what you strive for,' Dee observes from her vantage point today as a manager inside the music industry. 'You know those people are going to buy the concert tickets and the albums ... you know you've won.'

Dee was entering a potentially tense Stewart/Faces situation. With 'Maggie May' all over the radio in the States and *Every Picture Tells a Story* on release just as she met Rod, the vibrations that precipitated trouble were just beginning.

'It was pretty awful,' Dee remembered in an interview with John Gray. 'Rod couldn't stand all the messing around and standing still,' she says of the recording sessions, contradicting the views of producer Glyn Johns. 'He liked to go to work on time and make music rather than stay in the pub all night. I think he worked twice as hard as the others. For example, he wrote all

the lyrics. There was a tremendous amount of resent-
ment.' Even the Faces' wives were jealous: 'Woody
wasn't so bad. That's probably because he was more
involved with the solo albums, so financially and writ-
ing-wise he was better off. The rest didn't like it because
Rod was living in a big house, had more money and was
more recognized.' It upset Rod, Dee continued: 'They
made Rod feel bad for being good when they should
have been thanking him for the part he had played in
making them successful. There was added pressure in
that Rod had to write a Faces album a year plus a solo
album and also try to have some kind of life of his own.
I think he ended up working too hard. He was getting a
lot of grief.'

Two nights after that concert at Long Beach, Rod
and the Faces returned to Britain. Dee stayed in America for six weeks. When she returned to London, they
met for dinner and knew immediately that their liaison
in California had been no 'fling'. They felt good together. By then Rod had bought for £32,000 a four-bed-
roomed mock Tudor house in desirable Broad Walk,
Winchmore Hill, North London, and Dee moved in
with him to begin a four-year relationship. She soon
found herself ostracized by the Faces women. At home,
though, Rod and Dee were in perfect harmony. When
he composed songs and asked her opinion, he would be
petulant if she did not respond positively: 'He wouldn't
talk to me for two days! Then after a couple of days,
he'd say: "You're right, it's not that great."'

When his accountants told him that he should
invest in a more expensive property, the advice suited
Rod well. Star-spotters had discovered his home and
had begun to make life in Broad Walk difficult: there
was little security. What he needed was a more remote
property. In 1972 he and Dee moved into the splendid
Cranbourne Court at Winkfield Row near Windsor.
Bought for £89,000 from Lord Bethell, Lord-in-Waiting

to the Queen, and with thirty-six rooms and eight bathrooms, if offered the security from the outside world that stardom needed. Down the long drive were seventeen acres of gardens, a swimming-pool, stables, and a lodge. One wall at the Windsor mansion was covered with photographs of soccer star Denis Law, whom Rod described as 'my idol ... he sent me a Christmas card and a birthday card!' Rod had even met the great man.

With a horse and four bulls 'to keep the lawns trimmed', Rod joked, and three collie dogs for company, Rod enjoyed the spaciousness of his Windsor home, but it hardly changed his persona, probably because it had not come easily to him. Elton John was a neighbour and the two men met occasionally.

'The peaceful atmosphere is marvellous, just what I need after a tour,' Rod said at the time. 'I realize I've been lucky so I don't need to have it thrown in my face. Oh, yes, I get all that "Are you worth all that money?" routine and it's a question I often ask myself. Then I tell myself that nobody is forced to buy my records or see my concerts. I realize that a lot of guys can't do what I do.' Wealth used to worry him but 'I've grown out of it. It's no good tearing yourself to pieces. But I like to help people by being generous. I'll give a pound to a man selling matches'.

Visiting his new mansion for the first time, Rod's sister Mary was flabbergasted. Rod had driven her there in his Rolls-Royce, and as they entered the vast hallway, he lay spreadeagled on the floor, shouting with elation: 'It's mine, all mine!' Gradually, the whole Stewart clan came to inspect 'Roddy' in his new abode. His father was pleased to note that a tartan carpet had been placed in the snooker room; Roddy was 'enjoying his riches, and why not?' as his brother Bob observed. Immensely houseproud, Rod joined in the dusting and polishing of the extensive brasswork.

That year of 1972 was to be crucial in Rod's ascent. *Never a Dull Moment*, his fourth solo album, which would hurtle to the top in America, was not quite so strong on creativity as *Every Picture*. But Rod was proud of it: 'This album's much better than the last one: although I don't think there's anything as great as "Mandolin Wind".' His policy for the album was to make 'an album of singles'. But though it boasted his rapidly improving voice on such songs as 'Italian Girls', the album lacked the lyrical richness of his previous and future work. Since he was 'on a high' with the public, Rod had nothing to fear. It was a perfectly acceptable album. Once again his immaculate choice of other people's songs was spot-on: 'I'd Rather Go Blind', an old Etta James blues song, Sam Cooke's rollicking 'Twisting the Night Away', and Jimi Hendrix's 'Angel' were excellently reworked. The album enhanced Rod's career.

By far the stand-out track on the album was 'You Wear It Well', the jaunty song similar in texture and tempo to 'Maggie May'. Mickey Waller was again bustling away at the drums and the co-writer was again Martin Quittenton. When Rod went to perform it on *Top of the Pops*, featuring Kenney Jones at the drums, Waller would again sit at home seething as he watched. Fond though he was of Rod, he could never understand why he was required to be the studio drummer but was never invited to get the television glory he felt was his due when the record got moving. It had been the same, he mused, with 'Maggie May'.

Colliding with 'You Wear It Well' was the result of a recording session from three years previously, which he'd forgotten about. Rock stars were used to the exploitation of their work from earlier years, but Rod's experience was quite astonishing in the way it happened. In 1969 his friend John Peel, the disc jockey, informally asked Rod to help an Australian band called Python Lee Jackson by singing the lead vocal on the song 'In a

Broken Dream'. Rod was game. Peel had been a stout supporter of his work and was a fellow football fanatic. Rod did the recording session, and was paid … 'two carpets for my car!' Rod attempted to get a black sound on the ballad. He thought no more of it, believing the band and the album to have died. But the tapes had been sold and the record was eventually released on the Young-blood label. Though Rod was not formally named as the singer, his voice was unmistakable as the haunting song by Python Lee Jackson, with whirling Mellotron giving it an ethereal atmosphere, went to number three in the British chart. In America, it reached fifty-six.

• • •

In the aftermath of the pop explosion of the 1960s, when artists were courted for their views on everything from war to fashion, stars like Rod were still being interrogated at the start of the new decade. In a wide-ranging interview in the *Melody Maker* in 1972, Rod was asked whether, as an entertainer, he felt in a position to have some influence on society. He had never been a political thinker, preferring his lyrics to deal with personal relationships rather than international issues. This contrasted with the attitude of some of his contemporaries such as Bob Dylan, John Lennon and Pete Townshend of the Who, who fell into the role of seers, often with fatal results.

He thought that 'messages' from rock stars could be important, 'But I don't think it's down to me. I find it difficult to write songs about ordinary things like love, let alone things on social problems. Things like the Vietnam war wear a bit thin after eight or nine years. I feel for things like the Upper Clyde shipbuilders. I know how terrible unemployment is. I have contributed to their relief fund, but I wouldn't like to blow my own trumpet about it. I am not very aware of things that happen across the other side of the world, like Bangladesh, but I worry about what is happening in Glasgow because that is nearer home. It's more real to me. Every night I turn on the television and see the same thing about the IRA and the Irish situation. It does tend to drive you up the wall after a while. I wish they would have some good news.'

Did the ecology issue concern him? 'Yes, that is something I have often thought about. By 1983 there will be about 68 million people in this country. The ecologists say that at this rate we won't even be here by the year 2000, so there ain't no hope anyway.' Turning to what was then a controversial issue, the high price of tickets at concerts, Rod said: 'One thing that makes me angry is the seven dollars they charged for our concert at Madison Square Garden, but there is nothing I can do about that. If 40,000 people want to see us and there are only 20,000 seats, then everybody wants to make money. They printed the tickets first, before informing us of the price. They were sold out in five hours. This makes me really angry. There again, I don't lose sleep over it.'

Did it irritate him when people capitalized on his recent success by releasing early recordings such as 'In a Broken Dream'? Rod was phlegmatic, realistic. 'No, because I think that's what they are for, listening to. I don't think they are good but if people want to buy them they are welcome. The record company puts out records now because they think there is an audience for me now.'

Talking about his stage antics, Rod said: 'When I throw the mike around it's hard luck if anyone gets in the way. I don't get that carried away that I don't know what I am doing, though I've never once dropped the mike stand. Mostly, the act is very controlled. If we get a really big gig like Madison Square Garden the first three numbers will be frantic because everyone is trying so hard. That's the only time we would be out of control.'

Asked if, through his control from the stage over an audience, he ever felt that if he wanted to he could incite a riot, he declared: 'Yes, I'm bloody sure I could. If I told them at one point to go over there and stamp on the cops, they would. We've got songs that bring people to their feet and really get them at it, like "Plynth" and "Losing You" in which people get up and everybody runs to the stage.'

Wasn't that frightening? 'No, in America they have a real hatred for the police that does not exist in this country [Britain]. But it doesn't frighten me. It's a different kind of hysteria these days to what it was in the old, Small Faces days. I'd love to be in the audience and see how it feels. I think sex still plays an important part in music.'

Reaction to the Faces' music was: 'Unique. I would have thought the Who would have had a similar reaction of bringing people to their feet, but they don't, at least not when I've seen them, which was once at Boston and on TV. For me it's the hallmark of a good audience if they get up to their feet. You can feel then that they are really enjoying themselves.'

Had there ever been people hurt at any Faces concerts in America? 'Yes, at a couple of these big concerts a few people have got hurt. But that's not directly to do with us. The only time I've ever seen anybody hurt is when I swung the mike stand and the end came off and hit a geezer round the face.'

On the subject of politics, he was loyal in 1972 to his parental background. 'I'm a Labour man, and I did not vote in the last election because I thought Labour were going to walk it. Like a lot of people, I took too much notice of the opinion polls. I think really the difference between Labour and Conservatives is like the difference between tuberculosis and cancer. I'm

Labour by tradition really. I would call myself working-class.'

On his job of music-making he said: 'Music is very tiring. You also have to get in the right mental frame of mind before a big tour. After writing a song I feel flattened. I feel physically wrecked after working out a set of lyrics. In a strange kind of way, playing football is a kind of relaxation, especially afterwards having a pint of beer with the lads – can't beat it! Cornwall is where I usually go to. I always go in the winter if I get the chance, never in the summer, because it is so quiet in the winter and it is the warmest place in the country about this time of year and in January and February.'

Rod said he was fit to do a concert on five hours' sleep. Live shows were the cornerstone of his life and work. 'If I couldn't perform I'd give up. The recording side bores me stiff. I hate studios. I hate record company business. I hate writing songs. The only thing I get a buzz from is getting up and playing. When that goes, I'll go with it. Do like the pro-footballers, retire at the top.'

He was not merely working for the money, he said. At a mere twenty-seven he declared he did not have to work for the rest of his life. 'But not having that ninety minutes up there on stage any more! Phew, Christ, I don't like to think about it. I *don't* think about it. It frightens me.'

The music scene in the early 1970s was worthy but jaded. Heavy duty musicianship, which had mush-roomed out of the counter-culture of the 'under-ground', had left a vacuum in the star system. Magnificent music sometimes came from the giants like Pink Floyd (*The Dark Side of the Moon*) and Led Zeppelin (*Houses of the Holy*) in 1973. But it had taken Marc Bolan, with a string of jaunty hits like 'Ride a White Swan', 'Get It On' and 'Jeepster', to kick pop back to the people. It was, he declared, getting too dour.

With David Bowie, Bolan began the swing to Glam Rock. Decorated with mascara and festooned with a kaleidoscope of colours, they lifted the look of pop from the greyness of the late 1960s and the start of the new decade into a glistening new medium.

Bolan's music may have lacked the panache of Stewart's, but his message could not have been lost on Rod. In the words of one of Rod's friends, Steve Harley: 'Marc understood the star system and worked it. Brilliantly. Ceaselessly.'

Rod knew that to ensure true stardom, style was always a key ingredient in his armoury. 'Jagger might think he got into satins first,' he said in 1972, 'but he didn't.' But while he admired Marc Bolan and was a friend of the singer, he forecast correctly that the swing to Glam Rock would 'burn itself out ... groups are forcing themselves into that and when it becomes forced it doesn't work. Like Bowie's band; they so obviously don't belong in all that gear! It won't last. It'll get back to denims and jeans. Me, I'll stay the same because I've always been the same. I've never been through a humble phase, never been into denims and jeans. I think England is a little fed up with its stars being humble.' Reflecting on his old inspiration Sam Cooke, he said that when the singer had brought out a record called 'Chain Gang', 'that changed me; that's when I jumped into a mohair suit'.

From the crushed velvet simplicity of the Mod look, through the bare-chested boozer in the Faces, Rod always had eyes for the mirror. In the autumn of 1973, returning from yet another American tour with the Faces, Rod appeared to have changed. Always resplendent and extravagant, with a liberal dash of tartan to exert his quasi-Scottish personality, Rod now sharpened up his look. Gone was the often dishevelled urchin Face, in its place a more studied, glamorous appearance. Mascara and sequins were now more prevalent. And even his shoulder-length hair began to show signs of a swing to the pineapple-spiky look that would be part of his evolution, and appeal to women, in the years ahead.

The spring of that year was to prove another turning point. The balancing act between his own career and his role as a team player with the Faces was getting under his skin. One of the more endearing traits of Rod is his straight-talking honesty. In private he could be sulky, but never for long. In public, particularly through the press, he was abrasively honest.

Billy Gaff said at this time (1973) that the Faces had hardly changed. They had bigger houses, bigger cars and more money, but in temperament 'they're just as big bastards as they were four years ago. They give me just the same hard time'. Keeping their morale up was a central part of his job as manager, Gaff declared. He said that so many famous people descended into drugs 'and suddenly they are totally destroyed ... that really becomes the row when they get that big, because you can't dictate what they are going to do, although Rod is a marvellous listener'. Stewart, said Gaff, listened carefully to other views, never dismissing them merely because they were not his own.

There was nothing very deep about Stewart, the Faces manager continued. 'I mean, he's a very ordinary entertainer who happens to be quite clever at his craft.' Astutely, Gaff cited Rod as one of the three artists in rock's history who could brilliantly recreate other people's hits at least as well as – and sometimes better than – the originals. The other two acts were Joe Cocker and Janis Joplin.

Watching him at the pinnacle of his craft in 1994 it seems so easy as he takes a stage, cuts a new album or offers a freshly written song. But in the view of at least two of his former backroom team, Rod has always shown true grit off-stage as well as on. The skill of so many artists, like Stewart, lies partly in making their art look easy. In reality the stage show, as well as the strategy of the career, has been finely manicured. And that's what has pulled him through. 'He has a mind like a steel trap,' says Mike Gill, ex-managing director of Rod's record company, Riva. 'I thought he was as tough as old boots, an admirable quality,' says Peter Burton, ex-Faces publicist. 'That was a long, long slog with the Faces, going round America year in year out. But Billy Gaff had faith in the lot of them and Rod had faith in himself.'

Though he won the Best Singer award in both the British and World Sections of the *Disc and Music Echo* readers' poll in 1973, Rod was knocked from the top spot to second place in the prestigious *Melody Maker* awards. David Bowie won. As more of a populist artist than Bowie, Rod was rattled by this: 'I love to receive awards. That's because I'm a Capricorn and need to be reassured.'

It was an irascible Rod, therefore, who sat down with a writer friend in April 1973 to give the interview that would trigger the beginning of the end for the Faces. With Glyn Johns again at the controls, they had released the album *Ooh La La*, which spawned the strong number two hit single 'Cindy Incidentally', when Rod lit the fuse.

• • •

'Did you like the album?' Rod asked a sympathetic writer, Roy Hollingworth, who had gone to interview him for the *Melody Maker*. They were sitting in Rod's house in Windsor, munching ginger biscuits and drinking tea.

'Yes,' Hollingworth replied.

'Really?' Stewart responded with a puzzled look. 'It was a bloody mess,' he declared, his face turning stern. 'A bloody mess ... but I shouldn't say that, should I? I should say it in a few weeks' time. Not now. I mean, the public ain't gonna like me saying it's a bloody mess. It was a disgrace. But I'm not going to say anything more about it. All right? That's it.'

The conversation then proceeded through various topics, Rod perhaps realizing what he had said and diverting the conversation to football. He watched a film clip on TV of one of his idols, the Blackpool winger Stanley Matthews. 'Christ, I bet he felt bloody great,' Rod smiled as he admired the soccer star's rhythm. Often, Rod seemed to spring to life more enthusiastically when talking about football than he did with any other topic.

Picking up a copy of his parents' local paper, the *Hampstead and Highgate Express*, he showed off a photo of himself on a football pitch alongside former Spurs centre forward Bobby Smith. Rod said it was his proudest moment: 'A picture of me, in my footy gear, on the sports pages! It gave me more of a thrill than seeing my face plastered on the front of the rock papers. I was really moved.'

His mother brought him down to earth. 'Oh Roddy, what would you have been if you'd been a footballer?' More important than discussing the Faces seemed to be the news from his mother that his football socks, needed for that night's game, were mangled in the washing machine.

Soon, though, he had returned to the vexed issue of the Faces. Beyond his dislike of the new album, he seemed discontent. 'We're still doing the same bleedin' numbers [on stage] because we've got nothing else to do. I don't like the new album. One of the best tracks is one I don't sing on, [the Ronnie Lane composition] 'Ooh La La'. Then there's 'Borstal Boys' which we can't play on stage ... we went out of time four times with it. Terrible.'

He weighed into the lackadaisical recording

arrangements that surrounded the Faces and compared them with his own for solo work. 'We're our own worst enemies when it comes to getting into a studio. When I do my albums I say 7 p.m. until 12. And that's that. Now with the band, time agreed is at 9 p.m. The first one who rolls up is always Kenney. Then over to the boozer, closing time, and then we start. We've always done that. Honestly, we spend more money in the boozer than in the bloody studio – and it's £35 an hour in the studio.'

Slightly concerned by the trouble he must have known he was stoking up with the band, Rod then retreated slightly. Asked if he was thinking about his future more than that of the Faces, he answered: 'Er... Oh no. We're together for life. I don't think there's really anything else I could do. I just want to make good albums. When I make an album I want it to be some sort of event that people look forward to every year. If I can get into that position I'll be a very happy man.'

Against that ominous backdrop, the band began an American tour tensely. At a concert at Nassau Coliseum, the consensus view was that they were just going through the motions. In tight yellow silk trousers, flowered shirt and a red feather boa tied round his waist, Rod commanded the stage as ever. But the spirit was missing. The Faces, that most magical live band, were on autopilot.

When they returned to Britain, Ronnie Lane quit. For several months he had teased and warned the band that he was going, but few took him seriously. Finally, the polarization of Rod and the band could not be tolerated by the individualistic Lane. His departure was symbolically the beginning of the end – more than a bassist, Lane embodied the attitude and spirit of the Faces.

The problem for the Faces was always going to be Rod. They could not expect a well-organized, ambitious singer of his level and achievement to be happy inside a democratic organization. He had to be top dog. Most of the successful bands were dominated: the Stones by Jagger and Richards, the Beatles by Lennon and McCartney, the Who by Pete Townshend. Why should Rod not have run the Faces? Had they faced up to his clear-cut vision, they might have survived. But even with a new bassist, the band's days were numbered.

With Lane gone, Rod did exercise his unspoken leadership of the Faces. He went to Free, one of his favourite bands, and recruited their bass player, the Japanese Tetsu Yamauchi. 'Tetsu can down a bottle,' Rod smiled, 'so he was in!' Reflecting on Lane, Stewart said he was irreplaceable, not necessarily as a musician but as a character in the Faces. 'But we were getting very loose.'

A rumour that Rod was on the verge of marrying brought him apparent panic. 'That frightened me,' he said, and he left no doubt that his career came first. 'I wouldn't *not* get married because of me career. I think the days of that are gone. I'm not willing to get married because I feel there are some people who shouldn't ... Elvis Presley should never have been married ... if I got married I'd feel settled down, given away; I think it might even start affecting me music.' He reflected on the marriage of Paul and Linda McCartney (in 1969) and added: 'It might be just psychological with me. I'd think: "Oh Christ, I'm married now. I'm sick, finished..."'

Freshly ambitious for the new-look Faces, Rod made a statement that can now be seen as hilarious. 'My next solo LP will be my last so it's got to be a classic. Recording takes so much time and I've had virtually no social life for the last two or three years. I've been living and dying in the studios.' Mick Jagger had said tauntingly that Rod had saved his best material for his solo albums instead of giving some to the band. 'But the band never got into the acoustic things I did, and I've always been a folkie at heart.'

He felt at a crossroads at his career at that time in 1973. 'But I haven't lost interest at all. I've got to be honest and I'll be really self-indulgent as well, now. I've been riding the crest of a wave for three years and I think I've come through with flying colours.'

He quickly contradicted his statement that he was going to be a band member rather than a soloist. He loved being an idol. He had survived the popularity thrusts of such acts as Slade and Bowie. There was a sign, after all the touring, of the worries that would concern him later in life: he said he had been for medical checks to see if nodes had grown on his vocal cords. They were clear. 'My voice is as good as ever.' But, importantly, he revealed that he 'still can't sing more than four dates in a row'.

• • •

A new rock 'n' roll British aristocracy was born in the 1970s that would still be intact twenty-five years later. Jagger, Elton and Bowie, and even the more faceless bands like Pink Floyd, boasted such charisma and strong music that they could not be shifted by anything that followed in the 1980s and 1990s.

Conceding that he was 'in competition with people like Jagger', Rod Stewart occupied a well-carved niche. A people's star, he stayed unpretentious despite living the life of the nobility at his Windsor mansion. Not even the announcement of his engagement to Dee Harrington lost him any fans, as it might have done to pop stars a decade earlier. They stepped out together to the London clubs, but Rod was more often to be seen socializing with footballers when he was not working.

Jagger taunted Rod about his flash clothes: 'I see Rod is wearing the pyjamas I wore last year.' Elton John told Rod he remembered seeing him perform at a club near his home in Pinner, Middlesex – and he clearly recalled asking Rod for an autograph afterwards. 'I have very few friends,' Rod said as Christmas 1974 approached, 'but Elton and I have this much in common: we both came into the business through John Baldry, although I've been around longer than Elton.'

Still conceding that he worried about what his mother and father thought of him, and what he said, Rod reflected that when his first solo success came, he had cockily thought he had 'made it'. His parents and family had emphasized to him that 'a lot of people depend on you and a lot of people love you, and you can't let them down'. His big fear now was letting down his devoted audiences. This was to be a recurring concern.

Having pulled through the beatnik phase of his teen years, Rod's father had continued to instil into his superstar son the ethic of hard work and training, probably derived from the Stewart household's love of soccer. 'There are still challenges. I've still not made a classic album. It's got to be the kind of record that will sell a million copies in Britain alone,' Rod declared. Though he had yet to make enormous impact with ballads as a soloist, Rod showed his route to the future: 'I admire someone like Frank Sinatra who has been on top for years and has turned on three whole generations. Magnificent! In fact, I admire him as a man more than as a singer. He's done it all and when he goes on stage it's not as a museum piece but because people sincerely want to hear him.'

A firm step towards longevity came with the release of his new solo album. *Smiler* blended the drive of 'Sweet Little Rock 'n' Roller' with the taut beat of 'Bring It On Home to Me'; the flashback to his Dylan admiration with 'Girl from the North Country' to the tenderness of the surprisingly chosen 'I've Grown Accustomed to Her Face', a show song from *My Fair Lady*, firm evidence that Stewart would never be limited by the straitjacket of rock 'n' roll. That factor would separate him from the rest and help to guarantee his wide appeal and longevity.

Here, also, were two songs from his friends Paul McCartney and Elton John: Paul composed 'Mine for Me' especially for Rod, and Elton gave him 'Let Me Be Your Car', appropriate for the automobile-crazy Stewart, who now had a yellow Lamborghini Countach standing alongside his Rolls-Royce outside his Windsor mansion.

'My best so far!' Rod enthused about *Smiler*. But it was rock-star-speak. Later he would admit that *Smiler* fell below his usual standard, despite the inclusion of strong songs. It had been prepared at a time of maximum aggravation for him.

A boost for it came when Paul and Linda McCartney went to the Faces show at Lewisham Odeon on 18 November, 1974. 'I've got my brother and sister coming on stage with me now,' Rod told the bemused audience. 'My brother with a humped back, my sister with one leg. They're gonna come on and they're gonna sing a song.' The crowd erupted as Paul and Linda launched into a duet with Rod on 'Mine for Me'. In his early rock 'n' rolling years, Rod had been a Stones man. He seemed to swing towards fully appreciating the more melodic Beatles later, and loved McCartney's band Wings. Rod went on later to record Beatles songs 'Get Back' and 'In My Life'. It was, of course, for a song on a Stewart solo album rather than for a Faces album that such an illustrious event as the McCartney appearance had happened. It could only increase the envy of the Faces.

● ● ●

Always surrounding Rod was a highly professional team, and he wanted it that way, particularly when he was on tour. 'Since he's generating this huge income, he wants people to fetch, carry, be there, care,' says Mike Gill. 'He's like a Hollywood star, and he needs an entourage of hairdresser, secretary, manager, press agent.'

On some occasions he seemed to be pampered. During a 1974 solo promotional tour of the USA to support *Smiler*, Mike Gill recalls a hectic time flying from New York to Chicago and on to Los Angeles where he and Rod checked into the Beverly Wilshire Hotel. They were tired. As they awaited delivery of their luggage to their rooms, Rod said to Mike Gill: 'Do you know the time? It's four o'clock, tea time!'

Gill says: 'I said: "Yes, so?" He said: "Well?" I said: "Well, what?" He said: "Well, organize it!" I said: "Let me give you a little lesson. This is a telephone. You take this finger and put it in the '9' and when it stops, they will say: Room Service. And then you ask for what you want." Rod roared with laughter and said: "I can't do it with you, can I?"' Gill said: 'No, I'm just going to get changed. Order the tea. I will do most things for you. As a bloke I like you very much, but I am not your f—g valet. I am not going to be running around at your every whim, because at the end of the day we're only people. The fact that you've sold millions of records is irrelevant. I'm tired as well.'

Gill reflects: 'He was seeing how far he could push, without doubt. I have seen him do it to other people. I think one thing he detested was people tugging forelocks to him; he took the attitude that if people did that, why shouldn't he get them to do things for him? I've always found it very hard to put a handle on Rod. As a bloke, I was never frightened of him.' Dealing as a publicist with other stars, 'You stood back. Rod is a superstar, but always someone I could say this to: Come on, let's get *on* with it.'

Six   Sailing away

'MUCH AS I LOVE THE OLD COUNTRY, I JUST
CAN'T AFFORD TO LIVE THERE ANY MORE'
                    – Rod on his decision to live in the USA, 1975

Rod was ready for decisive change. And he met Britt Ekland. The year 1975 was to be the watershed in his life. His voice, his songwriting, his performing talent had never been in doubt. What lay at risk in the second half of the decade was his artistic integrity.

Against all the odds, the Faces were still intact, physically if not spiritually. After starting the year with concerts in Australia and Japan, they moved to the familiar turf of the USA for extensive tours during February and March. During this tour, the international media linked Rod romantically with Susan Ford, daughter of the US President, Gerald Ford. This was yet another piece of fabrication by Stewart's imaginative publicity team. Rod had been coaxed by them to write a letter inviting Susan Ford – a rock fan who had seen Elton John and George Harrison in concert – to the Faces' show at Washington's Capital Centre on 15 February. Afterwards she met Rod backstage. But despite an invitation to the White House, which followed, Rod demurred. He was, by then, in New York at a Led Zeppelin party. He sent a bouquet of red roses to Susan Ford by way of apology. The meeting never occurred;

but the thought of the rock star sitting at dinner at the White House with a President's daughter sent journalists into a frenzy.

Rod's meeting with Britt Ekland, by contrast, was a planned success. Her friend Joan Collins, with her then husband Ron Kass, invited Britt along to see the Faces at the Madison Square Garden, New York, on 24 February, 1975. Eighteen months older than Rod, the Swedish actress had two children: Victoria, then eleven, by her marriage to Peter Sellers, and Nicolai, then two, from her former relationship with Lou Adler, a leading record producer.

It was a fast love match. But back in Windsor was Dee Harrington, who often stayed at home running the mansion they shared while Rod travelled the world. She was elated when Rod unexpectedly phoned her to say that since he was *en route* to Los Angeles for a few days, why did she not fly in to see him? It was, after all, the city in which they had met four years earlier.

Rod's love of dating one girl while he was attached to another was well known. His sister Mary recalls 'one girl arriving at the front door at Archway Road while another was leaving through the back'. But the scenario that awaited his love life in California defied belief.

When Dee flew in to meet Rod at the Beverly Hills Hotel, they spent three hours together and then Rod said he had to leave … for 'an important business meeting'. Feeling tired after her flight from London, Dee said she would eat and then go to bed. But as the evening wore on, the time difference from the UK to the USA caused her to feel wide awake. She decided to go out, to the Troubadour, the hip night-spot where she and Rod had often been to see bands.

Driving along Santa Monica Boulevard, she stopped her car outside the club. Behind her came a limousine. When it halted immediately behind her, she

Visiting Dublin from his new
home in California in 1975 to
promote the album 'Atlantic
Crossing' (Vinnie
Zuffante/Star File)

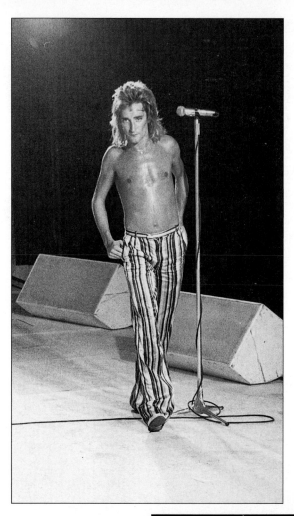

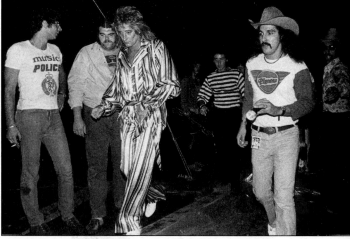

A sad end, a bright beginning:
on stage, and leaving it, during
the final Faces tour of the US,
October 1975 (Larry Kaplan
and Chuck Pulin, Star File)

Showmanship rules: touring
the US during the Footloose
And Fancy Free tour, 1977
(Richard E. Aaron/Star File)

The heavily-made-up look,
1977, during his American
tour (Jeffrey Mayer, Star File)

With Britt Ekland
(Rex Features)

The leopardskin pants look during a 1981 tour (Larry Kaplan and Bob Leafe, Star File)

On the road again, 1984 (Chuck Pulin, Star File)

Enjoying a British pint at his
local pub, May 1987 (Trayc
Stevenson/Smiler)

A zealous fan gets a ride from
Rod on stage at Madison
Square Garden, New York,
1988 (Dominick Conde, Star
File)

With his guitarist and close
friend Jim Cregan, January
1988 (Trayc Stevenson/
Smiler)

Performing at the Wiltern
Theatre, Los Angeles,
7 September 1990, at a benefit
concert for the Los Angeles
Aids Project (Vinnie
Zuffante/Star File)

realized that inside it was Rod ... and suddenly he was helping a blonde from the car. Could it be Chrissie Wood, wife of Ronnie? All the Faces ladies were in town. Dee tooted her car horn. Rod and the blonde did not appear to hear it and strode into the Troubadour.

Rod's four-year romance with Dee was about to end, at the bar. Following Rod and the woman in, Dee quickly realized that Rod was not partnered by a Faces lady, but by the recognizable face of Britt Ekland. So much for Rod's 'business meeting'.

Dee let fly. Rod and Britt could do little but face the righteous anger of a girl who felt humiliated. Back in their hotel suite, she fumed as Billy Gaff, who had heard about the scene, attempted to defuse her fury. But she could not be pacified; she packed her bags and returned to London the next day.

'BRITT EKLAND, ROD STEWART AND ME. BY HIS EX GIRLFRIEND' screamed *Woman's Own*. Dee pulled no punches in her detailed story, also told in the *Sunday Mirror*. And she said that she had always expected her formal engagement to Rod to end in marriage rather than tears. The episode marked the start of Rod's role as the rascal of the tabloid press. Handsome, daring, boozing and blonde-loving – and with a great voice thrown in – he was about to become every show-business photographer and reporter's favourite naughty boy.

• • •

Billy Gaff has a doll which Rod and the Faces gave him one Christmas. Specially made to look like Gaff, the doll has a printed quotation encased at its base: 'Have you got the readies, Bill?' That was what Rod asked the band manager after every show, in dressing-rooms all round the world.

Rod has often enjoyed lampooning his own well-known frugality with money. 'I don't mind buying a guy a drink, but I'm damned if I'll ever buy two!' was one of his favourite lines. But such flippancy was over-shadowed in the mid 1970s for millionaires by something more serious. With taxation at a crippling 83p in the pound, many rock stars, who had made big money very quickly, didn't see why such a huge proportion should be handed over to the government. They began to rebel.

Stars as diverse as Michael Caine and Tom Jones took the plunge by emigrating to the more lenient USA. Hoping for change, Rod shifted his political support from Labour to the Liberal Party (he was courted by its leader, David Steel). Saying he was hoping to persuade the Faces to do concerts to support the Liberals, Rod said he felt the Party was attracting people like him who 'felt they had to rebel in the 1950s during their teenage years, and are now fed up with the two-party system'. (Rod reaffirmed his support for the Liberals in 1986.)

But such a move could not swing the taxation issue overnight. At about the same time that he met Britt Ekland, Rod decided to go into tax exile in America. One report said that Rod faced a £750,000 bill from the Inland Revenue and he was bitter about this. 'Much as I love the old country, I just can't afford to live there any more,' Rod told the *Daily Mirror* by phone from Beverly Hills. He had flown there a month before that statement, in April 1975, on what he described as a working holiday. 'I have lived in California for a month now to see if I like it here. Well, I do. I have reluctantly made up my mind to stay and I am applying for American citizenship. I have also told my manager to sell up everything I own in Britain.'

Rod was careful with his money, perhaps because he was conscious that many show-business artists had made a lot, only to fall from grace and end up penniless.

'I've got short arms and deep pockets,' he once said to Peter Burton, the Faces' tour publicist, who adds, 'He would probably say: what do we get from tonight's concert? What's our cut of this?'

Once, while walking in Kensington, Rod saw an expensive antique chair. He said to Peter Burton, 'I like that. I'm going next door to the greengrocer to buy a bag of apples. Can you go in and beat them down?' Rod knew that had he walked in first to ask the price, it would have risen, probably tenfold, at the sight of him. 'I'd go in and beat them down, and Rod would walk in with the chequebook for the price I'd agreed,' Burton says.

The Windsor mansion was put up for sale at £300,000. Britt Ekland, who remarked that Rod was 'very unhappy' about having to quit Britain, was blamed by some as the reason for Rod's emigration. 'That was absolutely untrue,' Gaff says now. 'Rod very much made his own mind up. Sometimes he needed prodding, but he basically didn't want to go through this punitive taxation any longer. If anything, Britt would have been happier living in England. Britt had nothing to do with that decision.' She would, Gaff avers, have gone anywhere with Rod: 'She worshipped him.'

Now they were firmly set in their plans to set up home together in Los Angeles. Billy Gaff, who already had a house there, went shopping and found Rod the perfect property. At a cost of $750,000, Rod bought a twenty-roomed house in Carolwood Drive, Holmby Hills, the locale of stars from Barbra Streisand to Gregory Peck. Britt tore into the redecoration of the huge house with a fervour that pleased Rod. They shared the same taste in art nouveau and shipped in paintings and furniture from all round the world. 'We're desperately in love,' Rod said after a BBC television documentary showed their new home to the world. 'The boys in the band all love her.'

As he spoke, the slow, lingering death of the Faces took another twist. After Ronnie Lane's departure, Rod had driven one more nail into the band's coffin by crossing the Atlantic. Now came Ronnie Wood's contribution. Shortly after Rod's flight to California, Woody was asked by the Rolling Stones to become their temporary guitarist in succession to the departing Mick Taylor. Mick Jagger had once told Rod Stewart that he would never consciously poach Woody, though he was clearly custom-built for the Stones, the band he had adored since his youth. Rod had been reassured by Mick. Now, with no Faces work on the immediate horizon, Woody accepted. Everyone in the world of music agreed that Ronnie Wood was born to be a Rolling Stone.

The Faces were splitting, and messily. 'I feel pretty browned off,' Kenney Jones told the *Daily Express*. 'Ever since Rod moved to the States, everything's got disorganized. I now look on him as my friend who's gone astray.' With Rod's ascendancy, the atmosphere within the band changed from good, mischievous fun into a realization of a potentially serious situation.

'Ronnie Lane, not Rod, was the backbone of the Faces,' says their former press agent, Mike Gill. After 'a few barley wines', Lane was, says Gill, 'one of the most difficult people I have ever encountered in my life', but in his cogent moments, he was a bright under-estimated talent and held the band together for two years longer than it should have been a band. 'Because whereas MacLagan and Jones couldn't deal with Rod's success, Ronnie Lane could.'

Ronnie Wood, meanwhile, described himself as a part-time Rolling Stone. He swore loyalty to the Faces still; but with no recording sessions planned, according to Ian MacLagan, and with Rod setting up home in California, it sounded hollow. It was the most turbulent period in Rod's meteoric career since the Faces had begun. As well as developing his new life with Britt and keeping an ear on the Faces situation, he had to resolve complicated legal and business decisions.

The big problem, which had needed his attention just before he left Britain, surrounded his original Mercury Records contract. Billy Gaff found it an enormous benefit to have a solo singer on that label and the band on another, Warner Brothers. 'Mercury was very tight and would not spend any money on promotion; Rod was selling huge amounts of records for them while Warner, through the Faces, were spending huge amounts of money promoting them,' Gaff says. Warner outspent Mercury by ten to one, and by default the effect on Rod's solo albums was huge.

One of the biggest secrets of those years was that Warner sealed Rod's future with them by paying him a large sum to ensure that when his Mercury deal did expire, he would definitely go to Warner. 'It's not uncommon for people to come in when you have three albums to go with another company and say: let's make a deal for down the road,' Gaff points out. 'Three or four years before Rod's contract expired with Mercury, he knew we were signed to Warner [for the future]. But we didn't dare tell anybody. Only Rod and I and Mo Austin and Joe Smith [the American bosses of Warner] knew.' If the news had leaked, Gaff says: 'Mercury might have got angry and not worked' on his solo albums. In the High Court in December 1974, a judge freed Rod from his Mercury contract. Mercury, then an imprint of Phonogram and not the original Philips, appealed against that decision. This appeal was dismissed; the result was that Phonogram, who took over Rod's contract when Mercury was wound up in 1972, would not be able to extend their contract beyond the date of its expiry, 8 October, 1973.

Unshackled from that rewarding, career-building but messy solo deal with Mercury, Rod faced a new chapter in his life on many fronts. He had a glittering new woman and seemed to revel in the fidelity which he promised her in public interviews. He was exiled in America and enjoying the splendour, stepping out with Britt to the finest nightspots, where they were fêted. And he signed a solo deal with Warner Brothers. Gaff negotiated him a spectacular $25 million, ten-album contract, a stunning deal by any show business yardstick.

● ● ●

There comes a period in every major artist's life when the creativity inside is on the cusp of change, when it needs stimulus from fresh surroundings and people, in order to flower. For Rod Stewart at thirty, the self-imposed move to California with Britt triggered a crucial new chapter in his life and work.

Astonishingly, during the frenetic period of his Faces tour, his meeting with Britt, his migration to the States and the mentally draining business hassles, Rod managed to find time to write. So when Mo Austin and Joe Smith at Warner suggested he team up with the leading producer Tom Dowd for his next album, Rod was ready. Dowd's name alone was inspirational to artists of Rod's vintage. Like most artists of the 1960s, Stewart had weaned himself on the glorious sounds that Dowd had helped create, for he had been at the controls for records by legends like Aretha Franklin and Otis Redding. Only a year earlier, in 1974, Dowd had also worked wonders in the studio for a remarkable 'comeback' album by Eric Clapton, *461 Ocean Boulevard*.

It was the producer's job to surround the artist with the right musicians to suit the occasion and the songs. Rod was in the mood to cut with the past, shedding any songwriting link with his mate Woody (who was away touring with the Stones as Rod prepared the album). Since this was an American recording project, a break with his tradition of solo recording felt right: his writing with Woody had great moments and Rod had nothing against Mickey Waller or Martin Quittenton, but it was time for a fresh mood.

Flying to Alabama, Tom Dowd introduced Rod to the great musicians who formed the famed Muscle Shoals rhythm section, names whom Rod had known all his life from album notes: Al Jackson, Donald 'Duck' Dunn, Steve Cropper, Barry Beckett and Jimmy Johnson. Aghast to find that they were white men who had accompanied some of his favourite black artists, Rod soon struck up an empathy with them. The stage was set for the album that would become *Atlantic Crossing*. The title said it all: here was a spiritual as well as geographical statement of re-location.

'Sailing', which would stay with Rod for ever as one of his anthems, had a poor history before he recorded it under Tom Dowd's baton. It was composed by Gavin Sutherland of the cultish British group the Sutherland Brothers and Quiver. Released as a single on the Island label, it did not hit – but Rod was among the musicians who admired their work. He always had a feeling that 'Sailing' could be special, and he perceived it to be precisely what it became: a singalong anthem for the terraces. As the years passed, and the song became special to Stewart fans as well as to football supporters, Rod and his mother and father, who loved it, were immensely proud.

Surprisingly, Rod was not initially confident that 'Sailing' would be such a landmark release as a single. Returning from California with the master tape and artwork for *Atlantic Crossing*, Mike Gill played it to the staff at Rod's management offices. 'There were fourteen of us; we did a poll on what should be the first single. It was a close race between "Sailing" and "This Old Heart of Mine", but at the end of the day, "Sailing" won,' he recalls. Shortly afterwards, Gill was in the middle of making a speech of presentation of 'Sailing' and *Atlantic Crossing* to the Warner company's sales convention in Cambridge when a message was passed to him saying he was wanted urgently on the phone. It could not wait until he had finished speaking.

It was Rod calling from his yacht, *Riva*, in Cannes. 'Mike, I'm on the boat. I'm given to understand that "Sailing" is the first single off the album. I'm not very happy.'

Gill: 'I beg your pardon; didn't Billy tell you?'

Stewart: 'No, first I've heard about it. I'm very cross.'

Gill: 'Well, it's coming out next week. We've pressed 100,000 copies.'

Stewart: 'Well, I think the single should have been "Three Time Loser".'

Gill: 'No comment. I'll tell you what. If "Sailing" is not number one in four weeks, I'll resign.'

Stewart: 'OK, 'bye.'

'Sailing' shot to number twenty-four in its first week of release, went to number two the following week, and finally topped the chart for four weeks. Stewart rang Gill: 'Compliments to the chef! I was wrong, you were right. I won't argue in future.'

Judged by any yardstick in popular music, *Atlantic Crossing* as an album was a monumental triumph, a defining moment in Rod's career. He wrote – without any co-writers – three winners and delivered them with enormous verve and incisive arrangements, assisted by Dowd: 'Three Time Loser', 'All in the Name of Rock 'n' Roll' and 'Still Love You' (prompting people to think this might be an over-the-shoulder message to Dee Harrington). And although the ballad 'I Don't Want to Talk About It' wasn't written by Rod, the self-effacement of the song sounded as if it was, in fact, from his pen. It stands as one of his noted interpretations, perfect for its raw power.

Atlantic Crossing entered the British charts at number one. It stayed there for nearly two months. In the US, it reached number nine. 'Sailing' went to the top in Britain, but its peculiarly British attraction as a singalong song meant it didn't have the same appeal to American audiences. To them, Rod was, then as now, a rock singer – and 'Sailing' was almost 'easy listening'. It nudged the top fifty there. This was, in a sense, a pleasing irony; in his tastes in music and ear for a good song, Rod had clearly not lost his 'British ears'.

• • •

During the Faces tour of America in 1975, *Atlantic Crossing* earned Rod a gold disc. Flying into New York, Mike Gill had the actual gold disc to present to Rod, but the presentation ceremony was kept secret from everyone; Rod was told he was needed simply for a 'photo call'.

'Diplomatically it was an appalling move,' Gill remembers. 'Before I saw Rod I saw Ronnie Wood, Ian MacLagan and Kenney Jones. They asked what I was doing there and I said I couldn't tell them. But they knew there was some kind of press call that afternoon.' When Gill emerged with the gold disc for the surprise presentation to Rod, 'You could hear a pin drop. Suddenly the four other Faces realized that it was all over.'

Rod found it very hard, leading a double life as a solo star and band member. 'He felt very disloyal. But he is a consummate professional. That's why he endured,' Gill declares.

• • •

Many artists are content to be cosseted and told by their management and record company precisely what to do. But years of experience in the music business had given

Rod a fiercely independent edge. Better informed than most about the whims of the business, he was never going to be manipulated. Two examples of his assertiveness came shortly after his breakthrough with *Atlantic Crossing*.

Manager Gaff had been warned by promoters in the States that the Faces were a spent force. Against the advice of music business people in the States, they were taking to the road with no fresh album to stir interest in ticket sales. Their last collection, an uninspiring live album called *Coast to Coast*, had failed to deliver the raw excitement of their stage show. Even Rod's last album before the proposed tour, *Smiler*, was relatively weak.

To promote *Atlantic Crossing* in Germany, Rod flew to Frankfurt with Britt straight from the US after a Faces tour, and then on to Hamburg. There he met Mike Gill, who had warned the German representative of Warner Records that Rod was 'wiped out' from the flight and should not be shown his itinerary for the media as soon as he stepped from the plane. 'Five minutes out of the airport, the guy showed it to him and Rod took out a pen and said: "No, No, No, I'm not doing that." He arrived at the Atlantic Hotel in Hamburg in a real stink. He went to bed and I woke him later and he said: "Who's paying for dinner?" I said "Warner." He said: "Great."' A feast of caviare, steak and Château Margaux followed. Though they got drunk during dinner, Stewart showed his steely decisiveness and business acumen, even though he was jet-lagged. During dinner he pulled out the media interview schedule and said to Mike Gill: 'What will this [the media tour] mean to me?' Gill responded that it was the difference between selling about 20,000 albums and selling 150,000.

What, Stewart asked, did that mean in real terms? Maybe £100,000 worth of royalties extra, from doing the interviews, Gill told him. Rod said fine, he would do everything that had been lined up, with one exception. He would not open a Hamburg record store the next day, because he recalled that he had once sustained bruised ribs and nearly been crushed by a crowd when opening a store in Edinburgh. It was difficult to maintain security, he felt. Gill said fine, they had agreed twenty-three out of the twenty-four appointments.

But the record store opening had been fixed for ten o'clock next morning … and Gill forgot to tell the local Warner man, who arrived next day to escort Stewart to the grand opening. 'He was quite insistent: "You must do this, Rod," he said. Rod rightly said: "No, I won't do it; I already told Mike."' Ashen with remorse, Gill was chastised by Rod. 'You lied, didn't you?' Rod said to him. 'Yes,' Gill replied. 'I'm feeling very guilty.' Stewart said: 'Don't ever do that to me again.' Gill apologized, saying the media blitz in Germany had been a 'circus' and he had made a mistake.

During the promotional tour, Rod's industriousness and ambition surfaced. 'While we were doing a photo shoot, he pulled out three grubby bits of paper,' Mike Gill recalls. 'I said: "What's that?" He said it was a collection of songs for the next album. I said: "But you've only just finished this one. How many songs have you got on that list?" He said: "A hundred and five and I'm still looking for more."' Among the songs was 'I've Grown Accustomed to Her Face'. Rod described it as his 'shopping list'; whatever he was doing, he was constantly looking for new song material, according to his aides.

• • •

Described by Britt, but not by Rod, as the Richard Burton and Elizabeth Taylor of rock, the couple seemed inseparable, and she accompanied him on promotional interviews for *Atlantic Crossing*. As she did so, he was yet again part of the Faces touring machine as they stomped across America on what was to become the finale for the band. There was no 'kick' on which to launch the Faces in front of the crowds.

But Gaff was resolute. He had starved America of Faces concerts throughout 1974, firmly believing that fans were being drained of ticket money by British rock groups who were over-populating the USA. Two factors would, he believed, whet the American appetite for the troubled Faces. Rod was as hot as a pistol with *Atlantic Crossing* to promote; and Ronnie Wood's adoption by the Stones gave the Faces a kind of credibility. The plan worked. Twenty-thousand-seater stadiums of the size of New York's Madison Square Garden sold out within hours of tickets going on sale. Yet it could only be a hollow tour for the band: there was no new material to generate interest in their stage show, and Rod took the spotlight by presenting several songs from his *Atlantic Crossing* album. Effectively, this was a touring show for that new album, for the tour featured a fifteen-piece orchestra at Rod's request. Ian MacLagan considered that an absurd image for a band famous for unsophisticated rock 'n' roll.

And the atmosphere was turning very sour between the musicians. Any alchemy that had knitted them together musically was evaporating in a forest of uncertainty, distrust and envy. The signs of impending doom were obvious to Billy Gaff, who felt immense pressure. He knew Rod was the star but had no desire to be the one to signal the end of a band of old mates.

The Faces' tour lumbered along throughout September and October, Rod taking the stage in silk pyjama-striped apparel. As he prepared for Christmas with Britt in Los Angeles, he decided to confront the inevitable. By phone from Los Angeles to London, Stewart said to Gaff: 'You know, I'd really like to tour on my own. I don't know if I can take any more of touring with this lot.'

That confession hit a nerve with Gaff, who answered with the exasperation of a manager who felt he, too, had tolerated enough: 'I'm not sure I can do it any more, either. I can't take any more grief.' Touring with the Faces was hell for a manager, he reflected. 'I'm a very emotional person at the worst of times,' Gaff said to Stewart, 'but this is a nightmare ...'

Gaff takes up the story: 'I said: "Is touring on your own what you really want to do?" He said: "Yes, it is." I said: "Why don't you do it, because I don't think I want to do another tour with you and the Faces. I just don't know if mentally I can take it any longer." I said: "Can we make a decision?" And we did so on the phone. That was it: we decided to call it a day with the Faces. I said "Are you sure?" He said: "I'm absolutely sure this is what I want to do."'

Gaff then asked Stewart if he, as manager, could announce to the press the dramatic news that Rod Stewart was quitting the Faces and going solo. 'He said yes,' Gaff remembers.

Like Mike Gill and Peter Burton, Gaff knew that Rod had a habit of changing his mind on the subject of the media. Since his explosion to the *Melody Maker* over the *Ooh La La* album, Rod had become wary of the press, insisting on a tape recorder at interviews so that whatever he said was beyond dispute.

He had a habit, Gaff states, of denying that he had said what appeared in print. So Gaff phoned Stan Sayer, the *Daily Mirror* pop reporter. Gaff recalls: 'I said: "I don't want this to go out in the paper until you've heard it from Rod personally."' The news was what the media had waited for a year or more: that the star was leaving the Faces.

'So I gave the *Mirror* Rod's private number,' Gaff says. 'I lied to him about that, but it was the only way. The *Mirror* phoned him at his Los Angeles home and got him on tape.'

The *Daily Mirror* published its valuable exclusive story across the top of its front page on 19 December, 1975. Under the headline 'Why Rock Star Rod Is Quitting Faces', Stan Sayer wrote: 'Stewart told me from Los Angeles last night: "I have only just made up my mind, but I'm definitely quitting this time."'

In a strange twist, there was a tilt at Ronnie Wood. Tony Toon, Rod's personal publicist, told the *Mirror*: 'Rod feels he can no longer work in a situation where the group's lead guitarist Ronnie Wood seems to be permanently "on loan" to the Rolling Stones.' Gaff confirmed, however, that Rod 'thinks the world of Ronnie Wood'. At the time of the announcement, Wood was touring Europe with the Stones.

Tours by the Faces of Australia, New Zealand and the Far East for spring 1976 were being cancelled. Ian MacLagan told the *Mirror*: 'I won't believe he is leaving the Faces until I hear it from his own lips.' And Kenney Jones added: 'If this means the end of the Faces, I'm not bothered. I expect I will survive.'

Later that day, the media confirmed that Woody would join the Stones permanently. Describing the Stones as 'my idols, the ultimate rock 'n' roll band', Wood said that to play with them was a 'huge honour'.

Gaff says now: 'That's how it was engineered. From my point of view, if I had just said it, I think he would have changed his mind the next day. The band would have got on to him and he would have landed me in it. I was always the scapegoat. That's what managers are for! You have to look like a — half the time and take the fall. Hard as it is, if you can't do that, you can't be a manager.'

Of one thing Gaff is certain: 'I know the offer from the Stones was there for Ronnie Wood because Rod would never have upset Woody. But as Woody had the Stones in the bag, I don't think he lost any sleep over Rod's statement. If it had turned out that Woody didn't have the Stones, he would probably have gone with Rod anyway.'

As for the effect on Kenney Jones, Ian MacLagan, Ronnie Lane and the new man, Tetsu Yamauchi, Billy Gaff ruminates: 'I was the bad guy to the Faces anyway, so I didn't lose anything.' At the root of Rod's departure was his central core of discipline and ambition. While he might have appeared a casual guy, when it came to work he applied himself rigidly to a routine that produced the best possible results, particularly in the recording studio. 'We've tried it in the studio,' he said of his Faces years, 'and it's never really worked the way it should ... my albums have always been better than the Faces.' He even suggested that the band might ditch album-making and concentrate on making singles, instead.

The Faces' recording schedule was 'alien' to what he was used to. He went into a studio at midday and finished at seven o'clock. It was a creative clocking-on-and-off operation. 'On a Faces session, everybody falls into the public house. I can't cope with that.'

Artistically, Rod's departure from the Faces gave the world a classy entertainer. Financially, too, it was a correct move for him. Inside the Faces, he was part of a five-piece who would each collect between $50,000 and $70,000 net from an American tour. Shortly after he went solo, Billy Gaff remembers Rod picking up a cheque on two occasions for $1 million for his own solo tours of the States. Just two years after Rod left the Faces, Gaff negotiated a new solo deal for him with Warner in 1977 that sent Rod's income into the stratosphere.

To many, Rod had finally 'gone Hollywood'. Being seduced by the life in his mansion in Carolwood Drive, visiting the finest restaurants to be seen at in Hollywood, like Le Dome, creating an all-American album called *Atlantic Crossing*, and finally, ineptly, resigning from the Faces through the medium of the *Daily Mirror*, convinced Stewart-watchers that the rarefied air of Los Angeles, where millionaire stars are deified, had claimed his soul. He had lost touch with his roots. As Rod was spending a lot of time at his American home fascinated by the thirty-two radio stations that played rock for twenty-four hours a day, he could hardly be accused of opting out.

His most ardent fans were among his critics. They felt that Britt had been to the Faces what Yoko Ono had been to the Beatles through John Lennon: the catalyst to a split which the band's supporters had always feared. If that theory was accurate, that Britt had consciously or unconsciously pulled Rod away from the Faces, she is owed a debt of gratitude rather than criticism. Stewart had lingered far too long in a band that had peaked, whereas he had been pre-ordained as a star.

Coming from the world of film, Britt understood what made the star system tick. She gave Rod a confidence in himself that otherwise might always have eluded him. The parallel with Lennon and Yoko was strangely appropriate: the partnerships were not only romantic, but artistic.

Britt actually did Rod's make-up for him, and in Stewart circles she was nicknamed, disparagingly, 'the Max Factor lady'. But in Britain there was a backlash from Rod's fans. For the first time since his great career had begun, some of his fans felt alienated when, in October 1976, he flew to London to appear on a British television show, *A Night on the Town*, singing 'The First Cut is the Deepest', 'The Killing of Georgie' and 'The Wild Side of Life'. Caked in make-up, he affected mannerisms that appeared limp-wristed and effeminate; he preened far too much; his cocky, stylish rock 'n' roll edge had deserted him.

Commenting on the controversial TV show and its emphasis on anatomical camera work, Rod said: 'I had a feeling it would turn out like that. It was thrown together and came out very schmaltzy. It was very camp but you should always have a bit of mystery – keep the people guessing. I felt a bit risqué, very sensuous.' He had played football for Highgate Redwing the morning before the show was transmitted. And he could not but wonder what the people watching the programme would have made of the sight of him, 'up to me ankles in mud'. He did, indeed, look on the television show as if he had flown into London from a too-pampered lifestyle in Tinseltown USA.

'All of us who were Rod Stewart and Faces fans at the time were secretly hoping that Ronnie Wood would rush on stage and rescue him,' says John Gray, his fan club president. Gray was a fifteen-year-old schoolboy at the time. Watching the programme at his home, for the first time in his young life he felt 'embarrassed to be a Rod Stewart fan. Rod had transformed himself from one of the boys, going mad and getting drunk, into a playboy who posed. It may have been intended as tongue-in-cheek but it didn't come across that way. When he was pouting at the television cameraman, he looked as if he meant it'. Next day at school, Gray remembers, 'The other kids were blowing kisses at me as if to say: We *know* about *Rod!*'

And yet, though Rod might have been looking in the mirror too much at the start of the Britt years, his songwriting hit a remarkable peak. He must have been stimulated by his new life, for he began to compose both lyrics and melodies to his songs, hitherto a mostly shared arrangement. All the way back to his début solo album, *An Old Raincoat*, Rod had dealt with real life in his songwriting, as on the song 'I Wouldn't Ever Change a Thing'. Through 'Maggie May' and 'You Wear It Well', he dealt in direct 'message' lyrics, based on his emotional experiences. 'Three Time Loser', on *Atlantic Crossing*, had dealt with venereal disease. Now – on

A Night on the Town – came 'The Killing of Georgie'.

Since his entry into the rock 'n' roll world, Rod had been aware of its homosexual population. Some of the artists he had met in his earliest years in bands had been homosexual, and gays proliferated in the rock management field. Rod never had any problem with this factor because, as Peter Burton, the Faces' press agent, who is homosexual, points out: 'If a person is as secure about his heterosexuality as Rod is, he won't find homosexuals a problem at all. It's only when a person is insecure that an attitude develops.'

'The Killing of Georgie' was, like most Stewart compositions, based on reality. During a Faces tour of the States, in 1974, Rod met Georgie in New York. 'A few months before, he had left Denver after telling his parents he was gay,' Rod said in an interview with *Gay News*. 'Georgie was always saying that you should take every opportunity and make the most of every minute. I know it's a very corny expression but if you think about it, it's very easy to fulfil.' Hence the line in the song by Rod who says that youth does not last and should be lived long and fast. Rod said: 'I still firmly believe that.'

Describing the subject as 'fairly sophisticated' for a song such as this, Rod said: 'It's a brave attempt. I actually winced when I wrote the words 'cause I didn't think I'd get away with it. The lyrics looked trite on paper to me.' He explained how, when he was putting it together, he would wake up in the middle of the night and write another verse. 'It was such a hard song to write. Dylan probably hit it on the head when he said: "You don't write songs. You discover them." I mean, the thing was nearly thirty-eight verses. I thought: "Oh God, I'm gonna do another 'Sad-eyed Lady of the Lowlands'" [a classic, very long Dylan track from one of Rod's favourite albums, *Blonde on Blonde*].'

The story of how Georgie felt rejected by his parents and was forced to go to New York as 'a victim of these gay days' found Stewart dealing with human issues on a totally different plane from his previous work. Asked by *Gay News* about homosexual issues and what prompted the song, Rod was challenged that 'You felt much more for Georgie than for the girls ... is that fair?'

Rod answered: 'Yeah, I always think of that lovely song in *My Fair Lady* [adopts Rex Harrison voice]; "Why Can't a Woman Be More Like a Man?" I've never found that a relationship with a woman lasted longer than six or seven months [here he ignored Dee Harrington]. There was no one who kept me interested, mentally stimulated. I've found, not so much with Georgie but with others, that guys can expand you more. They make you think a lot more. Perhaps that's the reason.' Asked his preference in women, Rod said he liked his partner to be intelligent, 'But I couldn't bear a woman to be more intelligent than I am. I like to be taught a lot but not overpowered.'

Rod declared that homosexuals had been attracted to him back in the 1960s when he was in his Mod phase. It was a terrible blow to his masculinity to even think along those lines. 'I was all into football. I still think of football as all butch.'

In a show-business heavily populated with homosexuals, Rod never had a problem with their company, as the years unfolded and, as a major star, he worked alongside some in his management team. 'He almost has an empathy, is almost fascinated by them, while he is obviously completely heterosexual,' says Mike Gill. When 'The Killing of Georgie' was released, Gill ran into a battle at Warner Records: 'It was not a gay record, but a beautiful evocation of a story about a man who was gay. But someone at Warner tried to sabotage the release of the record. He thought it might damage Rod's career, hurt his macho image. I went apeshit.' Phoning Richard Robinson, then managing director of

Warner, Gill said: 'Bear in mind that you distribute our records. That's all you do. Any attempt to sabotage this record will be very unpopular.' One man with a homophobic reaction to the song had tried to colour other people's views. Both Stewart and the record company were vindicated when the record became one of the singer's most celebrated compositions. 'One of the curious things about Rod is that he is one of the least covered of writers,' Gill says, adding that perhaps it is because he 'writes in a way, and evokes his own songs in a way, that makes them almost uncoverable'.

Searing commentaries on Rod's relationships with women formed the core of the album entitled *A Night on the Town*, of which 'The Killing of Georgie' formed part in 1976, reaching number two in the British singles chart. The album, again with Tom Dowd at the production desk, kicked off with another wholly self-written song by Stewart. 'The Balltrap' was especially abrasive, Rod declaring that he wished the girl was dead with a rope around her neck and her thighs paralysed. He also wrote that a girl was so indifferent to him that she 'didn't even bother to ask his name, even when I came'. And the focal point of a sexually conscious album came with 'Tonight's the Night'.

One of the most sexually explicit songs ever written, addressing a young virgin who is to be deflowered, 'Tonight's the Night' tells the girl to get upstairs before the night's too old, to 'spread your wings and let me come inside'. The secret, Rod tells her, is about to unfold. Rod sang the song in a style similar to Sam Cooke's delivery, and Britt Ekland made her recording début on the song, uttering 'Mon dieu' at the end.

Not surprisingly, the BBC considered the lyrics of 'Tonight's the Night' too offensive for televising on *Top of the Pops*, but despite this it reached number five in the British charts in May 1976. In the USA 'Tonight's the Night', Rod's biggest US hit, was number one for eight weeks, the longest run since 'Hey Jude' by the Beatles achieved nine weeks in 1968. Saying he always tried to write about issues that had not been covered in songs before, Rod admitted that 'The Balltrap' was probably the worst example of his anti-female songs. Considering the reason he often took an anti-female stance in his songs, he said that when he was on the road with the Faces, 'I'd never let anybody stay the whole night … I'd kick them out. I'm sure that's where all my songs come from, because I've really used women.'

Night on the Town was generally well received, and was welcomed particularly for the emotional content of the ballads. He injected his soulful delivery into one of his oldest favourites, the emotional Cat Stevens composition 'The First Cut is the Deepest', setting an extraordinary pattern for the future: once he took 'possession' of other people's material, it invariably became irrevocably identified with Rod Stewart. One note of criticism came from an old ally of Stewart's work, Chris Welch, reviewing *Night on the Town* in the *Melody Maker*: 'While he's going out with a classy lady and here he is on the cover in a straw boater with a glass of champagne … the trouble is that he needs, perhaps, the iron boot of poverty and an empty belly to bring fire to his vocal cords.' Transparently off-target, Welch had failed to diagnose the true Rod that shone through in these songs. He had shed the strictures of a Faces rocker in favour of the versatile balladeer who needed to develop. Perhaps he was the new Sam Cooke of the 1970s.

Seven   Doing it his way

'HE LIKED TO KNOW ALL THE ECONOMIC FACTS
OF HIS CAREER. HE WOULD ASK: ANY EMPTY
SEATS TONIGHT? HOW'S THE ALBUM SOLD
TODAY?'
– Billy Gaff and Mike Gill, Rod's former executives

When Rod flew into London in the spring of
1976 for his first visit to Britain for a year, the word had
crept out: he had been experiencing voice problems. The
famous gravel edge had deserted him, he confessed, during the preparation of *A Night on the Town*, the album
he was in London to promote.

He blamed the Los Angeles smog for the difficulties he had encountered. Many British singers who visited California experienced similar difficulties and made
sure they were never far from a humidifier to offset the
dryness of the city. When Rod's voice packed up during
the recording sessions at Cherokee studios in Hollywood, Dowd moved him to Colorado. There, the Caribou studios, in idyllic surroundings, had been used
successfully by many successful artists from Elton John
to the Beach Boys. But the snag was that, at about 7,000
feet above sea level, Caribou felt airless. Finally they
moved successfully for Rod's vocals to be added to the
backing tracks at Criteria sound studios in Miami, Tom
Dowd's home territory.

Rod's voice had invariably caused him worry in
the often sultry atmosphere of Los Angeles. During a

Faces concert in 1973 he had been worried that it would fail on stage. It would be a recurring concern, yet his sound seemed to mature with age. Even so, Rod concerned himself that his singing came close to being eclipsed by his theatricality.

He was right to be wary, although he could have had little comprehension of how much credibility he had lost by the television appearance that had so irritated fans like John Gray. Pilloried by the British music press, he shot back that he did the show without a new band; and at least he had reappeared in Britain from his USA home to do a TV show. 'I can't win any more. I can't do a bloody thing right,' he groaned.

Rod had dyed his hair a reddish colour. It happened after Britt had dyed hers red, but the result was not successful; her hair turned a carrot colour. When she suggested she had a go at Rod's hair, he decided to go to the hairdresser. Explaining why he decided to abandon his blond streaks after so many years, Rod said: 'Well, they looked poofy, didn't they? Anyway, I thought this red colour would look good under the lights on the tour.'

Reassuring critics of the posturing Stewart on the TV show, Rosalind Russell wrote in *Record Mirror* that he was 'back to normal, far removed from the moody, unsmiling old ratbag that grumped around London a couple of months ago. Gone are the simple, dark-styled clothes and conservative image'. She reported him wearing bright green velvet jeans, red Inca sweater with leg warmers (wrinkled round the ankles) and furry possum jacket. 'Everybody goes through phases,' Rod remarked. 'I got this jumper in Ace in the Kings Road.'

It was imperative that his solo tour since quitting the Faces elevated him to a new level, but with the memory of that excruciating television show, students of Stewart were worried. A backlash was feared. His regular fans might be ready to punish him for posing too much for the magazines with Britt, looking smug, self-satisfied and embracing a Hollywood lifestyle. Watching his transformation, former Faces record producer Glyn Johns mused: 'He was always a likely candidate to "go L.A." – because he's a flash little git!'

Rod's tour opened in Norway on 1 November, 1976, travelling through Scandinavia and Holland before reaching Manchester for the British segment. This was a well-worn ploy by entertainers, 'running in' their new show before smaller audiences in less important markets before hitting the vital countries like Britain and the USA. Any theories that he had been too immersed in his love affair with Britt to concentrate on work were soon quashed. Rod had chosen his new band with immense skill: from Cockney Rebel, the musicianly band led by Steve Harley, came Jim Cregan, the guitarist who had contributed the trademark acoustic break at the beginning of that band's number one hit, 'Make Me Smile (Come Up and See Me)'. From a group called Strider, who had supported the Faces on the road, came another fine guitarist, Gary Grainger. From Chuck Berry's band came another, Billy Peek. Exemplary drummer Carmine Appice, who had worked with Jeff Beck and John Lennon, completed the line-up with bassist Phil Chen and keyboard-player John Jarvis.

To the public, these were hardly household names like those in the Faces. But they were stellar musicians who, in the years ahead, would fashion a fatter, punchier sound than Stewart audiences had ever heard behind him. The brilliant line-up would help Rod to crystallize his evolution. And, finally, importantly, he really was the boss.

His hair was reddish, long and flowing and strangely normal, almost an adaptation of the old Mod look, as he took to the road. When the Stewart spectacular reached London for four pre-Christmas concerts at Olympia from 21 December, the cynics were confounded. Rod was a million-carat star, and one duff television show and a flash public image was not construed by the British public to be artistic suicide. The reverse was the case – he was welcomed back as a hero. Tickets for the shows sold out instantly.* The Christmas Eve show was broadcast live on television to an estimated 3 million. The wanderer returned in triumph. All his stage movements looked brilliantly choreographed as he tore round from one side to the other, breathlessly enjoying himself. And his immaculate timing was evident as he went through 'Tonight's the Night' for the first time on a British concert stage. As he reached the lines, 'The secret is ... about to unfold', he stopped. The audience sang the next line immediately and loudly: 'Upstairs before the night's too old.' The deep voices at Olympia and elsewhere in Britain emphasized the difference in the audience's gender between Britain and America.

'Ain't seen you for two years. Let's see if you can still sing,' Rod roared to the crowd at Olympia. In a pair of baggy red bloomers tied around the waist by a yellow cord, Rod kicked a couple of footballs into the crowd, but it was a gimmick-free show in which the stage was bare, save white drapes and a smattering of imitation snowflakes. Writing in the *Melody Maker*, Chris Welch said: 'Maybe it wasn't quite the frantic madness of the golden years with the Faces, but there was sufficient cheering, scarf-waving and singing along to the greatest hits to show that Stewart remains a key rock idol even while his contemporaries have slipped, retired, or faded away.'

There was a fear, Welch continued, that Rod had

---

*Among the star-studded Olympia audience, which included Elton John and Paul and Linda McCartney, was former Prime Minister Edward Heath, a keen yachtsman probably attracted to Rod because of his hit 'Sailing'. Among the stars attending was Marc Bolan, a friend of Rod's who died in a car crash in September 1977. Rod attended his funeral in London.

overdone things on the national publicity stakes, becoming too removed from his roots. 'But once he was back on stage, performing with an expert and supremely confident band to give him necessary dynamite to the nether regions, he slipped easily into his role as a master front man.'

Supergroups in the 1970s looking for methods of making statements often did so by launching their own record companies. Most were contracted to the giant corporations, but for both financial and egotistical reasons, some wanted to create a name that had a little identity. Elton John had Rocket, Led Zeppelin launched Swan Song, Deep Purple had Purple. It was a flashback to the Beatles' company Apple; they were all licensed to the big companies who distributed them.

The hollow rivalry between Rod and Elton John was whipped up by the media during interviews Rod gave for his Olympia concerts. 'I don't think he was ever born to be a rock and roll star,' Rod said of Elton when asked at random for a comment on him. 'He was probably born to be chairman of Watford Football Club and now he's even beginning to look like a chairman of Watford as well.'

It must have been a tongue-in-cheek remark, for Elton's career was climbing well at that time. He enjoyed a number one duet with Kiki Dee in 1976 with 'Don't Go Breaking My Heart', and his album *Blue Moves* yielded the strong ballad 'Sorry Seems to be the Hardest Word'.

Elton responded tartly: 'I am capable of being a rock 'n' roll star and chairman of Watford FC ... and I sell more records throughout the world than Rod Stewart. Anyway, he should stick to gravedigging because that's where he belongs – six feet under!'

After a year in Los Angeles, Rod said he missed Britain but had no plans to move back. 'Even if they changed the tax laws overnight I would still stay in Los

Angeles. Most of the people who criticize it have never been there. It's no longer the film centre but the best rock 'n' roll town in the world. Living there hasn't changed me. I still catch colds like everybody else.'

He was always very self-conscious about the danger of tipping over the edge and appearing too flash. 'In 1971,' he said, 'I had a fleet of cars and a house at Windsor that was like a public library, but nobody accused me then of growing away from the fans. It's because of the word "Hollywood". They say: "He's gone 'orf to 'ollywood with an actress!"'

With *Night on the Town*, Rod appeared for the first time with an album on his own label, Riva, named after the manufacturer of a speedboat which he had been on during a holiday in the South of France; he was attracted to the name and told Gaff to call their new company by it. Gaff, who continued to manage Rod as a solo artist, now presided over an organization that involved music publishing and agency for several other acts as well as the career of a world star. With offices in New Kings Road, Fulham, it was a thriving company owned half by Rod and half by Warner Brothers with two substantial names under its umbrella: the Clash were signed for their music publishing and Status Quo were represented by the agency. Eventually, Gaff also would become personal manager of the successful US singer John Cougar Mellencamp.

Though the media was stacked with stories of his romance with Britt, Stewart's work schedule was as energetic as ever. 'He was certainly not lazy, ever,' Gaff says. 'There was a set routine. He made an album, which took three or four months, went on the road for three or four months, went to Australia, and then did Japan, Europe, the US. There were times when we should have taken more time off.'

Many artists were willing puppets. Rod was as single-minded and determined when he reached the pinnacle as he had been all his life. 'We had a meeting every day. He was very much involved,' Gaff recalls. 'In business affairs, he liked to know all the economic facts of his career. For any future projects he wanted to know "how much?"' And when Gaff would moot a sum he liked, Rod would say: 'Manager, if you get me that I'll give you a 5 per cent rise.'

While he enjoyed spending money on paintings, furniture, property and his beloved cars, 'He never had to spend money on vacations', Gaff says. 'He didn't have to; everybody invited him everywhere; and the record company often paid for dinner. He lived very well but was never extravagant. Anything he spent money on in those years, like property investments, is worth ten times what he paid for it.'

In Gaff's view, the criticism of Britt Ekland by outsiders for her influence on Rod was unfounded. 'She was the salt of the earth. She refined him. She introduced him to art' – and once that kind of introduction was made, Rod would quickly investigate the subject fully and learn a great deal about it, outflanking his tutors. 'Britt was a real lady,' Gaff adds. 'Her biggest problem was she didn't treat him badly enough; she was too easy-going. I think Rod liked his women to treat him a bit rough. I've never known Rod to be hurt by a woman.' For several years, the star and the manager socialized regularly and exchanged gifts on occasions. But sometimes there was an underlying tension. 'Close as we were,' Gaff reflects, 'we were very different. Many times I thought our association might end in tears.'

• • •

'He always wiggled his bum on stage, from the earliest days,' says one of Rod's fans. 'But the way he wiggled it when he was with Britt was, well, different.' The shaping of the 'American Rod' was perfectly captured on the cover photograph of *Night on the Town*. There he is, with a straw boater and glass of champagne, looking every inch like rock 'n' roll's answer to Fred Astaire. And the combination did not work. Stewart looked fey.

While his songwriting broke new ground, his private life was, as always, played out frantically in the newspapers. Rod's intense partnership with Britt drifted into a slow decline as he began to be seen out in Los Angeles with Elizabeth Treadwell and Bebe Buell. After two years together, he and Britt split. As a piece of imagery, the *Night on the Town* album cover was now scorned by Rod, who described the straw boater image as 'the most embarrassing thing I've ever done in my life'. After breaking with Britt in August 1977, his first solo tour of the US opened in October in New Haven, Connecticut. As on the European tour of 1976, the art work for the tour logo shows him punching his fist through the boater.

It was interpreted as a symbolic end to the posturing while he was with Britt, a look and a stance that he said with hindsight he regretted. And yet, while their passionate relationship had been at full tilt, Rod had been fulsome in his descriptions of her impact on him: 'I hated making records,' he told the *Sunday Mirror* in May 1976. 'If a studio was booked for 9 a.m. you could bet I wouldn't show up until noon, if at all. I had no direction in my life, my self-confidence was nil. Britt gave it all back to me. She disciplined me.'*

Describing her association with Rod as 'the last of the great loves', Britt considered them 'a contemporary Burton and Taylor ... with all the glamour but none of that diamond-buying drama'.

---

*This generous tribute to Britt seems a typical piece of Stewart exaggeration and self-effacement. Whatever forces were at work around him, Stewart has always been intensely motivated towards his work. For example, Britt supervised the decoration of Carolwood Drive while he went away on a long US tour; and 1976 was hardly a fallow period, with songs like 'Tonight's the Night' and 'The Killing of Georgie' being composed.

When their break-up became public knowledge, Rod's old love Dee Harrington pronounced on his amorous life: 'Rod is a nice guy but he hasn't learned how to deal with the Hollywood set. Underneath all that bravado he is a bloke who still wants to go down to the pub with his friends and take his girl to the super-market to buy frozen peas.' (Rod confirmed at least the drinking aspect of this view when he stated, in 1981: 'There's nothing I like more than standing at a bar, talk-ing about football, or swapping dirty stories with my mates over a few drinks ... away from the house I'm essentially a man's man.')

Dee Harrington, predicting that he would eventu-ally marry and have children, said: 'He'll make a good father. A child will give him a reason to live and I think that's why he's so restless now, moving countries, mov-ing homes, moving women. I still love Rod very much but I know that he is out of his depth. He is still a boy at heart.'

Pondering the split with Britt, Rod said: 'You just can't have a relationship living in Los Angeles. It's ten times worse than in London. I don't known what it is; probably just my lifestyle. There are probably millions of happy couples living in Los Angeles but I'm sure none of them is in rock 'n' roll.'

Of the songs on *Footloose and Fancy Free*, which he was working on when his affair with Britt broke up in the autumn of 1977, Rod said at the time: 'It was pretty much an attempt to explain my lifestyle. I find it much easier to put my thoughts in a song. I don't ever write letters or make phone calls'.*

A week after the break-up, on the last concert on his US tour, Rod slipped and fell on stage at San

---

*'I'd just moved to Hollywood and I was believing everything that was being said about me,' Rod told the London *Sunday Times* in March 1991. 'Britt was going: "Ah, you look lurvely, darling." How I survived all that, I have no idea. If I'd been one of my fans back in England living in a council flat, I'd have thought: f— you, I'm not buying any of your records.'

Franscisco's Cow Palace. Fans had thrown flowers on to the stage and Rod slipped on one, his face crashing into one of the drum supports. The audience of 15,000 gasped at the sight of blood pouring from his mouth, but he soldiered on bravely and continued singing for an hour. Then he went to hospital, where it was found that he had broken teeth and needed seven stitches in his face. A plastic surgeon was called in to ensure that his face was not scarred.

As he faced up to a court hearing in California, the news came that Britt sought $12 million from him, partly for what she claimed was a contribution to his career. The case was eventually settled out of court. Rod was shattered by the bitter nature of the parting although, displaying a chivalry he has shown towards his former loves, he did not speak negatively of Britt.

And almost twenty years later she was still reminiscing about the intensity of her love of him. She had never been so in love, and viewed the Rod she knew as a 'man-child', outwardly robust but inwardly 'shy and needy'. That was, she declared, tremendously appealing.

• • •

In Britain, 1977 was marked and marred by the arrival of punk. In tandem with a new look that presented shabby clothes, safety-pins through noses and acts spitting at their audience from the stage came a stream of attacks on the established rock names. Punks were not in the business of making fine music. Alienated from politicians and despairing at Britain's social decay, their primary aim was to strike an attitude. Hatred and anger spewed particularly towards the rock stars whom they could never match. There was a fundamental truth in their point that some acts had distanced themselves too much from reality. The punks targeted the giant bands who, with instrumental brilliance, had transported rock to a level far

removed from its roots. The emptiness of the punks'
attitude was that they offered no music to replace it.

Rod was very high on the punks' hit list – perhaps
even at the top of it. The Sex Pistols had been Faces
fans, even performing 'Three Button Hand Me Down'
in their rehearsals. But now he was perceived by the
punks as the prime example of everything that had gone
wrong with rock 'n' roll. He was, dammit, a millionaire;
he'd gone to Hollywood and posed with a series of
beautiful blondes on his arm. He was a self-proclaimed
tax exile, lived in a mansion, and drove an Excalibur
when he wasn't in a Rolls-Royce. Though he was a soft
target, Rod did not feel threatened by the punks. 'When
they attack me I take it as a compliment,' he declared.
'It's all very healthy for them to hate me. I think Johnny
Rotten is simply great. He's a real little show-off. And
I'm a show-off, too, so I like him. I hope it annoys him
that I like him, because he probably hates my guts.

'I suppose I can get up and sing "Maggie May"
until I'm seventy, if I want to,' said Rod. 'And if I
become like Frank Sinatra eventually, that's fine by me.'
He said that anybody who sang would like to be like
Frank Sinatra, bridging the generation gap. And watching people smile while singing to them was a lovely way
to earn a living. 'I went and saw Sinatra two, three years
ago. The guy wasn't singing that good. But there was
something about the way he carried himself. I mean,
music is physical. It really is. It's the love of it. It's as
corny and as simple as that …'

Asked by the American magazine *Circus* whether
he planned to be a rock 'n' roll star for the rest of his
life, he answered: 'Yeah. I can't do anything else. Too
old for football. It's really a state of mind – it's like an
old coat, you know? If the old jacket doesn't fit you any
more, then discard it. But if it still fits you, keep wearing
it until you wear it out. And I love rock 'n' roll. I think
it's totally physical.'

The start of the punk movement was ascribed by some observers to the split of the Faces. A people's band which attracted audiences mostly from the working class, its dissolution at the hands of big-time Rod Stewart helped to ignite the punks' revolt.

Throughout that uprising in 1977 Rod stayed in California. He went to see some of the newer bands like Graham Parker and the Rumour, and the Stranglers and he liked some of what he heard. But these were not hard-core punk bands. Over in London, punks continued to lambast Stewart. The jibes were irrelevant and pathetic: Mick Jones of the Clash, on a television documentary on the Sex Pistols by Janet Street-Porter, slammed Rod for taking a string section on the road. Unwittingly Rod played into the hands of his opponents, spreading himself liberally across the pages of women's magazines with stories of his life among women – but he did not talk to the music papers about his career.

In 1977, after being interviewed by Britain's *New Musical Express* and *Record Mirror*, he was not heard from by his fans talking seriously about his work until 1981, when he broke his silence to talk to *Rolling Stone* in the US. For four years he seemed preoccupied, in the eyes of those loyal to his records, by playing out that role as a big-time movie star. To his fans it appeared that he had decided the *Daily Mirror* was more important than any music paper.

Some rock stars of his era, like Pete Townshend of the Who, dignified the punks by hanging out with them in the clubs; it was embarrassing to watch such a great musician needlessly trying to justify himself. Stewart, quite rightly, virtually ignored the gang who derided him. In just one salvo, he put them precisely in their place. 'I come from the same background they do. In England, all rock 'n' roll comes from the working class. That's your only way of getting out of the rabble. I come from nothing. Then, all of a sudden, I'm faced with a lot of glamorous women.' What, he asked, was he supposed to do? Hide from them? And what was he supposed to do with his money? Not enjoy it?

The ugliness, the fatuity of the punks' platform would soon be demonstrated. Strong on polemics, devoid of music, the movement ignored the central asset of those like Rod whom they attempted to overwhelm. Stewart and those other so-called 'bores' like Pink Floyd, the Who, the Stones, Eric Clapton and Led Zeppelin had all paid serious dues as musicians. Stewart had truly struggled to reach the top. Nihilism and songs about anarchy would never be a substitute for stimulating and entertaining millions with the creativity of good songs. Punk was rooted in sociology, not rock 'n' roll or popular music.

Ironically, a commercial twist to the ugly punk saga came from a record from Stewart during his 'absentee' year in California.* In April 1977 he released two of his finest ballads on a single: 'The First Cut is the Deepest' was paired with 'I Don't Want to Talk About It'. Occupying the top of the charts for a whole month, it beat off competition from such future favourites as 'Hotel California' by the Eagles and 'A Star is Born (Evergreen)' by Barbra Streisand – and a slice of invective purporting to be music from the unspeakable Sex Pistols. Their 'God Save the Queen', even with a mighty hype, reached number two, held off by none other than Rod Stewart.

Sadly, Rod ended 1977 with a disgraceful performance aboard a jet flying from Los Angeles to London on 22 December. With some members of his team, he was reported to have run wild in the first-class section,

*Although he had left for his new base in the US, Rod was highly active in 1977, recording the album *Footloose and Fancy Free*, playing some British dates, visiting Japan, Australia and New Zealand, and ending the year with a gruelling three-month tour of the States.

scattering food, bottles and rubbish and damaging seats. Complaints from passengers alleged that they had been very noisy, drinking heavily and shouting abuse at other passengers. 'We sat up all the way singing and drinking,' Rod said of the ten-hour journey. 'I can't make any excuses for what happened. All I can say is we've been touring for a year and something had to give eventually. Maybe the Christmas spirit got out of hand, but nobody got hurt, so why worry?' (This was a piece of Stewart exaggeration. He had toured the USA and Australia for a total of nearly four months.) Stepping dishevelled from the plane, Rod was carrying a large glass of cognac and singing the words to 'My Mammy', the old Al Jolson classic from his childhood catalogue. He changed a word to suit his blonde-loving personality: instead of singing 'I'd walk a million miles for one of your *smiles*', he changed the word 'smiles' to 'legs'. It was not a pretty sight as the star flew into his homeland on the verge of his thirty-third birthday.

For its latest Stewart scandal story, the *Sun* newspaper had a change from his love life. Over an airport picture of Rod looking more than just jet-lagged, the front page headline was: Having a Brawl.

• • •

If Rod had been a stage-performing musician as well as a performer, in the style of pianists Elton John and Billy Joel, he might have been better recognized as a formidable songwriter. As it happened, his reputation as a philanderer towered over his artistic abilities in the eyes of the public who did not follow his work.

Throughout those years of notoriety in the tabloid newspapers, Stewart wrote prolifically and autobiographically, just as he had done since *An Old Raincoat*. His subjects were invariably drawn from the same wellspring: emotional experiences and confrontations, regrets, confessions, sexually implicit and explicit stories standing alongside straight shooting rock 'n' roll or power ballads. His appeal lay precisely in being 'one of the lads' and being able to articulate that role so precisely. From the unshaven scruff of the early Faces to the well-dressed superstar of the 1970s, 80s and 90s, Stewart remained totally accessible. 'The guys down the boozer won't believe my luck,' he wrote and sang in his 1986 song, 'A Night Like This'. Even in Britain, which usually despises success on his level, Stewart, the cat who got the cream, was welcome to it. He deserved it. His devotion to football, always paramount to his life, helped to 'ground' him in the eyes of the public.

To millions, sensitivity is hardly a word that sits comfortably on Rod Stewart. Yet his public face as a playboy of the 1970s was in sharp contrast to his lyrics and his voice, which always had an air of tender frailty. As the years passed and he built up experience, particularly with women, his inimitably soulful voice was able to wrench every vestige of passion from him. In America, he was the wild sex symbol whose extravagant stage show, kicked off by the introductory sound of 'The Stripper', was sheer escapism. In Britain, a more profound atmosphere had replaced that of the Faces years. In his homeland, Rod is considered much more the crooner, the troubadour, returning home with a bundle of stories and observations about life and love.

As a Briton touring America with Rod, his guitarist Jim Cregan has been able to observe the differences in audience reactions. Rod, he points out, 'still has a sense of the ridiculous, sending himself up a lot'. Rather like his friend Elton John, it is an endearing, peculiarly British characteristic of Rod's performance. Humour has always been a part of his visual strength and British audiences enjoy it. As Cregan says, Americans often react differently. Some are irritated by it 'or consider it is beneath Rod's dignity to run around the stage and act like a schoolboy'. They think he should be moving into some other area that he doesn't intend to. The real fans enjoyed seeing him 'rolling around the floor or waving his bum at the audience. They lap it up; everybody does, except the so-called serious music critics.'

Rod's concerts seem to gain their impetus from spontaneity. 'There are almost no post-mortems,' Cregan says. 'Nobody would bother going over the show note by note, song by song. From his history in the Faces, he has carried that right through. He's not at all heavy-handed, even though there might be a decision about the running order, changing it because some songs work better than others. And an improvisation passage might be too long, and the audience is losing attention; he will ask for it to be cut down. Or he will ask for a "fill" from the drummer to be removed, for example. "Don't put it there, I don't like it there."'

As Jim Cregan points out, some artists conduct four-hour sound checks before each show, followed by listening to a tape of each night's performance. 'We don't do any of that. So, the times you think you've played wonderfully you get a terrible review and the times you think it's been one of your worst gigs, people are ecstatic! So post-mortems are kind of pointless.'

Among his musicians and management team, Rod has always commanded immense respect for his standards. 'For things like sound checks, he's always been very much on the ball,' says Mike Gill. 'He's always determined to ensure that what you give on the night has to be right; the sound must be perfect. Painstaking attention to detail was always true of Rod. Nothing is left to chance. He does have a cavalier, ladies'-man image, but there's another part of him that's totally committed to his work. That's the testament to a great artist.'

He is also exceptionally loyal. The day after he had received a platinum disc for million-plus sales of

Night on the Town, Rod and several of his management team were having dinner at London's White Elephant. An executive of EMI, a rival record company, sitting near by, said to Rod: 'You realize, Rod, that if you didn't have Mike Gill running Riva Records, you could sell a lot more records on EMI?'

Rod: 'How many records to you think we've done, then?'

EMI man: 'You must have done 350,000 copies.'

Rod: 'That's interesting. Oddly enough I got a platinum disc yesterday for one million units. Could you do better than that?'

EMI man: 'Of course we could!'

Stewart convened another dinner at the same restaurant the next night. Nine people sat down. Rod asked Mike Gill if he had met the man from EMI. Yes, a few times, Gill answered.

Stewart said to Gill: 'Remind me how many copies of the new album we've sold.' One point one million, Gill answered.

'There you are,' Rod said to the critical EMI man. 'The next time you want to say anything about the guy who runs my record company, please do it to his face and not behind his back. And you're paying for dinner tonight.' The bill came to £965.

'Very bright on statistics,' Mike Gill says of Stewart. 'He could not be fooled. No way. You can't get away with anything with Rod. Anyone who runs away with the idea that he's feckless is a fool.' About his concert tours and his record sales, Rod stays on top of the statistics: 'Any empty seats tonight? How's the album sold today?'

• • •

Matching the turbulence of a life played out under the panoramic glare of the tabloid press, his albums *Foot-*

loose and Fancy Free (1977) and *Blondes Have More Fun* (1978) were radical shifts of emphasis in his work. At the time, Rod's staunchest fans thought the tone of the two records was too frothy, almost as if he had allowed the punks to derail him from his chosen path. But time has been kinder to these two controversial albums, made during his association with Britt.

'Hot Legs', which kicked off *Footloose*, suited Rod's reputation as a ladykiller, and the near-comic atmosphere of the song made it a perfect, highly popular stage vehicle. If some loathed its raucousness and its chauvinism, Stewart was always ready with a musical counterpoint. Two tracks later came 'You're in My Heart', a self-written song that stands as one of his finest. 'I Was Only Joking' continued that theme; when reflecting with a jocular jibe on his past and arriving at lyrics that millions can identify with, Stewart has been underrated through the years for his sheer power of observation of the human condition.

Talking of the album in the American magazine *Circus*, Rod said he had tried to sum up his whole life in one song, 'I Was Only Joking'. 'And the single ["You're In My Heart"], everybody thinks it's about Britt. It's not, really. It's about f—g football, soccer. The thing is, what I was trying to draw a comparison with, is that men, you know , especially in Britain, really love soccer, like I do. I mean, my first love in life is soccer. And music and women are a close second. Really,' he said in the years before he became a husband and father.

When he kicked footballs out to concert audiences from his stage, it was the only time he could act out what was in the back of his mind, 'of being able to play football in front of 18, 20,000-odd people. It's a fantasy. It's got nothing to do with music. All of a sudden I'm kicking footballs out … and they go, what the f—'s he doing? All I'm doing is living out a fantasy. It has nothing to do with the music. But all of a sudden I get someone to wake up 'cause a ball hits him on the head. I will do anything to entertain people, you know, I really will.'

So while the words to 'You're in My Heart' could be directed to women, they also stand as his reminder that football is forever central to his life. There, towards the end, are salutes to Celtic and Manchester United. The boy from Archway Road is never left far behind.

Describing the lyrics to 'You're in My Heart' as 'mind-blowing', his former colleague Mike d'Abo notes that Rod 'has never gone straight for rock or pop. There has always been a folk or country or Celtic touch to what he's done'. And d'Abo adds: 'The thing I've always admired about him was that he had the ability to think of Rod Stewart first and foremost to the exclusion of everything else. If he had to kick out the woman in his life, or a record company, or a record producer, he would. He would be prepared to make whatever move seemed right at the time for his own advancement. And I admire that because it's not a thing that I ever had in me.'

Discussing his attitude to marriage around this time, Rod said: 'I hope one day that one of my relationships is going to last more than a couple of years. I was fairly close to marrying Britt, but it was never really on. I think David Niven once said that the more you think about getting married, the more impossible it seems. You have got to really go in and do it or you'll avoid it for the rest of your life. It's the one thing that scares the pants off me. It's the idea of being domestic, you know.'

Describing himself as 'very much the sort of person Rex Harrison was in *My Fair Lady*', Rod said: 'I don't like being disturbed during the day by women.' He changed his women, because 'I think I've always had to be proving myself, proving that I'm sexually attractive to women. But I think I might have got over that by now,' he said. 'It's not that I know I'm attractive. It's just that you break too many people up by doing that. There has always got to be a loser.'

The songwriter inside the performer would, though, always be able to convert those highly publicized affairs into musical diaries of his life.

• • •

Back in 1964, Jim Cregan had been among the audiences watching Rod in his shows with Long John Baldry at Eel Pie Island. His arrival, twelve years later, into the Stewart band as a guitarist came after they had both collected wide experiences in the rock field.

After working in another Giorgio Gomelsky-managed group, the cultish Blossom Toes, Cregan found himself in the early 1970s with the popular Steve Harley and Cockney Rebel. A stylish guitarist, Cregan had similar tastes in music to Rod. 'I loved Sam Cooke, perhaps not quite so much as Rod did; Muddy Waters, Howlin' Wolf.' Rod offered him a job in 1976. Though Cregan was happy and in a successful band, 'Rod was a much bigger name. I said I was interested.' But when he didn't hear anything, he supposed Stewart had got someone else into the band and did not worry.

Then, in July 1976, Cregan happened to be in Los Angeles at a recording session with his first wife, the singer Linda Lewis. Back in his hotel, clicking his heels, he wondered if that Rod Stewart guitar chair was still open. He phoned Rod, who said: 'Oh yeah, can you come down today and play?' Cregan did, and his future was assured.

Quitting the Steve Harley band wasn't easy. 'I had great affection for Steve and playing with such people as Duncan Mackay and Stuart Elliott, but they accepted that a job with Rod Stewart was difficult to turn down.'

There was a special attraction for the talented Cregan. Whereas Steve Harley wrote all the songs, 'I was a songwriter too, and there was more opportunity to have my songwriting flourish with Rod,' This scope, in fact, represented an atmosphere of rare democracy inside the Stewart band – Cregan remembers entering the band as it took off on tour: 'Rod was extremely amicable, very much one of the lads, let's all go down the pub, anybody want to come round for a game of football?' To his new band, he behaved in a very 'non-star' manner, and it brought out the best in them. Says Cregan: 'He and Billy Gaff had set up a plan since the collapse of the Faces, that the new band would be a group of backing musicians which is traditional these days.

'Billy Gaff understood that the camaraderie and intertwining of personalities was healthy in a group that travelled so much together. To foster that is a smart move and we got off to a great start in that respect,' Cregan says: 'We travelled together. There was no separation of Rod and the band. Although he had the finest suites, naturally, we all travelled together in two or three limousines and we stayed around him; we flew on the same jet. I wasn't made to feel anything beyond a slightly unequal partner, which was ideal. You were encouraged to be creative and come up with ideas, as many as you wanted to.'

It was for the *Blondes Have More Fun* album that Rod was pilloried. The problem song was 'Da Ya Think I'm Sexy', which launched the album. At Rod's home in Los Angeles, among the records on his jukebox were 'Native New Yorker' and Chic's 'Dance Dance Dance (Yowsah Yowsah Yowsah)'. This hip disco field of the mid 1970s attracted Rod. The song, which he wrote with Carmine Appice, was a self-mocking piece of fun, similar in flavour to the Rolling Stones' hit 'Miss You'. It also merged well into the disco flavour of the period, but the critics were awaiting him with poison pens. Stewart had lost his marbles by 'going disco', they roared. He had displayed, in that one song, his artificiality.

Rod, however, pointed out that the song reflected his sense of humour towards disco. And the advantage of his doing the song was that it struck a firm contrast with some of his more thoughtful material. It was *not* meant as a first-person piece of conceit about his libidinous strength. 'Da Ya Think I'm Sexy', a huge disco hit, topped the chart in eleven countries including Britain and the USA and became one of the biggest-selling singles in Warner Records' history. Emphasizing that he was not writing about himself with the song, he said: 'I don't think I'm sexy, not really.' About his famous bum wiggle, he said: 'It really is the music that makes me do that. I don't do that for effect. I just get carried away. It's not done to please a female audience. I think I've always done that. I've always moved my bottom to the music. I see myself in the morning with nothing on and I know I'm not sexy!'

From his years with the Faces, Rod Stewart had always been about fun; as a soloist he had written and performed thoughtfully, but loud, smiling, energetic rock 'n' roll was always going to figure in his repertoire. 'Sexy' was the light diversion every artist is entitled to take. The public judged him right. It became a concert highlight as well as a transatlantic hit. And with his other work on the *Blondes Have More Fun* collection, Rod silenced those who alleged that he had lost his muse. 'Is That the Thanks I Get' sounded like a diatribe about his legal tangle with Britt Ekland; 'The Best Days of My Life' exposed Rod as the incurable soft romantic; while the chilling 'Scared and Scarred' was about a man committed to Death Row for murder. This was an extension of Stewart the commentator who had given us 'The Killing of Georgie'. So much for flippancy; and so much for the hollow taunts of the punks who felt that Stewart had lost his touch. For every lightweight song Rod could counter with either powerful romance or spine-tingling power.

Yet his public persona generated the image of the playboy. Now with a shock of dyed-blonde hair, he was still playing into the hands of those who, like the punks, saw him as a pampered irrelevance. While the two albums were slammed by some as an artistic decline, they properly reflected his ambience at the same time.

Blondes Have More Fun met a cynical response from several quarters, notably *Rolling Stone*, in which Janet Maslin wrote: 'Rod Stewart's best songs have always been full of assertiveness and insecurity, but until lately he's had a disarming way of acknowledging these traits before they could become unflattering. These days his work lacks the critical context he himself once supplied. The songs on the new record demand that the singer be both pitied and admired, but they aren't willing to compromise one bit of glamour to make room for real sympathy. The results are deeply unpleasant, with all the vanity and ill-advised manipulativeness laid bare.'

More in sorrow than in anger, Maslin added: 'No other pop performer has Stewart's talent for becoming his own favourite romantic hero and his own sharpest critic. Who else has a similar gift for leavening flamboyant, self-serving ambition with indisputable humanity? Right now, nobody. Here's hoping Rod Stewart retrieves it somehow.'

• • •

In March 1978 Rod began his relationship with Alana Hamilton, whom he met at a party. The former wife of actor George Hamilton, Alana lived in nearby Beverly Hills, not far from Rod, and seemed his perfect match. Blonde, with long shapely legs meeting his desired physical characteristics, she had another prime asset: a fertile mind. Their friendship proceeded slowly, but the signs of its seriousness were firmly in both their minds from an early stage. Rod adored Alana's stylish Texan drawl, and she discovered that, far beyond his image, Rod was a deeply thoughtful man. Both were thirty-three at the time they met, and agreed that a family should seal the marriage that they planned. For years, Rod had told the media that a marriage and children were certainly on his agenda when the time felt right. Passing thirty, and meeting Alana, who sprang from a similarly working-class background to Rod's, marked a turning point in his life. The man who had written the textbook for hedonism seemed to want a stable relationship, and so did she.

Unlike his previous partners, Alana joined the Stewart touring team, and, as he started a British tour in December 1978, the couple went to Plymouth docks for a somewhat sad visit to see the aircraft-carrier *Ark Royal*. Rod's version of 'Sailing' had opened the BBC television series *Sailor*, about life on the ship; now she was destined for the scrap-heap and Rod's symbolic visit touched the crew members, each of whom was given a special limited edition blue vinyl recording of Rod's anthem.

On 6 April, 1979, Rod and Alana's sudden marriage was the main news item on the front page of London's *Evening News*. Beneath the headline 'Rock Star Rod Weds', the paper trailered a background to his life on an inside page: 'The loves in the life of superstar Rod.' The blonde-loving Lothario had yet again supplied the world's media with a glitzy episode in his life, and to add some lustre, the wedding service was held at the Hollywood home of Frank Sinatra's daughter, Tina. Two children were born to the couple, Kimberley on 21 August, 1979, and Sean Roderick on 1 September, 1980.

A school of thought on rock 'n' roll insists that creativity takes a dive in any artist at the moment when prams and nappies arrive in his life. Deliriously happy at fatherhood, Stewart nevertherless knocked that theory cold. He continued his intense work schedule and seemed, as always, to have a biological need to write songs, make records, play concerts and travel the world. Always keeping an eye on his age to evaluate his career longevity, Stewart passed thirty and became a father with no concessions whatsoever to the change of gear that might have accompanied those events. It was nothing to do with making money any more; he had never faltered in staying the course as a singer and had not yet diverted into the rock 'n' roll artist's graveyard of the movies. Alongside the other titans who had survived the 1960s, men like McCartney, Clapton, Jagger, he was a compulsive and dedicated artist who had never fallen out of love with making music. If he looked for confirmation that his audiences remained loyal, it came just as the decade of the 1970s ended. Rod had six albums in the British Top 100 best-selling list surveying those ten years. *Atlantic Crossing* was at number sixteen. His total number of entries in the list of hundreds for the decade exceeded that of any other artist, a stunning statistic.

'He's always been very ambitious for his career,' notes Mike Gill, ex-managing director of Riva Records. 'He forgets nothing. He may try to lead you away into thinking it's all a bit vague, but it isn't. There was always a plan. And he has always known the time to drop excess baggage. He certainly does not suffer sycophants. He'll put up with them for a while, then pull in the line. I'm ashamed to admit that I've watched that happen many times. But his loyalty is quite breathtaking; I've seen that more than once.

'He was very loyal to Billy [Gaff] because he knew what a great job Billy was doing for him. Billy was without question instrumental in moulding that career and in making Rod do things he didn't want to do. A great example was at the Grammy Awards in 1976. Billy said to Rod they wanted him to sing "Tonight's the Night" on the Grammy Awards show. Rod said: "I don't want to do that." Billy said: "It has the biggest audience, it's the record industry's Oscars, millions and millions of people watch it; you must do it. It's the hottest track on *Night on the Town*! You'd be insane not to do it."'

According to Gill, Rod then phoned Elton John for his opinion. Elton reportedly said: 'I wouldn't do it if I were you.' After a 'huge argument' with Gaff, Rod relented and sang the song. 'Their rows were legendary, but Billy's rows with everybody were legendary,' Gill smiles. 'And Billy was right. The Grammy Awards were a key component in making *Night on the Town* so successful.'*

'If you commented on his personal life you were slapped down,' Mike Gill remembers. 'He'd say, "None of your business," and quite rightly. He wanted separate lives in three compartments: professional, personal, and "out with the boys for a drink".' There is a deeply private side to him: one Christmas, while living at Windsor, the star contemplated the grand festive season facing him and decided to pay for some under-privileged, physically debilitated children to have some gifts and a dinner. When someone close to the charity blew the news to a newspaper, Rod was furious. He said he would never have done it for the publicity; he wanted it to be a private affair.

*With the impact of Rod's televised performance of the song at the Grammy Awards, 'Tonight's the Night' went to the top of America's Billboard Hot 100 chart, staying there for an extraordinary eight weeks.

Eight   Soccer in the sun

'AS A FOOTBALLER, ROD IS A VERY AGGRESSIVE,
ATTACKING, UPFIELD FULLBACK. VERY FAST AND
PRECISE'
     – Lionel Conway, President of Stewart's team, the Los
                                          Angeles Exiles

Rod seemed equipped to weather all manner of hurdles. Just as the record buyers ignored the punks' exhortations to bury him, so he rode some dangerous turf with lyrics. Contrasting with the sensibilities of 'Mandolin Wind' and *Gasoline Alley*, he offered up in some of his songs blatant lines that were hardly terms of endearment. In 'Three Time Loser', he sang 'While I'm jacking-off, reading *Playboy* ...' In 'Oh God I Wish I Was Home', he sang: 'Keep your legs closed tight'. In 'Tora Tora Tora (Out with the Boys)', he sang about 'thirteen guys and a packet of three'. In 'Dirty Week-end', he sang: 'I'm gonna rock you till your pussy's sore.' And he reached the apotheosis of explicitness in popular song with 'Tonight's the Night', telling the virgin child that the secret was about to unfold ...

Some writers and performers would have been denigrated, castigated, annihilated by the public for such sentiments. But apart from a ban by television and radio for 'Tonight's the Night' (which survived that, anyway, by becoming a huge record and stage success), Stewart has *enhanced*, rather than hindered his reputation with such material. Comedians have often run into trouble because of innuendo in their scripts. There was often no *hinting* from Rod. His words were often uncensored – and yet he got away with them.

The vaudevillian inside him knows how to work an audience. But he never seems to have striven for the 'bad boy' image that such songs might have engendered. They came, however, as part of an irresistible package that struck a chord for men and women alike in his core audience. He was the teenage drifter, the beatnik, who had drifted into rock 'n' roll with a guitar and harmonica slung around him. He had sailed through bands to serve his apprenticeship well in the epochal 1960s. He dated a bevy of leggy blondes. He launched a solo career while still in the Faces, then struck out alone and went to California, hanging out with the beautiful people. He lived in mansions and drove Rolls-Royces, Lamborghinis and Porsches. But, importantly, he always came back, and his parents, brothers and sisters were never far from his side. And he was rarely out of the tabloid papers, which enjoyed splashing headlines like:

WILL MARRIAGE SPOIL ROD STEWART? (*Daily Mirror*)
HE JUST CAN'T FACE SLEEPING ON HIS OWN (*News of the World*)
DOUBLE MATCH OF THE DAY (He plays football after shock wedding) (*Sunday People*)
I GET AWAY WITH NOTHING NOW – You see, Alana is very short-tempered (*Daily Mirror*)
BRITT SLAPS ROD IN PARTY TIFF OVER SUSAN GEORGE (*Sun*)
INSIDE BRITT AND ROD'S LOVE NEST (*Sunday Mirror*)
ROD WILL STAY WITH ME FOR EVER – Britt (*Daily Express*)
MARRIAGE? I CAN'T AFFORD IT SAYS ROD (*News of the World*)
OH BEBE! ROD'S GIVEN YOU THE ELBOW (*London Evening News*)

HOT ROD'S SEXY SECRETS by Dee Harrington (*Sunday Mirror*)
BRITT MOVES OUT WITH £500,000 (*London Evening News*)

And yet, through all this and more, Rod Stewart retained every ounce of street credibility. Outside his family and music, football remained the love of his life and he jetted to see Scotland play as often as possible. He prospered as an artist simply because he played the deck of cards to the full; and he was honest. The image that could have worked against him became his ace. Women who might have recoiled from his lyrics saw them as Rod being what he has always has been: utterly forthright about life as he saw it. Rod Stewart never came shrink-wrapped; what you saw and what you heard was all there was. As for the armies of men who loved him – the rascal had it all, said it all, and did it all, and he came to represent a million men's fantasy life at centre stage. Beautiful women, millions of dollars, fast cars, fancy restaurants, mansions, and happy families ... all in the name of stardom.

Even though Rod might not have consciously planned it that way, he retained a mesmerizing appeal to both men and women. Together with his looks and his stagecraft, those audacious songs would help ensure his longevity. John Gray, his fan club president, helps to pinpoint that aspect of Stewart's appeal: 'I can remember being sixteen or seventeen years old and looking in the newspapers to find that Rod had about five different girls on his arm in the space of five months. And I was really impressed. I thought: "Good old Rod, get rid of her and get another one." That is definitely where a lot of his appeal lay to young men ... as a hero, living the kind of life a rock star should. On top of all that, he had the advantage of being very talented and making brilliant records. He couldn't fail.'

'I think he likes the fact that he's considered sexy by the girls,' says his thoughtful guitarist Jim Cregan. 'Most men who would like that kind of attention would enjoy that.' But, as Cregan points out: 'It's a difficult thing to deal with if you aren't going to be mature about it.'

Nor did marriage to Alana diminish his appeal. Two decades earlier, a rock star was expected to be a bachelor, to be 'available' in the eyes of his female fans. John Lennon's first marriage, for example, was kept secret on the orders of his manager, Brian Epstein, in the belief that the news would harm the Beatles. As Rod stepped out with his beautiful girlfriends and now with his wife, it actually rounded out the portrait of him as a normal guy. Alana had resented his rather British habit of enjoying a night out drinking with the boys, but Rod balanced that with demonstrations of paternal pride many rock stars would have shied away from. He took their children, Kimberley and Sean on stage in Los Angeles, both dressed in leopardskin pants to match his own ensemble. Before the 20,000 audience at the Forum in December 1981, and millions watching on television, Rod the family man said to his fans: 'Meet the kids!' Kimberley was two and Sean only one year old at the time. No other rock star would parade his life so proudly to the fans. The crescendo of screams proved that Stewart's human touch had, as always, worked well.

• • •

The drubbing Rod received from the critics around 1977 did him a power of good, he declared. In truth, no creative singer-songwriter could expect to have a clear run of success without a blemish. Rod's 'sin' in the view of many was to succumb to a pleasurable lifestyle to the detriment of his art. While it was true that *Blondes Have More Fun* and *Footloose and Fancy Free* did not have the spark of *Every Picture Tells a Story* or *Atlantic Crossing*, what could? And those who went cantankerous over Stewart overlooked this fact: in the heat of the New Wave/punk explosion, Stewart at his nadir was offering music more substantial than most of the challenging rock acts. Heard now, tracks like 'Standing in the Shadows of Love', 'I Was Only Joking' and the ignored classic 'Scarred and Scared' stand up well to being replayed.

By 1981, when Rod had weathered the storm, he was able to reflect positively on the period when he had been under attack. 'I deserved a lot of the knocking that I got,' he told Robert Palmer in an interview for *Rolling Stone*. He felt he had gone through a period of losing contact with rock 'n' roll, and was more interested in his self-image. But he had now returned to what he did best, 'shoutin' rock 'n' roll'.

Foolish Behaviour had been another patchy collection the previous year: the song 'Oh God I Wish Was Home Tonight' was vintage Stewart, a narrative in the tradition of his powerful observations. The title track followed a similar theme, putting man's wanderlust under the spotlight. The album featured the song 'Passion' – Elsie Stewart's least favourite song of her son's career.

Like a prizefighter who had been on the ropes, Stewart bounced back. *Tonight I'm Yours*, his 1981 album, found his rediscovering his earliest strength as a fine lyricist. 'Young Turks ('Young hearts be free tonight')' would prove one of his finest raunchy concert tracks, a combination of the hard-driving rock which he loves and dealing with the subject of pregnancy in teenagers; a memorable version of Bob Dylan's magnificent 'Just Like a Woman' was read with tenderness by Rod; and there was a flashback to a smooth golden oldie, the Ace hit 'How Long'. Yet again Rod proved that if he has temporarily been sucked into the California sunshine a little too much, his memory for wonderful songs of yesteryear would never desert him.

Ultimately he was, and is for ever, a song man rather than a playboy. 'He can pull out amazing things from his memory,' Jim Cregan confirms. 'He has an amazing memory for riffs, things that might have been written four or five years ago. He'll say: "That will fit in here." If he wasn't such a flamboyant performer, with such a wonderful and distinctive voice, his songwriting would be noticed more. But the other things are so much larger than life that people are inclined to overlook the fact that he wrote 'Maggie May', 'You Wear It Well' and many other wonderful sets of lyrics.'

The magic on *Tonight I'm Yours* was the song 'Only a Boy'. Few singer-songwriters can touch as melancholy a note as Stewart when he's reflecting on his youthful adventures, and here, as he writes about the rock 'n' roll that was in his veins, and the 'football fields and teenage feels', he was at his most tantalizing. Somehow, he manages to employ sentiment in his work while always stopping short of the maudlin, and 'Only a Boy' was a reminder, from the fleshpots of golden California, that the scuffling Highgate years would never be expunged from his memory. Nor, thankfully, had humanity deserted him. The most poignant moment on the album came with the song 'Never Give Up on a Dream'. This had originated from a newspaper report which Rod saw about Canadian-born Terry Fox, who had lost a leg through cancer when he was only eighteen. Fitted with an artificial limb, he ran 3,339 miles across Canada in 144 days. His run was cut short on 1 September, 1980 when pain from his spreading cancer became unbearable. He died on 28 June, 1981, aged twenty-two. The plaintive song about Fox's courage and plight ended the album; with Rod's vocal showing his natural sentimental strength, it stands as one of his most moving renditions, enough to bring a lump to the throat of anyone who doesn't have a heart of stone. Royalties to the song went to aid cancer research; and eight years later, Rod was still working for the cause. On 5 August, 1989, in Boston, he performed a concert to raise funds for the American Cancer Society. At the request of Terry Fox's mother, Rod sang 'When Irish Eyes Are Smiling'. The event raised about $175,000. 'Terry Fox and Otis Redding are two guys I wish I'd met,' Rod told a press conference movingly.

Although there was cynicism for *Tonight I'm Yours* from British writers, American writers considered it a step forward. Paul Nelson, writing in *Rolling Stone*, said the album showed that Stewart had examined his recent history 'and decided to apologize for it'. He pointed to the words 'let's turn it all around', in the opening song, as evidence that Rod had reapproached his career. 'In addition to the philosophical gear shifting,' Nelson wrote, 'getting rid of the band he'd used since 1977's *Footloose and Fancy Free* was a terrific idea. What's immediately apparent on *Tonight I'm Yours* is that Stewart's current crew (guitarist and co-producer Jim Cregan is the only holdover) can really play.' Among Nelson's astute observations of the Rod Stewart style was that 'Tora Tora Tora (Out with the Boys)' showed a rabble-rousing, night-on-the-town rocker that Rod seemed to retool for every album; and that 'Young Turks' seemed like a cross between a Dire Straits track and Rod's own 'The Killing of Georgie'. But so what? It worked; the theme held up.

• • •

Among the aspects of Rod's off-stage personality, his family life with Alana seemed to have given him a new focus. Of their children, Kimberley and Sean, he said: 'They've opened up my life so much. I feel a huge emptiness when they're not around.'

His career, however, remained of tremendous importance to him as he prepared for his 1981 tour. 'For the first time in my career I'm really scared,' he told the London *Sunday Mirror*, somewhat puzzlingly, just before the trek began. 'I'm absolutely terrified of failure, that one day I'll make a hash of things and the fans will turn nasty. That's my big fear, letting down the punters. I worry like hell about the fans who flock to my shows. I couldn't bear them to regard me as second best. I must go out and prove how good I am. Not once but night after night.'

Such apprehension is both natural and healthy, probably generating the tension that helps lift the level of a concert. He need not have worried about his prowess; as he began that tour, the signs were all there. At one show, a blonde threw her knickers and he picked them up and wiped his brow, to the delight of the crowd. When a black bra landed at his feet, he picked it up and stuck it on the microphone stand.

●　●　●

Rod would fly virtually anywhere to see Scotland play football, and in October 1981 he and a tartan-clad Alana were photographed at Heathrow airport. 'I'm really here to see my Mum and Dad and launch my new record, *Tonight I'm Yours*,' Rod told reporters. 'But there just happens to be the Northern Ireland versus Scotland World Cup match going on, which I want to see.'

Within two months, the seeds of discontent in their marriage began to infiltrate the British newspapers. Under the headline, 'Rod Tells the Wife: Tonight I'm Not Yours', the *Sun* reported: 'Rows over trips to the pub ... Rod's "boozy nights out with the boys are putting a strain on his marriage",' John Hiscock wrote from Los Angeles. 'Rod and Alana "constantly row about his trips to the local", the singer admitted ...' 'If there's one thing wrong with our marriage it's that she doesn't understand that I enjoy men's company,' Rod was quoted as saying. 'I like to go to bars and drink and that's not going to change. There's something that a man can give you – when you're talking to other guys – that a woman can't.' Rod frequented a small British-styled pub in Hollywood. 'What a pity,' he explained, 'that my dear wife doesn't understand my boozing habits.'

The story had every component a British tabloid newspaper could wish for: a millionaire rock star, booze, a marital hiccup played out in public, a beautiful blonde wife and children. The *Daily Mirror* chimed in: 'Go out boozing, Rod tells Alana.' Here, Rod was said to be urging Alana to go out drinking with the girls, so that she wouldn't complain about his nights out with the boys. 'My drinking with the boys is what Alana and I row about consistently. I think she is beginning to understand me a little now.' He said that after he suggested she went out with some girlfriends, she did so. 'But you know what they drank? Four Perrier waters. And they were home in bed by ten o'clock.'

Rod's rationale for his nights out with men friends was that he did not want to lose touch with the reality of a rock 'n' roll lifestyle completely. And this helped. Life in California, more so than anywhere outside one's homeland, can cocoon a person, and a millionaire even more so. The seductive, heady atmosphere, where show-business dominates and too many congratulations are flying, is utterly different from the British background that had fuelled Rod's art. Perhaps subconsciously, he was trying to resist being drawn into that circuit for twenty-four hours a day. And drinking with his mates in a British-styled pub on Sunset Boulevard, with beer on tap, helped provide an answer.

Manager Billy Gaff found Rod a demanding artist – 'very much so; but that's what you're there for: it's a twenty-four hour job and I was at his beck and call night and day. I remember once going on vacation to Spain. I'd been there one day and got a call from California saying Rod wanted to see me. I was told he was very down and low. I got on the next plane from Málaga to New York to Los Angeles and went up to the house that afternoon.' When Gaff arrived he wondered why he had been summoned. 'He was in great form!'

Any accusations that Rod had lost his rock 'n' roll raunch often met with a swift response. After seeing Tina Turner appearing at the Ritz, a New York club, Rod went backstage and what resulted was her guest appearance with him on the US networked TV programme *Saturday Night Live* in October 1981. Together they duetted on 'Hot Legs', a highly appropriate song for Rod to be singing alongside the best pair of legs in rock 'n' roll. The energy, excitement, and infectious happiness of the two stars on stage continued in a show at the Forum, Los Angeles, on 19 December. Televised worldwide, the show attracted an estimated international audience of 60 million and gave Tina's career a neat boost.

The early 1980s were, however, about to become a pressure, professionally and personally. In the spring of 1982, Stewart split with his manager, Billy Gaff, the man who had been in at the birth of the Faces and had worked with Stewart the solo megastar since the Faces had finished. Problems between the two men had been developing throughout the tour of the US to support the album *Tonight I'm Yours*. Gaff's inner feelings through the years that their association 'might end in tears' came true. Rod announced: 'Gaff was fired strictly on the basis of his performance as my manager and business adviser.' Gaff, confirming to me that the split was at Rod's instigation, added: 'Basically what happened was, Rod and I fell out. I was not fired. I quit. I basically said I can't take this any more. I walked off and that was the end of it. I was given forty-eight hours to make up my mind and I'd made up my mind and I really didn't want to go back.' Psychologically and emotionally, Gaff says now, it was a 'very traumatic period' which he had tried to put out of his mind. The dispute between Stewart and Gaff went to a court hearing, but was eventually settled out of court, with millions of dollars being cited in settlement figures. Billy Gaff says he has 'nothing derogatory to say about Rod'.

● ● ●

The ritual of making a record, choosing the single that would act as a commercial trailer for it, then touring to promote it never seemed to lose its attraction for Rod Stewart. A diversion to the world of movies was always a possibility, but he has wisely stuck to what he does best. As an actor, Rod would irrevocably be Rod Stewart, and would always find it hard to submerge his strong identity into the character of anyone else.

Reaching Britain in June 1983 for concerts that culminated in three nights at Earls Court, the sheer weight of his two decades of recording were rammed home. On stage he could choose from a veritable armoury of material, settling on winners like 'I Don't Want to Talk About It', 'Tonight I'm Yours', 'You're in My Heart', 'Gasoline Alley', 'Maggie May', 'You Wear It Well', and, inevitably 'Da Ya Think I'm Sexy', plus others. The show ended, of course, with 'Sailing', which converted the bleak arena into the atmosphere of a football match, bodies swaying, tartan scarves waving.

For this tour, Rod had realigned his band. Jim Cregan, by then a close buddy of Rod and the nearest anyone could come to succeeding Ronnie Wood, was still on guitar; he was joined by Robin Le Mesurier, guitar-playing son of *Dad's Army* actor John Le Mesurier and actress Hattie Jacques, Tony Brock (drums),

Kevin Savigar (keyboards), John Corey (keyboards and guitar) and Jimmy Zavala (harmonica and saxophone). It was 'a pretty snazzy band', Cregan says, 'because a lot of people liked each other and played that difficult combination of half tight and half loose, which is so difficult for rock 'n' roll. The Rolling Stones are the finest exponents of that. It can't be too tidy because if it's too slick it doesn't sound right. And if it's too loose it doesn't sound right either. It's a very difficult line to tread.' Allied to the high standard he has always kept in musicians, Stewart's stage choreography would tax the demands of anyone half his age. 'He has a huge amount of energy,' Cregan observes. 'He's very fit from all those years of playing soccer.'

While the success-hating British critics were lying in wait for him – one even suggested he should retire because his career was finished – Stewart answered them as ever with a hit: he soared to the top of the British charts with the rocky 'Baby Jane'; it also reached number fourteen in the USA.

Only Carol Clerk, writing in the *Melody Maker* about Rod's Earls Court concert, hit a positive note: 'He didn't put a foot wrong all night. No one could deny that this was a remarkably triumphant return.' It should have been a euphoric period for Rod, and he certainly appeared to have his self-image boosted when he appeared at the Glasgow Ibrox Stadium during that tour swathed in tartan, with a kilt, too.

But as stories persisted that his marriage to Alana was on the rocks, *Body Wishes* presaged a mysterious loss of impetus in his recording career. *Body Wishes* and *Camouflage*, the albums of 1983 and 1984, marked a change of direction, a creative dip that depressed Stewart fans. In the view of Jim Cregan, the problem was traceable partly to Rod's lifestyle.

'*Body Wishes* was a confusing time,' he told me. 'There was a moment there that lasted about two years when Rod got really sucked into the Hollywood night life. I remember we were rehearsing and we'd start at 2 p.m. and he sometimes wouldn't show up until four or five or whatever. We would all get pissed off because it was a waste of everyone's time. It would be very hard to get hold of him. His wife, Alana, not such a bad sort I discovered later on, was very much the Hollywood hostess and his house was full of whoever the biggest celebrities in film and music were at that time. He would party until late in the night, then come all battered and shabby to the rehearsals, and not much would be going on.

'I feel that played a certain part in his not working hard enough on the records, or taking it quite seriously enough. Maybe we tried to do too much. We tried to do a double album [*Body Wishes* ended up as a single album]. Perhaps we were diluting the effort by concentrating on a double. Then there was a decision that Rod should have a change of producer and the first choice was Michael Omartian, who had come off the Donna Summer hits. I think we fell victim to the synthesized, drum-machine-driven, strange kind of record that didn't reflect Rod's roots. It ignored his blues, or folk, or Scottish roots, even.'

Body Wishes reached number five in Britain and thirty in the more sceptical US; aside from the pleasing 'Baby Jane', there was little to commend the record, which his press release fanfared as 'rich with the uptempo sounds of such new songs as "Ghetto Blaster", "Dancin' Alone" and "Baby Jane"'. The following year's *Camouflage* was weak, too, and it was difficult to reconcile the great voice of Rod Stewart with such thin material. The loyalty of Rod's fans gave the album respectable positions: eight in Britain and eighteen in the US, but serious Stewart-watchers were disappointed. These were untypical records from him, and he needed to rethink – and, preferably, return in part to his basics of great ballads and rock 'n' roll. He seemed to have been derailed into an effort to sound rhythmically trendy, whereas he had always set his own musical style in a combination of, quite simply, good lyrics and melody.

• • •

It was a salutary time for him in the domestic area, too. Among the difficulties in his marriage to Alana was her reported unwillingness to accept the company of Rod's male friends. At Christmas 1983 Alana joined Rod, who had flown into Britain ahead with their children Kimberley and Sean; it was a last-ditch attempt to see if the five-year marriage could be saved. But there were clearly too many differences. Flying out of Britain, Alana told the press: 'Right now, it's up to Rod. He has to decide if he wants to be a man with a wife and kids or a freewheeling bachelor.' Rod faced up to the trauma of separation from the children he adored, and, as he headed for his thirty-ninth birthday, his first marriage headed for divorce. Rod's mother spoke with her usual clarity of her son's situation: 'I could never understand why he married her in the first place.' Elsie added that her husband wished Rod had married a girl from Scotland. 'He'd have been a lot better off.'

Although he had broken with many girlfriends in the past, Rod must have been sore about the collapse of his marriage. Not merely because it signalled a breakdown, but because he cared deeply about ensuring that Kimberley and Sean were not hurt.

In the spring of 1984, Rod was stepping out publicly with blonde Kelly Emberg. A Texan who had moved to New York to become a highly successful model, she gave birth to a child by Rod, named Ruby Rachel, on 17 June, 1987. In a happy relationship that would last several years, they spent much time together at Rod's Malibu beach home; in Britain he bought a huge new property in Epping, Essex, where he would eventually build a football pitch in the grounds. In the Californian sunshine, Rod might have been forgiven if he had forgotten about the football of his homeland. But the sport that had been embedded in his psyche since his youth remained his passion right though his monumental work schedule and his tempestuous private life.

Among the British population of around 300,000 in Los Angeles, Rod discovered many kindred spirits. They swapped visits to enjoy cooking roast lamb and steak and kidney pie; and gradually, they drifted into Sunday morning knockabouts in a park. Thus was born in 1985 the Los Angeles Exiles football team. It began casually but soon developed into something deadly serious, fielding its team in the tough Pacific League. The team's president, Lionel Conway, a Londoner with a zeal for soccer similar to Rod's, ran Island Records' music publishing division in the US at the time. Today he is president of Madonna's company, Maverick Music. 'We used to meet in the British pub on Sunset Boulevard in the earliest days,' Conway recalls. 'Rod was always very sincere about the ambitions for the club, and about his playing. I'd describe him as a very aggressive attacking upfield fullback, very fast and precise.' As the years passed, Conway noted, too, a Stewart speciality: an exceptionally accurate 'dead ball' technique.

'Originally it was a British gang,' Conway says, 'but it grew into a team of many nationalities and people from all walks of life, not at all show-business based. I believe that aspect of it appeals to Rod. We have power lunches to discuss strategy for the team and he's always been very ambitious for the Exiles.' When in 1993 they came top of the league, Rod invited the whole team to his home for a celebration. 'He loves having guys over for a black tie dinner and traditional speeches,' Conway adds. The Exiles, Rod's 'baby', are as strong as ever and Rod is ambitious about the club's future.

Of his involvement with the Exiles, and his fitness to play, Rod has said: 'Most of the guys are in their early twenties and super fit and I have to keep up with them, I have to train them. And I have found the only way to do that is to certainly stop a lot of drinking and get some early nights, which I do.'

In the same manner that teenage fans idolized him, so Rod looks up to some professional footballers as his heroes. He has exchanged some of his gold discs, awarded for million-plus sales, for footballers' mementoes like a Scottish Cap belonging to Sandy Jardine and the shirt Sunderland's Billy Hughes wore for their Cup Final against Leeds. During the soccer season, he will phone his family in London to have the phone placed next to the radio as the League results are read out by the BBC. And he has spent thousands of pounds on journeys from all parts of the world simply to watch a Cup Final.

Considering his age, Lionel Conway declares, Rod displays stamina as a sportsman. It is a word that would always apply to the Stewart career, for as much as he continued to be mainstay of the journalists' diet, his attention to music and to keeping a packed schedule, year on year, has never wavered.

The surprise twists to his career kept coming. The Apollo Theatre in Harlem, the wellspring of so much black talent that inspired Rod and hundreds of British acts in the 1960s, was the venue in 1985 for a remarkable concert called *Motown Returns to the Apollo*. Rod, one of only four white acts to perform on a bill including such legends as Diana Ross, Stevie Wonder, Smokey Robinson, Little Richard, the Four Tops, the Temptations and Wilson Pickett, offered his reading of the Otis Redding classic 'Sitting on the Dock of the Bay'. That year, too, he guested with Elton John at Wembly Arena.

Their friendship dated back to the early 1970s when Rod was living in Windsor and Elton's home was

nearby. Both were hugely successful by then, and they
shared a similar 'apprenticeship', having worked with
Long John Baldry in their early years: Rod with the
Hoochie Coochie Men, Elton with Bluesology. 'We
lived within fifteen minutes of each other so we both
kept each other company when we were sad,' Rod told
Janice Long in a BBC radio interview in 1986. He
recalled a 'huge argument' at the time Elton planned to
become a tax exile. 'I was playing him *The Last Night of
the Proms*. [Rod has always had a fondness for that kind
of pomp and nationalistic pride.] I was saying: "How
could you leave this marvellous country, Elton, what *are*
you doing?"' Within a couple of months, Rod recalled
amusingly, *he* had left for California as an exile – while
Elton stayed in Britain.

In a wide-ranging interview, Stewart seemed
entirely at ease as he surveyed his career. In a year in
which the pundit Jonathan King attacked Rod as 'mut-
ton dressed as lamb ... appalling ... a prancing poser',
Stewart showed that it was music, rather than preening,
that truly mattered to him. 'I love music and I don't like
to be imprisoned by any style of music so I just record
anything I want to record,' he told Janice Long. Lyrics
were very important to him on cover versions. Bob
Dylan was 'fabulous, still the best in my book. He just
paints such marvellous images with words. It's not just
black and white, it is images, which is so difficult to do
that many songwriters can't'. Among the lyricists he
admired were Bruce Springsteen, Steve Harley and Kate
Bush.

Ten years after the punks had arrived, Rod had
time to review their impact. 'I think it was a very, very
healthy thing for us all, really. It gave us a kick up the
bum. I think a lot of us were getting rather complacent
about that time. Personally I wasn't influenced either by
the fashion or the music but I admired the raw energy
and just the fact that anybody should be able to get up

With his daughter Ruby who
was born to his then partner
Kelly Emberg on 17 June
1987 (Trayc Stevenson/
Smiler)

On his American tour, 1984
(Jeffrey Mayer/Star File)

With Kelly Emberg
(Rex Features)

The showman in pink satin,
on the Blondes Have More
Fun 1979 tour of the US
(Lydia Criss/Star File)

Rock 'n' Roll raunch as Tina
Turner joins Rod during his
concert at the Los Angeles
Forum, 19 December 1981
(Larry Kaplan/Star File)

Rod alone; and his brother
Don and their father Bob
during a visit to him in
California (Vinnie
Zuffante/Star File)

With his daughter Kimberley
who was born on 21 August
1979 (Vinnie Zuffante/Star
File)

The pensive look, 1983
(Vinnie Zuffante/Star File)

The love match: Rachel and
Rod in 1991. They were
married in Los Angeles on
15 December 1990 (Jeffrey
Mayer and Vinnie Zuffante/
Star File)

The 'Unplugged . . . and
Seated' television show and
album reaffirmed Rod
Stewart's status. This picture
shows him beginning the
'Unplugged' tour at Los
Angeles Forum in 1994
(Dominick Conde/Star File)

Resplendent in red suit at the
American Music Awards in
1994, at which Rod received a
Lifetime Achievement Award
(Vinnie Zuffante/Star File)

and play. But I was too far away from it. I was in California. I was not at the hub if it, which was London.'

Relating an amusing anecdote about Rod Stewart lookalike clones, he seemed amused. 'There's still a great deal of it in the States. Guys in the States are getting away with murder looking like me.' In New York, one had actually managed to buy a Ferrari. 'Got the car out of the shop and got it down the streets before the police suddenly realized … he was driving it down Fifth Avenue and they stopped him for some traffic violation, otherwise he was away with this car. He'd fooled the people so easily. British accent and everything!' There was a serious, irritating side of it. Rod related the story of one lookalike, 'who is being rude to everybody and I get a phone call: "I saw you in New York and you didn't even say hello," and I say: "I wasn't *in* New York! What are you talking about?"'

Introspection as well as flamboyance has always been part of Rod Stewart's appeal. Steeped in family values, he said they really managed to keep his feet on the ground, 'especially my elder brother. I need that every now and then, a smack round the head'. Without a trace of cockiness, Rod ruminated: 'I really did want to be famous when I was young. I didn't necessarily want to be *rich* and famous but I wanted to be famous. I wanted to be able to show everybody.' He felt that out of about every two or three thousand people whom God put on earth, 'I think one in there is meant to be famous.'

Told by Janice Long that he was a 'bit of a Peter Pan; you don't seem to have aged', Rod replied: 'People don't buy records for looks, anyway, hopefully not. Elton's not a beauty and neither is Phil Collins but they are two of the most talented people in the business.' Of retirement, he felt that time should come 'when you don't enjoy doing it any more and you embarrass yourself. I think a bell rings: that's when you say: stop'.

That seemed an eternity away as Rod declared

quickly: 'I have got so much music I want to make right now. I have passionately fallen in love with making music again.'

Nine   The wedding

'HE'S MATURED IMMENSELY WITH THIS
RELATIONSHIP. HE FELL MADLY IN LOVE WITH
RACHEL. THEY SEEM VERY WELL SUITED AND
ENJOY EACH OTHER'S COMPANY.'
        – Jim Cregan, Rod's friend and guitarist in his band

By 1986, British fans of Rod Stewart had good
reason to feel restless. For three years he had not toured
his home country. The gaps between his British tours
were, in fact, starving British fans of what they loved
about him: the celebration of him on stage. There had
been no UK tour between 1980 and 1983, and during
the three-year intermission there had been two dubious
albums, *Absolutely Live* and *Body Wishes*, to test the
patience of the faithful.

Wafting across the Atlantic came news of American tours – and of Rod's marital difficulties. There was
word of his reunion in 1984 with Jeff Beck for a projected five-month tour which Beck quit after only one
week. In 1984 and 1985 he toured the US extensively, as
well as Japan and Australasia. There was news, too, of
his regrettable concerts in South Africa during
apartheid. And there was news of Rod staying cool
when he faced a gunman on Sunset Boulevard, Hollywood, who demanded possession of the star's Porsche.
Rod had Kimberley with him at the time, and the police
praised him for his aplomb under pressure.

There was always plenty of 'colour' around Rod's

activities. But he needed to return to active service on the road in Britain. The show-business maxim that runs, 'You're only as good as your last hit record' seemed strangely appropriate ... which was ironic, since Rod has maintained an overall image as one of the hardest workers in contemporary music. From old colleagues like Mickey Waller to newer colleagues like Jim Cregan, Rod is regarded as conscientious and insatiable for work.

But despite all that had happened since the 1960s, the top-calibre artists of that decade, like Paul McCartney, Elton John, the Bee Gees, Pink Floyd and many others, were built to last, despite any threats from newer acts. Rod Stewart was about to show, in 1986, his innate talent, even if it had not been quite visible enough recently. Talking of the period 1977–9, Rod said at that time: 'I started getting wrapped up in believing in my own image. Definitely. I would even put that down to between 1977 and 1979 when I did think I was God's gift to women.' He was not aware of the change in his music on the albums: 'It was the same musicians who had played on the last two albums. That's probably because I moved to California and there were millions of blonde birds walking about and I started writing songs about them, and why not?' he told BBC interviewer Janice Long.

For his first British tour in three years in that summer of 1986, Rod played before a crowd of an estimated 66,000 at Wembley. There had been times when he might even have preferred to have been on the famous turf as a footballer, but that was to come later. At the end of the show, fans were thrilled to see on stage, for the first time in eleven years, the reunited Faces. Wheelchair-ridden Ronnie Lane, who had done so much to give the great band its infectious character, went on stage to sing one song – and many of the audience were in tears. He was crippled by multiple sclerosis and, at this time of writing, is in a hospital in the US. In his place for the actual concert, Bill Wyman, the bassist with the Rolling Stones notorious for his dour appearance on stage, was seen to smile happily as the band rocked through 'Stay With Me' and other Faces classics.

Stewart was back, for as he took that stage, 'Every Beat of My Heart', the title track of his new album of the same name, was released. (The album was called simply *Rod Stewart* in the US.) Destined to reach the number two spot in Britain, it led the album as the stand-out track marking Rod's renewal. The album was produced by Bob Ezrin, respected for his work with Pink Floyd and many other major acts.

The title track, with words by Rod and melody by his band keyboardist Kevin Savigar, was immediately branded as mawkish by some. There was always a view that Rod should have stayed as the Jack the Lad in the Faces, forever singing rock 'n' roll and not touching sentiment in his songs. The real Rod was more flexible. He had been a child of the rock revolution, but melancholia was never far away in his definitive interpretations, from 'Reason to Believe' through 'I Don't Want to Talk About It' to 'The First Cut is the Deepest'. The beauty, the enormous strength of his work is that he could combine the role of modern troubadour, singing autobiographically, with love ballads that anyone could identify with.

And he had matured. *Every Beat of My Heart* found him confidently bouncing from his own 'A Night Like This', with its neat self-deprecating line about the boys in the boozer not being able to believe his luck; through the poignancy of his composition 'Who's Gonna Take Me Home', into the brave rendition of a John Lennon classic, 'In My Life'.

'Every Beat of My Heart' was vintage Stewart; he would later admit that there was an element of home-sickness within the heartfelt lyrics. One reason that song, and others that followed, would be sniped at by the self-appointed hip crowd is that they managed to articulate general feelings. Stewart's stories have often been self-analytical or remorseful, but cynicism and the woes of the world were not part of his baggage. A populist writer he remained, and now, having come out of the tunnel of glitz, he was about to prove that, floppy pink suits or leopardskin trousers notwithstanding, he could not be consigned to the history books. Proof of this was the fact that his *Every Beat of My Heart* tour was the biggest he had ever undertaken in Europe, opening in Belfast in June and ending in Brighton in November.

Out of Order, two years later, found Stewart thundering back with a tantalizingly fresh approach, his creative juices at full throttle. Produced by Rod together with Bernard Edwards and Duran Duran's Andy Taylor, the wide-ranging songs included the rocky 'Lost in You', the dramatic 'Dynamite', and the catchy, popular 'My Heart Can't Tell You No', which was written by Simon Climie (now managed by Rod's former girlfriend Dee Harrington).

Although the album was not the smash it deserved to be in Britain, its American sales went through the roof, notching up four hit singles. 'Try a Little Tenderness' and 'Forever Young' were the clinchers, and as Rod took to the road to promote the album, that summer in America, 'Forever Young' emerged as the new 'singalong' track, a big favourite with the audience. Within only a few months of its release, *Out of Order* had sold millions in the US and catapulted Rod before an entirely new audience as well as retaining his old fans. Intimacy and vibrancy had continued to present a truly rejuvenated Rod. A dramatic shift in emphasis from *Camouflage* and *Body Wishes*, it was just the spur needed to silence the sceptics.

Reporting in his fan club magazine, *Smiler*, John

Gray said of Rod's concert at Jones Beach, New York State, on 18 September, 1988: 'I've seen Rod live over sixty times and the show certainly surprised me. His performance as always was superb, although more mature than usual. A lot of the ass-shaking has stopped and Rod seems to be putting more effort into his singing. That's not to say he's lost his sense of humour; he still loves twirling mike stands and kicking footballs around the stage.' For many icons of Stewart's size, strong-arm bouncers and the star's own inaccessibility erect a real barrier at concerts, but, astonishingly at Jones Beach, Rod literally had a party with his fans on stage. One excited female got up there alongside Rod during 'Twistin' the Night Away', and when others followed her, Rod helped them up. Eventually there were about twenty fans doing the conga. 'The security hated it,' John Gray wrote, 'but the look on Rod's face said it all. He looked extremely happy. "I like it when people come up on the stage and have a dance," he told the ecstatic crowd.'

With more than twenty US top forty entries to choose from, Rod is surely among the few artists who could devise a concert repertoire entirely from his own hits; but new and old material was included in that tour. From the new album came 'Dynamite', 'Forever Young' and 'Lost in You', while there were tips of the hat to the past with 'Mandolin Wind', 'First Cut is the Deepest' and 'Reason to Believe'.

John Gray had met Rod for the first time a year earlier, at his local pub in Epping. As a fan, but not a fanatic, Gray was slightly apprehensive. 'I thought that knowing him might take away from my enjoyment of his music,' Gray told me. 'But I talked to him for two and a half hours and he was the Rod Stewart I'd always expected: down to earth, not perfect but a normal, average guy. He's simply a nice geezer. I could never imagine, say, David Bowie being as down to earth or as friendly. In the pub, with people going up to him for autographs, he always made conversation, found time to talk. There was Kelly Emberg over at the fruit machine with Kimberley ... it could have been any ordinary man out for a drink in his local.' He even accepted a drink from Gray: 'Toby Ale, which can't be bought in America.'

• • •

On 8 September, 1990, Rod's father died in his sleep at the age of eighty-six. While it was not entirely unexpected, since Bob Stewart had been in declining health, the shock to Rod and his whole family was profound. An unpretentious, close-knit and large family, the Stewarts respected Bob for his down-to-earth outlook, his hard-working ethics. Moralistic and a disciplinarian, he had won Rod's heart, and he was predictably unfazed by Rod's fame and fortune.

'His father was the closest person on earth to him,' says a family friend. Flying in for the funeral at the same Highgate cemetery where he had worked twenty-seven years earlier, Rod, together with his brothers Don and Bob, arranged floral displays such as a football pitch with a Scottish flag. That year was to be one of the most important in Rod Stewart's life. For while his father's passing hit him hard, 1990 was also to be contrasted with unprecedented happiness. He and Rachel Hunter discovered each other.

On 8 September, 1968, when Rachel Hunter was born in New Zealand, Rod was already on course to becoming a star singer. At twenty-three, he was playing in clubs in Britain the week she was born, and, after the triumphant first tour of the US by the Jeff Beck Group, he was *en route* to dates in Scandinavia. His life in the Faces had yet to come to ordain him as a fully-fledged megastar of the future, but he was certainly on his way.

While his career headed inexorably for the summit, so did that of Rachel as the 1970s and 1980s passed. She emerged as a hugely successful and conscientiously ambitious model, moving to the US. Her stunning looks, with tumbling reddish-blonde hair, were matched with a bubbling vivacity. During 1990 Rod caught sight of Rachel's lithe figure and winning smile as she appeared on CNN cable television in *Sports Illustrated* magazine's "Super Shape-Up" commercial.

They met by chance shortly afterwards at a Hollywood club. The chemistry between them was clearly not diminished by the twenty-three-year age gap. Within six weeks of that meeting they became engaged, and as Kelly Emberg and Rod Stewart's daughter Ruby moved out of his house, Rod prepared to wed Rachel Hunter.

After a whirlwind period of engagement, Rod and Rachel were married at the Beverly Hills Presbyterian Church on 15 December, 1990. Among the 250 guests was John Gray, who had been flattered to receive a surprise invitation that began: 'Good morning. Are you sitting down? Rachel Hunter and Rod Stewart request the honour of your presence at their marriage.' Flying down from London to California for the big day that had astonished millions of Stewart fans around the world, Gray was struck by the generally un-glitzy nature of the assembled guests. The bride and groom's families occupied pride of place but the wedding and reception afterwards at the Four Seasons Hotel was certainly not an exclusive occasion for the Hollywood glitterati. Rather, footballers from all walks of life and members of the Exiles club rubbed shoulders with musician friends of Rod ... plus John and Sheila Padget, mine hosts at the local pub near Rod's home in Epping.

There was a distinctly British flavour to the wedding reception, with tables being assigned names of UK football teams. The food, too, was the kind of fare Rod had grown up with rather than Californian cuisine. Rod opted for roast lamb with mint sauce and roast potatoes with sprouts, while the three-foot-tall wedding cake was a replica of the Houses of Parliament with Big Ben. Rachel was honoured with a huge kiwi on its roof.

Forty-five at the time of this, his second marriage, Rod Stewart had a reputation on and off the stage as a lady-killer. From his years as a young man, through his millionaire lifestyle, he had demonstrated a healthy heterosexual appetite. But friends detected signs of a very different man in the company of Rachel. Her zest and personality seemed to refresh Rod, and he particularly liked her unpretentiousness. His friend in the Los Angeles Exiles, Lionel Conway, says that her casual style, allied to her intelligence, suits Rod's temperament. 'She's very into football and rugby,' adds Conway, whose wife, Victoria, has become friendly with Rachel.

Says Jim Cregan: 'I think he's matured immensely with this relationship. At a certain point in your life you have got to analyse what's going on and I think with Rachel, he fell so madly in love with her that he realized that if he was ever going to make a success out of the marriage he would have to behave himself and be loyal, modest and responsible. I think that's been very good for him. Rachel travels around with him on the tours; they seem to enjoy each other's company and be very well suited. Hopefully this will be a marriage that will keep for ever.' In 1991 Rachel accompanied Rod at most of the concerts on his exhaustive tour of the world.

Rod has said that others are welcome to the sex-symbol crown. And friends have noticed a different approach to life since his second marriage. 'He doesn't go out with the band as much as he used to,' says Dominick Conde, a New York photographer who is the cousin of Rod's musical director, bassist Carmine Rojas. Among the gang of guys who used to hang out at the China Club in Manhattan after a show, Conde was part of the clan. 'He was always the star but also a great mixer,' Conde says. 'I started taking pictures of him around 1988 and grew to like him a lot on that year's tour. He's also a very funny man.' A young veteran of rock photography, Conde 'could not believe the show he put on in 1988 at Jones Beach. He made girls come on stage and dance with him during the encore; there would be about fifty girls there'. But by then, the kicking of footballs into the audience seemed to have stopped. Carmine told Conde it had become too dangerous. 'People might have been sitting there waiting for the ball to come down and hit them on the head. Then they could say: Hey, I'm suing Rod!'

• • •

Jim Cregan, who has assumed a level of friendship within the Stewart coterie akin to Ronnie Wood, describes his boss as a 'complicated person … but he has very good qualities. He can be very generous'. At the time he was breaking up with Alana, Rod went to live in Cregan's house for four months. 'When I married my wife Jane in August 1990, he gave me the ballroom of his house for our wedding reception. He has a reputation for being fairly stingy and in some departments he can be. But he can also be very generous with his time and with the warmth of his friendship. Anything he has, houses, cars, access to anything, he will always give or lend to you. We've been on holidays together and his house in Spain was mine to use whenever I felt like it; he had a boat and said: "Take it out, any time."' While Rod Stewart has never hidden his attachment to money, he probably faces the eternal millionaire's difficulty of not wanting to be exploited financially simply because he has a lot of it. More relevant than what he does with his cash is the spirit of the man. He is, avers the thoughtful Jim Cregan, 'very open-hearted'.

As Rod and Rachel enjoyed their honeymoon in Britain, the airwaves were alive with an extraordinary new Stewart single. With one of the other great acts in rock, Tina Turner, Rod had teamed up to release the effervescent 'It Takes Two', from his forthcoming *Vagabond Heart* album. Speaking of her admiration for him, and the way he had helped lift her career when she was struggling a little in 1981, Tina Turner declared that Rod 'still has a voice that knocks you dead'.

The brilliant union of two of rock's most identifiable voices went to number five in the British charts. Twenty-seven years after he joined his first band, Rod Stewart was still in a dominant position in that most precarious and fickle of professions: rock 'n' roll.

● ● ●

A heart-rending disaster that hit one of Rod's fans deeply moved the singer, and also demonstrated his stout heart. On 25 June, 1983, at Rod's concert at Earls Court, twenty-four-year-old Colin Jones plunged thirty feet from a balcony, head-first, from temporary seating. After three weeks in a coma, he spent three months in a hospital neurological unit with brain injuries that have caused him to be epileptic. A fan of Rod's for many years, Colin would point to a poster of his idol every morning when he awoke, saying: 'Rod, Rod!'

Stewart's response to a tragedy which has afflicted Colin Jones for life was swift and compassionate. He went to the home of Jones and his parents in Bethnal Green, East London, taking his daughter Kimberley, posing for pictures with Colin. He then invited him to tea in Epping when he flew in six months later with girlfriend Kelly Emberg. 'Colin was thrilled,' says his mother, 'to meet Rod's mum and sister and we were given free seats for his Wembley shows as well as a portable television set.' There was an offer of a free holi-

day at Rod's home in Spain, which could not be accepted because of the need for medical attention. 'He even
gave Colin his gold disc for "Maggie May",' says his
mother. 'After his marriage to Rachel, Rod took his wife
to see Colin and presented him with a silver-framed
photograph of their wedding.' Stewart's music pervades
the Jones house all the time, but while he received
£625,000 in damages for the injuries sustained, nothing
compares with the pleasure Colin has derived from
the therapy of Rod Stewart's friendship, concern and
support.

● ● ●

With a happy new marriage to enjoy, Rod Stewart, this
far into his life and career, could have been forgiven for
taking a deserved break from touring and album-making. But a glance at his exhaustive schedule shows him
to have imposed on himself one of the most gruelling
quarter-centuries of anyone in his field.

Amid the never-ending stream of stories about his
romantic exploits throughout the years, comparatively
little notice has been given to the very reason he is interesting: his voice, his songs, his charismatic personality.
Ultimately, it has been Stewart's unerring ear for great
songs that has attracted his audience, much more so
than his activities away from the recording studio or the
stage.

Rod's intuitive 'feel' for a song had never deserted
him, but by the end of the 1980s, the lines between the
sounds that his American audiences liked and what the
rest of the world wanted from him were becoming
blurred. He wanted to regenerate his appeal outside the
US. He was fortunate that the chief of Warner Music in
Britain was Rob Dickins, who had known Rod inter-
mittently since 1971 when he was the social secretary
at Loughborough University, booking the Faces for

dances. Dickins had met Rod and the Faces during a 1973 tour, when he had begun his climb within the British music industry as a publisher. No particular friendship was struck on that occasion. 'Backstage in America is a celebration,' Dickins points out. 'Radio programmers and all kinds of people hang out and it's a party. Backstage in Britain is more solemn.' Visiting them at BBC television's *Top of the Pops* studio, Dickins felt unwelcome. He thought to himself as he left: 'I don't ever want to feel like this again.'

By 1983, when he took over at the helm of Warner in Britain, Dickins recalls: 'This company was in a little bit of a shaky state. Then, as I walked in, "Baby Jane" was at number one.' It was an omen that the fortune of the company was about to change. 'They had not had a number one for years and this was nothing to do with me.' He could not guess that the name on that single, that of Rod Stewart, would be such an important part of his life in the years ahead.

As his first few years at the top passed, Dickins met Stewart occasionally, 'but we were not particularly friendly. I got on with Arnold Stiefel [Rod's manager]. We had a big hit with *Every Beat of My Heart* [in 1986]. That was Arnold's first major record that we worked together on and went to number two for weeks on end.' Gradually he met Rod more frequently, both in London and Los Angeles, and a kinship developed. Rod chided Dickins: 'How come you've never come backstage all these years?' Dickins replied that he had at the beginning, but after feeling frozen out at *Top of the Pops*, he had not done so again. Stewart said to him: 'You're very silly, over-sensitive. We like to see people. You should have …'

Rod's relationship with his British record boss was to develop naturally with tremendous results for his recording career. Part of Rob Dickins's job was to have a total grasp of the differences in world markets. 'It's always been a bat and ball thing with Europe and America,' he says, analysing Rod's different appeal. '"Sailing" wasn't really a hit in America of any consequence but was one of the biggest records ever in the UK. "Sexy" was a hit in the US but it didn't do him any good; over here in the UK it did him wonders.' There is, Dickins explains, a different view of Rod in the two countries: 'In America they see him as a *rock singer*. In Europe and the rest of the world we see him as a great *singer/performer*, an *entertainer*.'

During a conversation in London, Rod turned to Rob Dickins and asked him with the directness everybody has come to expect from him: 'How come I don't sell records in the UK any more?' (For UK, says Dickins, read outside of America.) 'I said, "Do you really want to know?" Here I am, the head of a record company, and he is asking me why he doesn't sell records. He said: "Yes."'

Dickins replied succinctly: 'Well, you're a great singer of great songs and a not-so-great singer of not-so-great songs. Because we see you over here as particularly an entertainer and a performer, your material is absolutely vital. Now whether you write it or whether you find it [the song] is irrelevant. No one's really bothered about that at all.' (Here, Dickins points out that in America, audiences do care a little more about whether a song is self-written: the 'cover' syndrome is not quite as popular in the US as elsewhere in the world.)

'So,' Rod Stewart said to Rob Dickins, 'you think if I did a great song I'd have a big hit record, do you?' 'Yes, I do.' Stewart: 'And you can find me a great song?' Dickins: 'Yes.'

As a follower of Stewart's work down the years, Dickins knew Rod had a fine ear. As well as writing good songs, Rod also recognized compositions by others that he could make uniquely his own. As Dickins points out, Danny Whitten's 'I Don't Want to Talk

About It', Cat Stevens's 'The First Cut Is the Deepest', Tim Hardin's 'Reason to Believe' and Bob Dylan's 'Mama You've Been on My Mind' were nuggets which fans lapped up without caring whether Rod had written them or not. Rod had taken possession of certain songs and decisively made them his own.

'Then,' says Rob Dickins, 'I think he went through a period when he wasn't in touch any more. There was the social Rod Stewart, the Britt Ekland/Alana Hamilton/Beverly Hills period when I actually think a Tiffany lamp was more important than a song. His career was kept going but he wasn't digging for those nuggets any more.'

And yet, by the end of the 1980s, Rod's career had been running for twenty-five years and he was entitled to take a diversion, of whatever kind he chose. Despite the fact that it did not prove quite so rich for the fans as *Every Picture Tells a Story*, his track record was no shame. To knock him for failing to repeat that is like castigating the Beatles for not writing another *Sgt Pepper's Lonely Hearts Club Band*, or Bob Dylan for not recreating *Blonde on Blonde*. Every artist has landmark albums, and to Rod's eternal credit, his volume of work on the road and in the studio has been gigantic. Small wonder that there has been work of varying standard.

● ● ●

Rob Dickins was a committed fan of Bob Dylan, as was Rod. Dickins also had a passion for the writer-singer Tom Waits, who constructed wonderfully quirky songs but didn't have the vocal power of Stewart to make them hugely commercial. Hearing the Waits song 'Downtown Train', Dickins felt: 'What a fantastic structure! What a wonderful song! If only someone with a more acceptable voice to the public would sing this.' His mind turned to Rod who, surprisingly, since Waits is Dylanesque in his compositions, was unfamiliar with his work.

The long-term wish of Dickins as Stewart's record man was to get the star to return to more intense song-writing. That year of 1989, Rod was at Epping and had an appointment to visit Dickins at the office of Warner Brothers in Kensington, London. 'He cancelled the trip into town, but said: "I'm in on Saturday,"' Dickins recalls. The record chief's adrenalin was flowing as he considered the prospect of 'selling' a song idea to Stewart: 'Once you've got an idea going and get frustrated, you become obsessed by it.'

Worried about not getting his man, Dickins went to Epping that Saturday, armed with his tape and a ghetto-blaster. He takes up the story: 'I put this tape on of "Downtown Train". I looked at him and saw this slightly perplexed concentration on his face. I'd been a publisher for twelve years and got lots of covers and could sell a song. I got to the end of the song and said, "Don't say a word." I re-wound it and played it again. And again I said: "Don't say a word." And I played it for the third time. And then I said: "What do you think?" He said: "*I absolutely love it*. I love the song. I love the lyric. We have to do this. How are we going to do it?"'

At that time, Stewart's record company was closing the compilation that became the four-album collection called *Storyteller*. The title alone was a perfect evocation of Rod's work, and the package, a subjective summary of his career, carried his own amusing, informative and often self-deprecating notes alongside each song. Rod was destined to be in Britain for only a few days before returning to California, and Rob Dickins sorely wanted 'Downtown Train' to figure on the *Storyteller* album. The clock was ticking away.

Dickins called up producer Trevor Horn. 'How would you like to produce Rod Stewart?' 'Hmmm. I'm not sure,' Horn answered. He was working on a project in Scotland as they spoke. There was a pleading tone in Dickins's voice: 'Trevor. It's for *one song!*' Dickins's fear was that his pet project could not be completed in time. They were speaking on Friday night; Rod was due to leave the UK the next Wednesday. 'I thought that if Trevor couldn't do it in that period, the whole idea would have gone.' Horn asked: 'Will we have a laugh?' 'Of course we will!' Dickins replied. 'OK. I'll do it. Send me the song. If it's great I'll believe you.' Dickins then sprang the problem: 'The only trouble is, it's got to be done by Wednesday. Rod's here for three days.' Horn: 'Oh my God!'

The timetable proved the least of their problems, as the drama unfolded around the song that was destined to revitalize Rod's recording career and open the door to more hits.

• • •

After getting a tape of 'Downtown Train' by courier, Trevor Horn flew down to London. He and Rod quickly went into the studio to cut a working track. Rod went into the studio fairly cold; he had not been recording lately, and Trevor was working with a basic machine at this early stage in the project. Then the first bombshell hit Rob Dickins: Trevor Horn phoned him to say that he needed an orchestra on the track. 'I said, "Trevor, do you mean strings?" He said: "No, I mean an orchestra."' Dickins was now concerned. 'Nobody had cleared a budget with this. And here I was rushing into making a record with an artist and I'd got a couple of phone calls saying: What do you think you're doing? If this doesn't work, it is not our cost. I was sitting thinking: This is a big mistake. And now Trevor is asking for an orchestra! I said to Trevor: "Is an orchestra going to make any difference?" He said, "Yes."' Dickins continues: 'I had to make a decision: I was in so much trouble here anyway!' After Horn had added an orchestra to Rod's guide vocal, the final vocal had to be put on it in Los Angeles. Then another difficulty arose. It was discovered that the level of Rod's voice had changed in California. 'When he is singing cold [as he was in London] it's a semitone lower,' Dickins says. 'So now we have this huge expense of this huge orchestra in the wrong key.'

Trevor Horn was by now in Los Angeles and feeling 'really depressed' in the studio, from where he told Dickins in London by phone that the guide vocal presented Rod's voice as too low: 'If he goes and warms it up for a few hours …' Dickins reflects: 'I had a dog! I had a cut-off time of thirty-six hours and I'd brought Trevor down from Scotland where he was busy and now he's in Los Angeles with a track that doesn't work that cost a lot of money.' So they worked through the night, starting with the drummer, to get the musicians to replay the song in a new key. 'There was an electronic gadget in the studio where you can transfer strings, only a semitone or a quartertone. So you can take the string part and transpose it up to the right key!'

That did the trick. Rod went in next day to the studio to sing the vocal that the world finally heard. And a crucial hit was finished. With an impressive video, the song soared to number three in the *Billboard* Hot 100 and ten in Britain's chart, and in the nick of time got on to the *Storyteller* album.

The nerve-racking operation for the record-making trio of Stewart, Dickins and Horn had paid off. In the view of Rob Dickins, the song marked 'an incredible turning point' for Rod Stewart. 'The most important thing about Rod singing "Downtown Train" was that the critics, who had been lukewarm or down on him, started saying Rod was a wonderful interpreter, a great vocalist and performer. There was this wonderful new thought about him. And it was all done on a ridiculous history of maybe, couldn't have been, wouldn't have happened and this terrible time problem."

• • •

The Rolling Stones toured America in 1989 for what was then statistically the biggest tour in rock history. They went on to tour Japan and Europe. And Rod Stewart's 'Downtown Train' topped the Adult Contemporary chart section in *Billboard* magazine. By May 1990, Rod was top of that section again with a re-recording of his 1985 hit 'This Old Heart of Mine', a remarkable feat. (He duetted with Ronald Isley of the original Isley Brothers.)

The bleatings of the punk rockers, some thirteen years earlier, never looked more hollow, as the Stones, Elton John, Pink Floyd and Rod Stewart settled in for their fourth decade of, quite simply, pleasing their audiences. Incredibly, Elton John, the same vintage as Rod, had scored his first British number one with the haunting 'Sacrifice/Healing Hands'. The older acts like Rod, laughed at and written off by the critics, showed that music, not posing, was what counted.

And the age of such rock stars became increasingly irrelevant. The appeal of Rod Stewart at forty-five stretched right through from fifteen-year-olds to young married couples who had followed him for years, from people who were not born when he was making his first impact, to adults who spanned the generations.

The message of 'Downtown Train' was that, away from the ballyhoo and the newspapers, whether Rod sported a new haircut or lived in a mansion was not an issue to record buyers. What they demanded from him was a good song. When he wrapped that extraordinary voice around a winning composition, everything fell into place. Rod's stage power, originally stimulated by the great Al Jolson, would always be a huge part of his appeal. But he would always need strong songs to refresh it.

The matching of songs to artists had always been Rob Dickins's stock-in-trade. Long before his close association with Rod as boss of his London record company, Dickins had received demonstration tapes from songwriters offering stereotypical Stewart songs. Some were sung in a phoney Stewart style; others were *so* Stewart-styled that they were over the top.

Back in 1986, as Rod was all over the world's radio with 'Every Beat of My Heart', Rob Dickins had received a song from a Canadian writer, Mark Jordan. It was such a quintessential Stewart song, Dickins believed, that Rod could not possibly consider it at the same time as 'Every Beat of My Heart'. So it joined cassettes of interesting songs lining the bedroom wall at Rob Dickins's home. Through the years, he would play it, and even mimic Rod Stewart impersonations to it. 'It was long before I had any relationship with him; I would put it on when I was with my girlfriend and do the whole Rod Stewart schtick to it,' he smiled.

Flying into Los Angeles while Rod was preparing the album that would become *Vagabond Heart*, Dickins felt that perhaps enough time had elapsed since 'Every Beat of My Heart' for this new one to be considered. The song was called 'Rhythm of My Heart'. Since the 'Downtown Train' success, Dickins had established a good rapport with Rod and his manager, Arnold Stiefel. Previously, Dickins says he had 'always been one pace away from Rod Stewart but now we got to know each other more. I really liked him, found him very funny and really warmed to him. I really liked Rachel and really liked the Rod that came from being Rod and Rachel'.

Hearing the songs for *Vagabond Heart*, Dickins felt it 'was a really good Rod Stewart album and I'm sure in America it would be a strong record', but it somehow lacked that big Stewart smash hit for Europe.

Dickins said to Arnold Stiefel: 'I've got a song. It will be the last time he can ever do a song like this. This is the ultimate Rod Stewart song. He won't be able to do any more like this because he's done 'Every Beat of My Heart', and 'Sailing', the big anthem-like bagpipe things. But he hasn't done them for five years!'

Dickins and Stiefel were in Los Angeles, driving back from lunch. Warily, since it was such a classic Stewart track, Dickins played it to Stiefel, saying: 'You might think I'm taking the piss if I play you this.' But the manager was impressed. Says Dickins: 'He called Rod from the car and said to him: "Meet me at the house. He just played me a smash for you."' Dickins was now apprehensive, fearing that Rod would judge the whole context of the song against the well-worn background of tartan and bagpipes atmosphere.

'Rod came over to Arnold's house. I put the song on and I thought: "I'll do the Rod Stewart schtick, you know, what I do when I'm playing this song. I acted the song a little bit, like an old-time music publisher. I could mimic the words. I was like Phil Silvers in *Cover Girl*. I went through the song, slightly embarrassed because this was such a Rod Stewart song. And I am playing it to Rod Stewart.' But Dickins felt he had to lighten the load here, make it a little more tongue-in-cheek than the deadly serious 'sell' he had applied to 'Downtown Train'. 'I was trying to say: it could be great if you cut this song, but I also wanted to be a little tongue-in-cheek with the whole thing. And he was *blown away*: it was completely different from "Downtown Train". He just said: "I could kill for this song. This is uncanny, the way this song is for me."'

Although it was not immediately apparent, 'Rhythm of My Heart' was a song which recalled a soldier's homesickness during the Vietnam war. The emotional commitment of the song, however, made it perfect for Rod – but as the Gulf War happened,

Dickins began to have reservations. 'It was quite a heavy lyric, but Rod connected with the lyric and loved the song, the atmosphere of it, the coming-home aspect to it.' Fascinating, here, was that the war aspect of the song was totally overwhelmed by the majesty of Rod's vocal. If nobody told you it was a war song, it was a Rod Stewart song about the rhythm of his heart, and words like 'I love you' triumphed over the sound of military helicopters. The ears of Rob Dickins for a Stewart song, and Rod's unerring instinct for other people's compositions that were right for him, was vindicated as 'Rhythm of My Heart' bounded to number three in the British charts and number five in the US.

The single was his most successful in Germany for many years, staying on the chart there for forty weeks. The album *Vagabond Heart*, from which it came, further boosted Rod's reputation, loaded with songs like 'The Motown Song' (again provided by Rob Dickins, who says: 'The Americans didn't get that one at all; everybody tried to stop him recording it. You had to be British to get it. Rod did.') Still, Rod was proving that as an interpreting singer, he has few equals in his field.

With a gorgeous American love song, 'Broken Arrow', written by Robbie Robertson, and its other winning tracks 'Have I Told You Lately That I Love You' and 'You Are Everything', the *Vagabond Heart* album catapulted to number two in Britain and number ten in the US. There was an example of the curiously British attitude to its superstars when Rod appeared on the Michael Aspel TV show to sing 'Rhythm of Your Heart'. Reflecting the condescending British attitude towards people successful in the arts, Aspel seemed grudging towards Rod's extraordinary history, and even contrived to forget Rachel's name. In America, artists of Stewart's level are treated respectfully for their achievements in reaching the public; in Britain, as ever, flippancy and tabloid thinking reigns. Always, Rod is

British/Scottish and proudly so, but the country's lack of generosity of spirit – as well as the dollars – sends artists like him scuttling to the USA where their endeavours and successes are taken seriously.

• • •

As Rod began his first European tour for more than four years in the spring of 1991, in a tour that would reach well over a million concertgoers, he had a revamped band to invigorate his stage sound. In came Carmine Rojas (bass), Jeff Colub (guitar), Chuck Kentis (keyboards), Dave Palmer (drums), Jimmy Roberts (saxophone), Rick Braun (trumpet/keyboards), Nick Lane (trombone), Don Teschner (mandolin and violin), and backing vocalists Darryl Phinnessee and Dorian Holley.

For his four-night stand at Wembley Arena from 1 April, the fans' excitement was feverish, whipped up by a week of Stewart quizzes and music on London's Capital Radio and news that tickets had sold out months in advance. A Scottish pipe band paraded the aisles before the concert, and when the curtains parted, Stewart kicked the first of many footballs into the crowd to signal that the 'match' had begun. The audience was on its feet instantly, and in a two-and-a-half hour set Rod demonstrated the breadth of his music, from 'Mandolin Wind' and a particularly moving 'Reason to Believe' right through to his newer hits and upbeat tracks like 'Sweet Little Rock 'n' Roller'. As he swung into 'Sailing', there were lumps in the throats of thousands of fans singing along with Stewart yet again. The song remains the favourite of his mother, who sat watching his Wembley show, but alas, the death of his father the previous autumn tinged the night with sadness. Rod dedicated the *Vagabond Heart* tour to his memory, noting in the programme that if it had not been for his

Dad's foresight, buying him a guitar rather than a station for his model railway on his fourteenth birthday, 'I'd still be standing on platform three.' Touchingly, Rod added: 'Thanks for the Tartan Pride, Dad.'

An hilarious April Fool's Day joke gave the show an unexpected twist. Rod was aghast when Elton John walked on stage to sit astride his knee during his singing of 'You're in My Heart'. Wearing a black and gold frilly dress, stockings, high heels and a blonde wig, Elton served him brandy from a silver tray. As Elton made his exit, Rod seemed genuinely astonished, telling the crowd: 'What a convincing performance. For those of you who didn't know, that was Elton John.'

Rod's voice sounded as strong and as inimitable as ever at those Wembley shows. But before long, as the tour moved across Europe before returning to Britain in the summer, his voice gave cause for concern. Three years earlier, Rod had been forced to postpone concerts in Canada because of throat problems. His voice had more of a sandpaper sound than ever; some found it attractive. But at times he clearly found it hard to hit some of the high notes in his repertoire. At that time, Rod stated: 'I'm a very unhappy man when I lose my voice. In fifteen years I've only cancelled about half a dozen concerts out of thousands and thousands.' Observing also that the pitch of his voice had changed, getting higher, he jested to the American magazine *Creem*: 'Perhaps someone's cut off my bollocks and I haven't noticed!'

Now in Europe in 1991, vocal problems loomed again. After the Wembley shows, the *Vagabond Heart* tour moved happily through Europe before shows in Cologne, Germany, and Lyons, France, had to be postponed. In May before recommencing the British leg of the marathon world tour. Rod checked into the London Bridge Hospital and an American throat specialist flew in to investigate his difficulties. Recent bouts of hayfever and food poisoning had certainly not helped, and specialists diagnosed an allergy to pollen and dust, perhaps exacerbated by his exposure to ragweed and pollen at his home in Epping.

The shows proceeded successfully through Europe and Britain, Rod playing a series of football stadium dates supported by Joe Cocker and Status Quo. But when he arrived in the North of England, his vocal troubles recurred. After postponing a show at Gateshead, his Sheffield concert on 5 June was a mere eighty minutes. Rod later explained that he had been prescribed cortisone, a steroid, which had caused his throat to swell up. He was supposed to have taken the pills on a full stomach with a glass of milk, 'But I'd been taking them on an empty stomach! I was bleeding internally for an hour and a half while I was on stage. I shouldn't have gone on,' he told his fan club magazine, *Smiler*. 'It was one time I should have said to everybody: "Go home."'

The appalling spring weather in Britain, when the tour had begun, had not helped, but as Rod pointed out: 'My voice is my life and it has taken a terrible pounding.' A virus infection had affected the vocal cords. Happily, although Rod confessed to *Today* newspaper that, 'I have had a terrible time worrying about my voice,' the concern was soon allayed and his uncompromising schedule on the road and in the recording studio continued to put acts half his age to shame.

Ten Tears and cheers

'IT WOULD BE VERY *BRAVE* IF I DID THIS ... LET'S
DO IT!
  – Rod, when he first heard the song 'Tom Traubert's Blues
[Waltzing Matilda]'

Taking the stage at Wembley Stadium on 15
June, 1991, Rod proudly announced to the cheering
crowds that he had been married to Rachel for six
months. His mother, watching the show, displayed the
dry sense of humour that her son and indeed the whole
Stewart family exhibit. From her wheelchair, the hard-
of-hearing Elsie asked a family friend to tell her what
Rod had said that had caused so much noise from the
crowd. 'He said he's been married six months,' the
friend told her. 'Well,' Elsie said. 'He never told me.
Does Rachel know this?'

Elsie had not been able to travel to Los Angeles
for the wedding, but Rachel accompanied Rod on most
of his 1991 concerts and got to know Rod's mother at
that time. Elsie's humour surfaced when she asked Rod
what he had been doing lately. 'I've been working, on
tour,' he replied. Elsie said that Rod's sister Mary had
been to see her. 'She's got a full-time job, works every
day, doesn't work *every few years*,' Elsie told her son.
The humour of his mother's aside was not lost on Rod,
unarguably one of the hardest-working entertainers.
Rachel, too, had always been a hard-working model and

her industriousness continued, as if to demonstrate that marrying a rock star millionaire would not eliminate her work ethic.

By the time the couple arrived in Epping to settle in for Christmas 1991, there was exhilarating news: Rachel was pregnant. Rod proved the doting, totally involved father-to-be when she went into London's Portland Hospital. On 1 June, 1992 she presented Rod with their 8 lb 4 oz daughter, Renée, named to immortalize a favourite song of Rod's called 'Walk Away Renée', first cut by the US group Left Banke and popularized by Tamla Motown's Four Tops. Describing Rod's presence throughout the birth, Rachel said: 'He couldn't keep still. One minute he was down one end of the bed, next he was up at the other. He really didn't have a clue what to do next.' Rod began singing to the new infant immediately. He pointed out that since Rachel had been to so many of his concerts the previous year, the baby had been listening to his voice extensively from inside her tummy. 'So singing to her the minute she came into the world seemed like the most sensible way to help her get her bearings.' Their second child, son Liam McAllister was born, weighing 7 lb 14 oz, in the same hospital on 4 September, 1994.

• • •

Like Bob Dylan, Stewart was a wordsmith for whom rock 'n' roll was the vehicle, while some acts worked in the reverse order. Dylan's genius was to tumble out memorable lines that left the head reeling with the originality of his perspective. Rod had never lost his wonder at Dylan's art. So when he got together with his record company chief, passionate Dylan student Rob Dickins, in London, the air would often be thick with quotations from Dylan songs. One that stuck in Rod's head, from Dickins's immense knowledge of gem-like Dylan lines, was: 'What's a sweetheart like you doing in a dump like this?'

'Rod said he couldn't get that line out of his mind; such a brilliant idea for a lyric,' Dickins says. Since 'Downtown Train' and 'Rhythm of My Heart' had touched a nerve, Dickins had gently said to Rod that he ought to start writing again more prolifically; he was such a natural talent, and his audience would love to hear more words from his own pen. Rod made the point that has earliest writing had been created in different circumstances from the lifestyle he now enjoyed. 'I'm so happy,' he said to Dickins. 'I get up in the morning, I love my wife, I love my children, I love where I live. When I wrote those songs, they were kind of diaries,' he reflected, referring to the autobiographical works such as 'Maggie May' and 'Cindy Incidentally'. Stewart asked Dickins the rhetorical question: should he write a song saying he got up this morning to see his wonderful children and he was happy with his life? That, he said, was not a song! It wasn't lack of inspiration, but changed circumstances. 'It's much harder to write a song now,' Rod said. 'It's much easier to *connect* with songs,' implying some other people's compositions that touched his heart and soul. The producer Trevor Horn suggested he should go to Scotland with an acoustic guitar, separate himself temporarily from his family, the clubs and restaurants, and, like many another creative soul, 'rent a cottage and write an album'. 'Rod was there when Trevor said it,' Dickins remembered. 'I looked at Rod … and I said: "You've got to be joking. He can't change his life *that* much!"'

Dickins, however, was a militant song merchant. Faced with the reality, he said, 'My theory was that as long as I kept bombarding him with interesting lyrics and melodic songs, whether he recorded them or not, it was back to him hearing them again.' When he reiterated to Stewart that 'You've got to write,' Rod retorted once: 'If you keep saying that, you're like a black cloud over my head.' Yet he was still looking for songs, specially for the album planned under the title *Lead Vocalist*.

Rachel left Rod in Rob Dickins's office while she went off to buy a dog. Two and a half hours later, Dickins had played Rod about forty tracks. 'Some he liked and connected with; there was a Dylan song called "The Groom is Still Waiting at the Altar", which has a fantastic lyric and Rod really liked. Basically it was a twelve-bar R & B song. I was getting a fix on the songs he'd like and those he didn't. It was also a process of education for Rod because he was hearing things, and some writers he'd never heard before.' Dickins recalls, 'We picked about six songs during the whole afternoon. I'd made notes of his comments and said I could make up his favourite tape from the songs played; in fact he could have several tapes showing his different levels of interest.' Stewart, ever the song man, said: 'That'll be great!'

'I don't think we can listen to any more,' Dickins said to Stewart. 'Our heads . . . !' They chatted generally. The session, reflects Dickins, was like the old days of any true music fan going over to a friend's house to enjoy playing record after record. At one point, Rod thought they would still be playing tapes when Rachel returned. Luckily, as it turned out, she was slightly longer than expected looking for that dog.

Stewart: 'Got anything else?'

Dickins: 'There's one I've got and I keep thinking about it. But actually I think I might be taking you too far down that road; that's not really fair and not what you're about.'

Stewart (always a man for directness): 'What is it?'

Dickins: 'Oh, I don't want to get into it.'

Stewart: 'Come on, play it to me!'

Dickins: 'Well, it's another Tom Waits song.'

Stewart: 'What's it about?'

Dickins: 'Well, it's about whatever you want it to be about; very complicated lyrics …'

The record man says: 'I didn't deliberately set out to intrigue him, but he was intrigued. I said: "It's called 'Tom Traubert's Blues' and it's got 'Waltzing Matilda' in it." He kind of looked at me strange and I said: "But it's beautiful, the way it's done. It's not kind of hokey at all. All right, I'll play it to you." And it had this incredibly bizarre lyric with this "Waltzing Matilda" chorus.'

Before the Tom Waits song had reached its end, Rod turned his head as he sat in the black leather chair in Dickins's office. Dickins was at his desk. 'It would be very brave if I did this, wouldn't it?' Rod said.

'It sure would,' Dickins admitted.

'Let's do it,' Rod said.

• • •

'Tom Traubert's Blues (Waltzing Matilda)' stands as a classic reading by Rod Stewart of a song that might have been exquisitely tailored just for him. Though he has lived the definitive rock 'n' roll life, it is for his tenderness, rather than his raucousness, that he will always be remembered. Words like 'wasted and wounded/innocent victim' and the lachrymose air of Tom Waits's song are just perfect in Rod's voice of brooding melancholy. But, like 'Downtown Train', the story behind the making of the record was one of high drama.

Rod had recorded the song under the production of Trevor Horn, who had added an orchestra to what Rod had originally worked with, a guitar and piano. In a six-and-a-half-minute version, there were one or two lines that Trevor wanted to re-record. On a beautiful Los Angeles day, Rod met Rob Dickins at the studio at the prescribed time of 5 pm. But Trevor Horn was delayed at another studio, working on a different Rod Stewart track. 'We chatted a bit and he was a bit restless, looking at his watch,' Dickins recalls of Rod.

Dickins was in the control room, Rod with his headphones on, ready to re-work the lines which Horn wanted. To pass the time as they awaited the producer, Dickins asked Rod if he wanted to hear the latest version, since he had not heard it since the orchestra had gone on. 'I said: "Do you want to come in?" – meaning, to the recording control desk.' Rod replied no, Dickins should play it through the cans. 'And it absolutely *got* to him, there was almost a tear in his eye. He was listening to the song with the full arrangement objectively for the first time, hearing it like we hear it. I think it was quite an emotional moment.'

It was also a frustrating moment for Dickins. 'I thought: I wish Trevor was here now because Rod is now in the grips of this song.' Then came a phone call saying Horn would be delayed a further hour. Rod said to Rob Dickins: 'You *know* this song, don't you? I can sing this song; we've got the engineer here; I'll trust you; just tell me if it's right or wrong.'

Rod sang it a couple of times. 'We were dropping in the last few lines of the song, where the melody slightly changes,' Dickins says. 'We had to make a subtle change at the end.' He flinches at the memory of his own voice, on talkback. 'Me, who can't sing a note, sounding absolutely awful, singing it through for Rod and he said: "Yeah, I've got it."' Rod pronounced it fixed, and left for a dinner date, leaving Dickins reeling at the responsibility. 'When Trevor Horn came in, I said: "We've done it."'

Coming in at six and a half minutes, the song was the only conceivable reason for anyone to buy the 1992 compilation album called *Lead Vocalist*. This truly bizarre collection, originally called *Once in a Blue Moon*, could hardly have been aimed at serious Stewart fans, since seven of the tracks were already on release, many of them years earlier. Significantly, the album went unreleased in America. But the single, trimmed down to four minutes to make it more accessible for disc jockeys, was a stunning success. It jumped to number six in the British chart and has become a perennial radio favourite.*

Rod was in Ireland, recording tracks for the *Lead Vocalist* album, when a phone call told him that the father of his guitarist Jim Cregan had died. Cregan was not working on Rod's album, but by the time he got to London for the funeral he was touched to find that his boss had flown in to be by his side. 'I will always be fond of Rod for that alone,' Cregan says. 'It was a very sweet, special gesture.'

● ● ●

Among the many awards that have piled on to his walls in his thirty years, the two that marked the start of the 1990s were certainly among the most significant. On 28 June, 1991, the Nordoff Robbins Music Therapy Centre for Handicapped Children's annual Silver Clef award went to Rod. Recognizing outstanding service to British music, the award was presented to Rod by his friend Elton John. Rod had won the coveted Living Legend Award in America's Grammys in 1989.

And on 16 February, 1993 came the Brit Award for Lifetime Achievement, presented to him in London

---

* The album *Lead Vocalist* was lambasted by Rod's always vociferous fans as a piece of shameful exploitative marketing. Typical of the irate reactions of loyal Stewart people, writing to the fan club magazine *Smiler*, was the view of Mary Roberts of Cleveland: 'I never thought I would ever write this, but Rod's new album is a bloody disgrace. I eagerly awaited the release of *Lead Vocalist* only to find it a compilation of seven previously released tracks! Of the five others, I already had the two singles so I was left to hear three new tracks for £12.99. How can Rod or Warner Records justify this? All genuine Rod fans will feel cheated by this effort.' Another letter described the album as 'a deceit', and a fan of twenty-two years' standing protested: 'Please, Rod, don't do this to your fans again. Surely we're worth more than this? Get your old pen out, mate, and write us some more of your great songs.'

by another name from Rod's celebrated past, Long John Baldry. Addressing the crowd at Alexandra Palace, so near Highgate Village where he was born, Rod struck his usual note of fact and humour: 'When I started out at nineteen I made myself three promises. To stay in a job for more than six months, to save £300 to buy a sports car, and to pull as many birds as I could. All those dreams have come wonderfully true!' he told the cheering crowd.

Adding modestly that he still felt he had to create the definitive Rod Stewart album, he recalled how, all those years ago, his brother Don had taken him to the Gaumont State, Kilburn, to see Bill Haley, sparking off his long journey to the apogee of this night, when he was being fêted by his contemporaries from all sides of the music world.

Rod performed his latest single, 'Ruby Tuesday', before being joined on stage, to the surprise of the audience, by his old friends Ronnie Wood, Kenney Jones and Ian MacLagan. It would have been a full Faces reunion, but for the sad absence of Ronnie Lane. In Ronnie's place was Bill Wyman. As Rod led them into a rousing version of 'Stay with Me', that finest moment of the Faces' recording history, Mick Jagger, who was in the audience, noted that Bill Wyman's traditional poker face inside the Stones had been replaced by a beaming smile inside the Faces line-up. To Jagger's surprise the infectiousness of what was happening on stage caused him also even to join in the singing. 'Never been known,' said Mick of his ex-bassist.

● ● ●

'I think his voice is a little sweeter than it used to be,' says his guitarist and pal Jim Cregan. 'I don't think he has the raspy edge he had twenty years ago, probably because he looks after it better and knows a little better how to use it. Instead of getting weaker as he gets older, it gets better; it's as good now as it's ever been.' Rod took some singing lessons in Los Angeles in 1992, Cregan relates, 'And it gave him a couple of extra, high notes, which is unusual. Normally what happens is that as you get older your vocal range diminishes in power.'

For the 1993–4 *Unplugged* tour, Rod also received the aid of high technology. 'It's rather like a hearing aid and you get a belt pack and you get a stereo mix wherever you go on stage,' Cregan says. 'He can sing as softly as he wants to; he can hear himself singing and he gets a stereo mix of what the band's doing; it's great for his pitching as he's not shouting and blowing his voice out, which used to be a major concern. If his voice was in trouble he'd be very apprehensive about the show. It would ruin the whole day for him and after the show he'd go straight to bed and rest; he wouldn't be able to go out anywhere and have fun. He was solely dependent on the strength of that muscle. Whereas with this new wireless headphone technology, he doesn't have any problems with his voice.' As Cregan points out, postponed concerts were disappointing for fans and also caused lost revenue. 'The tour would have to be extended to make up for lost dates. It was a Catch 22 situation: what he really needed to do when his voice got bad was rest, but you've got seven trucks, and two planes and four buses on the road, a lot of money going out every week. So cancelling is an expensive operation.'

Concerns about postponed concerts have now diminished. Years earlier, Rod would have thought nothing about port and brandy mixed, or even half a bottle of Bacardi and Coke before taking the stage. Now, he drinks great quantities of Evian water and is fit and strong for the rigours of travelling and performing a particularly athletic stage show.

That voice has always been the most powerful asset, and it continues to improve as the years pass.

Once, he tilted it, and his stage work, towards hard driving rock 'n' roll. But while there are many hundreds of fine rock 'n' rollers, there is only one Stewart voice. As he passed forty-eight, perhaps the biggest test of his career, and his vocal abilities, awaited him.

In the US, the brilliantly conceived MTV series *Unplugged* had attracted many substantial artists into a studio where, stripped of amplification, they were invited to prove not merely that their repertoire had stood the test of time, but because their instrumental and vocal prowess was matched by lyrics that could actually be enjoyed with no amplification. Musicians of the calibre of Paul McCartney, Eric Clapton and Neil Young had all appeared on *Unplugged*, reminding their old fans of the strength and beauty of their songs, while also tapping into a new generation.

When Rod Stewart took the stage at Universal Studios, Los Angeles on 5 February, 1993 for his televised-and-recorded appearance on *Unplugged ... and Seated*, as he would call his album, there was no amplification, but the atmosphere was certainly electric. In an emotional session, Rod teamed up with Ronnie Wood and an eleven-piece band to delve into his golden oldie catalogue, providing a rich harvest of great lyrics and powerful melodies, set off by a voice that seemed, even after all those years, freshly plaintive and more determined than ever to enrich the stories in the songs.

Running parallel with the performance was Stewart's self-mocking chat. Writing of her attendance at the session in the magazine *Smiler*, Adele Adams noted that both the spiky-haired Stewart and Ronnie Wood wore spectacles. 'There's spectacles everywhere,' Rod said, commenting that he and his old mate were getting old. 'Rod's rapport with the audience was unique,' wrote Adele Adams, 'and on several occasions he teased Ronnie about his job with the Rolling Stones: "Here's a song we used to do before you went and joined that other band.'" Launching into 'Reason to Believe', Rod said: 'We haven't done this together since we recorded it twenty-two years ago. Most of the band weren't born and my wife was only one.'

The material spanned the whole range of Rod's most articulate songs. But there were two significant differences between the old versions and the *Unplugged* sessions. Remarkably, his voice was better equipped (undoubtedly through his maturity) to resonate with the tenderness of the lyrics, and, with such a spare and sensitive line-up of musicians, every nuance of every song could be heard.

The *Unplugged* philosophy is the opposite of forced showmanship. The songs stand naked. With the emphasis firmly on his work rather than acrobatics, Rod truly got inside some of his vintage work. 'Maggie May', which originally hit us all as a light swinger, suddenly sprang into a new life as a tender ballad, with every line in the song of Rod's youthful experience standing up well to this sudden glare. 'Handbags and Gladrags' was beautifully read, and when Rod dedicated 'Have I Told You Lately' to Rachel, who was sitting in the audience with their eight-month-old daughter, Renée, he was overwhelmed with emotion. 'His voice cracked near the end of the song and he dissolved into tears,' noted Adele Adams. Later Rod said it had indeed been a genuine tear ... 'And why not?' he asked.

The star who came from a non-tactile family – 'The only time my Dad and I ever hugged was when Scotland scored a goal against England' – has become visibly demonstrative with his own children. 'My kids hug and kiss me so much ... it's taught me to do it with my own parents now,' he said in 1986. 'I don't ever remember telling my mum and dad how much I loved them, but I do now.'

While Stewart is not known for being publicity-shy, he has been quietly philanthropic in charitable areas. Committed to the battle against AIDS from the beginning of the epidemic, he has given generously to the Aids organizations and to the Terence Higgins Trust in London. And in the 1994 Los Angeles earthquake, partly as an expression of relief, since his mansion was unaffected, he and Rachel bought tents and sleeping-bags to distribute to homeless victims, as well as buying food and hiring trucks to distribute it around the city.

Most of the gems of his career were in his set: the irony of 'The First Cut is the Deepest'; the gentleness of 'Mandolin Wind'; the reminder of his break-through with 'Every Picture Tells a Story'; and more. 'Tom Traubert's Blues (Waltzing Matilda)' topped off a stunning, highly charged performance. In a sphere of the entertainment world noted for exaggeration, Stewart's *Unplugged ... and Seated* was a true triumph, demonstrating that his work as a singer and composer could stand the toughest of tests.

The album *Unplugged ... and Seated* was a colossal commercial, as well as artistic, success. It arrived straight into the US magazine *Billboard*'s Hot 100 Album chart at number two, the highest chart entry for any Stewart album in the US. Staying there for five weeks, it was held off the top spot by Janet Jackson. But it was still the top position Rod had achieved in the US album charts since he hit the top in 1979 with *Blondes Have More Fun. Unplugged* also reached the number two spot in Britain.

Rod's voice and the sheer power of those songs reached across the generations with *Unplugged ... and Seated*, touching fans who were certainly not born when he started out, right through to those of his own age. It was a pivotal moment in his life and career. In conversations with Rob Dickins, the two men had sometimes discussed the future. Can the peak Rod has reached be sustained when, say, he heads into his late fifties? Frank Sinatra has certainly done it with dignity.

It is a challenge that, after the revelation of *Unplugged*, Stewart can face confidently. It might be too much to see him lurching about singing 'Da Ya Think I'm Sexy'; but in 'Tom Traubert's Blues' and 'Reason to Believe', to name but two, he has guaranteed timelessness.

'He could have been a huge star in the East End of London in the music hall in the 1920s,' Dickins points out. 'He has that persona, the charisma of the loved entertainer in the loud check suit, rather like Max Wall. Part of his unique success is that he has taken that into the 1970s, 1980s and 1990s. He's wedded to music hall, performance, entertaining, whereas others were 1970s or 1980s rock boys. Others were of a moment. Rod was never "of a moment".'

Declaring that he was never an intense fan of the rock 'n' roll giants like Chuck Berry or Jerry Lee Lewis, Rod has stated that he was originally 'a folkie at heart'. As for his love of Jolson, whose performance might sound terribly dated and irrelevant to some of his young followers, Stewart drew an analogy between him and Michael Jackson, who projected himself with white socks and glove. Such flamboyance was being demonstrated, Rod pointed out, by Al Jolson in the 1950s as a crowd-pleasing entertainer. 'Jolson was a white Jew who dressed up as a black man, really weird,' Rod said. But he knew how to communicate with his audiences. In show-business, very little is new.

Fuelled by the universal applause for the acoustic set, Rod took to the road in 1993 for the *Unplugged ... and Seated* tour. At Madison Square Garden in November, the years rolled away for the 20,000 New York crowd as, resplendent in a mauve suit and white frilly shirt, he looked and sounded rejuvenated as he launched into 'Reason to Believe'. As a violin introduction took him into a light, swinging version of 'You Wear It Well', he took off his jacket to reveal a purple waistcoat. Clearly, the pared-down simplicity of an *Unplugged* collection was not going to stifle the theatrical side of Stewart. Soon he was running around the stage, preening with the mike, tantalizing with 'Tonight's the Night' as flowers arrived at his feet from admiring fans.

The crowd went wild at his sexiest lyric before 'Maggie May' was unveiled. In reality, Rod does not need to sing much at his own concerts; his crowds know every word of every song and join in at the vital moments. And Stewart knows precisely when to encourage that to happen. In 'You're in my Heart', the huge crowd was there, waiting on cue, to join in chanting 'You are my lover, you're my best friend'. And then, the young reprobate from Highgate is back. As he evokes in his lyrics the memory of Celtic United, he's down on one knee, with arms outstretched. Just like Al Jolson.

Discography 1964–1994

Compiled by John Gray, President of the Official Rod Stewart Fan Club and editor of the Rod Stewart magazine *Smiler*. For membership and subscription details send SAE to: P.O. Box 475, Morden, Surrey SM4 6AT, England.

The following discography is the most comprehensive listing of Rod Stewart's UK work ever compiled. It is intended to reflect his recording career as he planned it and therefore omits reissued singles and the many compilation albums released without his consent. Following Rod's career on record can sometimes be confusing, as he has recorded for many different labels over his thirty-year career. However, this discography is probably the first ever to list every single version of every single track Rod has ever recorded. Also included for the first time in any Rod Stewart discography is a list of songs Rod is known to have performed live on stage but has not committed to record, and also a list of Stewart written or co-written songs which have been covered by other artists.

As a general rule, this discography does not include promotional discs, twelve-inch singles, re-releases, re-packages or picture discs except where they contain previously unreleased tracks that are not available elsewhere. *Songs either completely written or co-written by Rod are printed in capital letters.* Catalogue numbers refer to vinyl releases up until 1987; thereafter, track details and catalogue numbers refer to compact disc releases. All track details are listed as they appear on the record even if they are incorrect (see notes 5 and 6 below).

*Denotes tracks which Rod did not appear on.

NOTES:
1. The single versions of 'It's All Over Now' (1970) and 'Had Me a Real Good Time' (Faces: 1970) are different versions from the album tracks.
2. 'I Wish It Would Rain', B-side of 'Pool Hall Richard' (Faces: 1973) was recorded live at the Reading Festival, 25 August 1973.
3. 'Shine' (Ted Wood: 1975, B-side) also features Gary Glitter and Bobby Womack.

4. 'I Just Want to Make Love to You', featured on the cassette version of 'Foolish Behaviour', was recorded live at the Los Angeles Forum, June 1979.

5. 'Hot Legs' [live] on the single 'It Takes Two' (Rod Stewart and Tina Turner: 1990) does not feature Tina Turner despite the label credit.

6. 'I Don't Want to Talk About It' [newly recorded] (1991) on the B-side of 'Rhythm of My Heart' is not the newly recorded version but the original from 1975s *Atlantic Crossing*.

7. 'Sweet Soul Music', featured on the single 'The Motown Song', was recorded live at Wembley Arena, April 1990.

Singles

1964	June	'You'll Be Mine'*/'Up Above My Head' (United Artists UP 1056: Long John Baldry and the Hoochie Coochie Men)
	October	'Good Morning Little Schoolgirl'/'I'm Gonna Move to the Outskirts of Town' (Decca F 11996)
1965	November	'The Day Will Come'/'Why Does It Go On' (Columbia DB 7766)
1966	April	'Shake'/'I Just Got Some' (Columbia DB 7892)
	October	'I Could Feel the Whole World Turn Round Underneath Me'/'Curtains' [instrumental]* (Columbia DB 8025: Shotgun Express)
1967	July	'Tallyman' [instrumental]*/'Rock My Plimsoul' (Columbia DB 8227: Jeff Beck)
1968	February	'Love Is Blue' [instrumental]*/'I've Been Drinking' (Columbia DB 8359: Jeff Beck)
	March	'Little Miss Understood'/'SO MUCH TO SAY' (Immediate IM 060)
1970		'In a Broken Dream'/'Doing Fine' (Youngblood YB 1017: Python Lee Jackson)
	February	'FLYING'/'THREE BUTTON HAND ME DOWN' (Warner Bros. WB 8005: Faces)
	September	'It's All Over Now'/'JO'S LAMENT' (Vertigo 6086 002)
	November	'HAD ME A REAL GOOD TIME'/'Rear Wheel Skid' [instrumental]* (Warner Bros. WB 8018: Faces)
1971	August	'Reason to Believe'/'MAGGIE MAY' (Mercury, 6052 097)
	December	'STAY WITH ME'/'Debris' (Warner Bros. K 16136: Faces)
1972	August	'YOU WEAR IT WELL'/'LOST PARAGUYOS' (Mercury 6052 171)
	November	'Angel'/'What Made Milwaukee Famous (Has Made a Loser out of Me)' (Mercury 6052 198, 1972)
1973	February	'CINDY INCIDENTALLY'/'Skewiff (Mend the Fuse)' [instrumental]* (Warner Bros. K 16247: Faces)
	April	'DISHEVELMENT BLUES'/'Ooh La La Preview'(NME Flexi: Faces)

	August	'Oh No Not My Baby'/'JODIE' (Mercury, 6052 371: B-side Faces)
	November	'POOL HALL RICHARD'/'I Wish It Would Rain' [live] (Warner Bros. K 16341: Faces)
1974	September	'FAREWELL'/'Bring It On Home – You Send Me' (Mercury, 6167 033)
	November	'YOU CAN MAKE ME DANCE, SING OR ANYTHING'/'AS LONG AS YOU TELL HIM' (Warner Bros. K 16494: Rod Stewart/Faces)
1975	August	'Sailing'/'STONE COLD SOBER' (Warner Bros. K 16600)
	September	'Am I Blue'*/'Shine' (Penny Farthing PEN 891: Ted Wood – Rod sings back-up on B-side)
	November	'This Old Heart of Mine'/'ALL IN THE NAME OF ROCK 'N' ROLL' (Riva 1)
1976	April	'Skye Boat Song'/'Skye Boat Song' [instrumental]* (Riva 2: The Atlantic Crossing Drum & Pipe Band)
	May	'TONIGHT'S THE NIGHT'/'THE BALL TRAP' (Riva 3)
	August	'THE KILLING OF GEORGIE' (Parts I & II)/ 'FOOL FOR YOU' (Riva 4)
	December	'Get Back'/'Trade Winds' (Riva 6)
1977	April	'The First Cut Is the Deepest'/'I Don't Want to Talk About It' (Riva 7)
	October	'YOU'RE IN MY HEART'/'YOU GOT A NERVE' (Riva 11)
1978	January	'HOT LEGS'/'I WAS ONLY JOKING' (Riva 10)
	May	'OLE OLA (MULHER BRASILEIRA'/'I'd Walk A Million Miles for One of Your Goals' (1. 'Que Sara Sara' 2. 'My Mammy') (Riva 15: B-side Rod Stewart & The Scottish World Cup Squad 1978)
	November	'DA YA THINK I'M SEXY?'/'DIRTY WEEKEND' (Riva 17)
1979	January	'AIN'T LOVE A BITCH'/'SCARED AND SCARRED' (Riva 18)
	April	'BLONDES (HAVE MORE FUN)'/'THE BEST DAYS OF MY LIFE' (Riva 19)
1980	May	'If Loving You is Wrong (I Don't Want to be Right)'/'LAST SUMMER' (Riva 23)
	October	'PASSION'/'BETTER OFF DEAD' (Riva 26) 'PASSION' [extended version]/'BETTER OFF DEAD' (Riva 26T, 12")
	December	'MY GIRL'/'DANCE WITH ME' (Riva 28)
1981	March	'OH GOD I WISH I WAS HOME TONIGHT'/'SOMEBODY SPECIAL' (Riva 29)
	October	'TONIGHT I'M YOURS (DON'T HURT ME)'/'SONNY' (Riva 33)
	December	'YOUNG TURKS'/'TORA TORA TORA (OUT WITH THE BOYS)' (Riva 34)
1982	February	'How Long'/'JEALOUS' (Riva 35)
1983	May	'BABY JANE'/'READY NOW'/ (Warner Bros. W 9608) 'BABY JANE'/'READY NOW'/('If Loving You is Wrong)

		I Don't Want to be Right' [live version] (Warner Bros. W 96564T, 12")
	August	'WHAT AM I GONNA DO'/'DANCIN' ALONE' (Warner Bros. W 9564)
	December	'SWEET SURRENDER'/'GHETTO BLASTER' (Warner Bros. W 9440)
1984	May	'INFATUATION'/'THREE TIME LOSER' (Warner Bros. W 9256)
	July	'Some Guys Have All the Luck'/'I WAS ONLY JOKING' (Warner Bros. W 9204)
	December	'TROUBLE'/'TORA TORA TORA (OUT WITH THE BOYS)' (Warner Bros. W 9115)
1985	June	'People Get Ready'/'Back on the Street'* (Epic A 6387: Jeff Beck and Rod Stewart)
1986	May	'Love Touch'/'HEART IS ON THE LINE' (Warner Bros. W 8668)
		'Love Touch'/'HEART IS ON THE LINE'/'Hard Lesson to Learn' (Warner Bros. W 8668T, 12")
	June	'EVERY BEAT OF MY HEART'/'TROUBLE' (Warner Bros. W 8652)
	July	'EVERY BEAT OF MY HEART' [Tartan Mix]/'TROUBLE' 'Some Guys Have All the Luck' [live]/'I Don't Want to Talk About It' [live] (Warner Bros. W 8625TE, 12")
	September	'ANOTHER HEARTACHE'/'YOU'RE IN MY HEART' [live] (Warner Bros. W 8631)
		'ANOTHER HEARTACHE' [extended version]/'ANOTHER HEARTACHE' [edit]/'YOU'RE IN MY HEART' [live] (Warner Bros. W 8631T, 12")
	December	'In My Life'/'IN MY OWN CRAZY WAY' (Warner Bros. W 8489)
1987	August	'In a Broken Dream' [remix]/'The Blues'/'Cloud Nine' (Bold Reprise Records BRM 004T, 12")
	October	'Twistin' the Night Away'/'Let's Get Small' [instrumental] (Geffen RODS 1)
1988	May	'LOST IN YOU' [fade]/'ALMOST ILLEGAL'/'LOST IN YOU' [extended remix]/'BABY JANE' (Warner Bros. W 7927CD)
	August	'FOREVER YOUNG' [LP]/'DAYS OF RAGE'/'FOREVER YOUNG' [remix]/'EVERY BEAT OF MY HEART' [LP] (Warner Bros. W 7796CD)
1989	April	'My Heart Can't Tell You No'/'THE WILD HORSE'/'PASSION' [live] (Warner Bros. W 7792CD)
	October	'This Old Heart of Mine'/'AIN'T LOVE A BITCH'/'TONIGHT I'M YOURS (DON'T HURT ME)' (Warner Bros. W 2686CD)
1990	January	'Downtown Train'/'STAY WITH ME' [with Faces]/'HOT LEGS' (Warner Bros. W 2647CD)
	November	'It Takes Two' [extended remix]/'It Takes Two'/'HOT

LEGS' [live] (Warner Bros. RODICD: Rod Stewart and
Tina Turner)

1991 March   'Rhythm of My Heart'/'MOMENT OF GLORY'/'I Don't
              Want to Talk About It' [newly recorded] Warner Bros.
              W 0017CD)

     July   'The Motown Song' [remix]/'Sweet Soul Music'
              [live]/'Try a Little Tenderness' (Warner Bros. W 0030)

     August   'Broken Arrow'/'I WAS ONLY JOKING'/ 'THE KILLING
              OF GEORGIE (PARTS 1 & 2)' (Warner Bros. W 0059CD)

     October 'My Town'/'The Tragedy of Love'*/'Don't Forget Me
              (When I'm Gone)'*/'Diamond Sun'* (EMI EM 212:
              Glass Tiger)

1992 April   'Your Song'/'Broken Arrow'/'MANDOLIN WIND'/ 'The
              First Cut is the Deepest' (Warner Bros. W 0104CD)

     November 'Tom Traubert's Blues'/'NO HOLDING
              BACK'/'Downtown Train' (Warner Bros. W 0144CD)

1993 February 'Ruby Tuesday'/'You're in My Heart'/'Passion'/'Crazy
              About Her' (Warner Bros. W 0158CD)
              'Ruby Tuesday' [alternative version]/'STAY WITH ME'
              (Warner Bros. W 0158X – limited edition 7")

     April   'Shotgun Wedding'/'Sweet Soul Music' [live]/'Every
              Beat Of My Heart' (Warner Bros. W 0171CD)

     June   'Have I Told You Lately' [live version]/'Gasoline Alley'
              [live version]/'Let the Day Begin' (Warner Bros.
              W 0185CD1)
              'Have I Told You Lately' [original version]/'Love
              Wars'/'One Night' (Warner Bros. W 0185CD2)

     August   'Reason to Believe' [live version]/'It's All Over Now'
              [live version]/'Love in the Right Hands' (Warner Bros.
              W 0198CD1)

     December 'People Get Ready' [live version]/'DA YA THINK I'M
              SEXY?'/'Sweet Little Rock 'n' Roller' [live version]/
              'Baby Jane' (Warner Bros. W 0226CD1)

1994 January 'All for Love' [album version]/'Straight from the Heart'
              [live]*/'If Only'/'Love is Stronger than Justice' [live]*
              (A&M 580 477-2: Bryan Adams/Rod Stewart/Sting)

Original albums

1968 October   **Truth** (Columbia SCX 6293: Jeff Beck)
               'Shapes of Things'; 'Let Me Love You'; 'Morning Dew';
               'You Shook Me'; 'Ol' Man River'; 'Greensleeves'; 'Rock
               My Plimsoul'; 'Beck's Bolero' [instrumental]*; 'Blues De
               Luxe'; 'I Ain't Superstitious'.

1969 September **Beck Ola** (Columbia SCX 6351: Jeff Beck)
               'All Shook Up'; 'SPANISH BOOTS'; 'Girls from Mill
               Valley' [instrumental]*; 'Jailhouse Rock'; 'PLYNTH
               (WATER DOWN THE DRAIN)'; 'THE HANGMANS KNEE';

'Rice Pudding' [instrumental]*.

1970 February **An Old Raincoat Won't Ever Let You Down**
(Vertigo VO4)
'Street Fighting Man'; 'MAN OF CONSTANT SORROW';
'BLIND PRAYER'; 'Handbags and Gladrags'; 'AN OLD
RAINCOAT WON'T EVER LET YOU DOWN'; 'I
WOULDN'T EVER CHANGE A THING'; 'CINDY'S
LAMENT'; 'Dirty Old Town'.

March **First Step** (Warner Bros. K 46053: Faces)
'Wicked Messenger'; 'Devotion'; 'Shake, Shudder,
Shiver'; 'AROUND THE PLYNTH'; 'FLYING'; 'Pineapple
and the Monkey' [instrumental]*; 'Nobody Knows';
'Looking out the Window' [instrumental]*; 'THREE
BUTTON HAND ME DOWN'.

September **Gasoline Alley** (Vertigo 6360 500)
'GASOLINE ALLEY'; 'It's All Over Now'; 'Only a
Hobo'; 'My Way of Giving'; 'Country Comfort'; 'Cut
Across Shorty'; 'LADY DAY'; 'JO'S LAMENT'; 'I Don't
Want to Discuss It'.

1971 March **Long Player** (Warner Bros. K 46064: Faces)
'BAD 'N' RUIN'; 'Tell Everyone'; 'SWEET LADY MARY';
'Richmond'*; 'Maybe I'm Amazed'; 'HAD ME A REAL
GOOD TIME'; 'On the Beach'; 'I Feel So Good';
'Jerusalem' [instrumental]*.

July **Every Picture Tells A Story** (Mercury 6338 063)
'EVERY PICTURE TELLS A STORY'; 'Seems Like A Long
Time'; 'That's All Right'; 'Amazing Grace'; 'Tomorrow
is a Long Time'; 'Henry'; 'MAGGIE MAY';
'MANDOLIN WIND'; '[I Know] I'm Losing You';
'Reason to Believe'.

December **A Nod's As Good As A Wink** (Warner Bros. K
56006: Faces)
'MISS JUDY'S FARM'; 'You're So Rude'*; 'LOVE LIVES
HERE'; 'Last Orders Please'*; 'STAY WITH ME'; 'Debris';
'Memphis'; 'TOO BAD'; 'THAT'S ALL YOU NEED'.

1972 July **Never A Dull Moment** (Mercury 6499 163)
'TRUE BLUE'; 'LOST PARAGUAYOS'; 'Mama You Been
on My Mind'; 'ITALIAN GIRLS'; 'Angel'; 'Interludings';
'YOU WEAR IT WELL'; 'I'd Rather Go Blind'; 'Twistin'
the Night Away'.

1973 April **Ooh La La** (Warner Bros. K 56011: Faces)
'SILICONE GROWN'; 'CINDY INCIDENTALLY'; 'FLAGS
AND BANNERS'; 'MY FAULT'; 'BORSTAL BOYS'; 'Fly in
the Ointment' [instrumental]*; 'IF I'M ON THE LATE
SIDE'; 'Glad and Sorry'*; 'Just Another Honkey'; 'Ooh
La La'*.

1974 January **Coast to Coast/Overtures & Beginners** (Mercury
9100 001: Rod Stewart/Faces)

'It's All Over Now'; 'Cut Across Shorty'; 'TOO BAD';
'EVERY PICTURE TELLS A STORY'; 'Angel'; 'STAY WITH
ME'; 'I Wish It Would Rain'; 'I'd Rather Go Blind';
'BORSTAL BOY'; 'Amazing Grace'; 'Jealous Guy'.
[Cassette version contains extra track: '(I Know) I'm
Losing You']

October   **Smiler** (Mercury 9104 001)
'Sweet Little Rock 'n' Roller'; 'Lochinvar'; 'FAREWELL';
'SAILOR'; 'Bring It on Home to Me – You Send Me';
'Let Me Be Your Car'; 'A Natural Man'; 'DIXIE TOOT';
'Hard Road'; 'I've Grown Accustomed to Her Face';
'Girl from the North Country'; 'Mine for Me'.

1975   August   **Atlantic Crossing** (Warner Bros. K 56151)
'THREE TIME LOSER'; 'ALRIGHT FOR AN HOUR'; 'ALL
IN THE NAME OF ROCK 'N' ROLL'; 'Drift Away';
'STONE COLD SOBER'; 'I Don't Want to Talk About It';
'It's Not the Spotlight'; 'This Old Heart of Mine'; 'STILL
LOVE YOU'; 'Sailing'.

1976   June   **A Night On The Town** (Riva RVLP1)
'THE BALLTRAP'; 'Pretty Flamingo'; 'Big Bayou'; 'The
Wild Side of Life'; 'Trade Winds'; 'TONIGHT'S THE
NIGHT'; 'The First Cut is the Deepest'; 'FOOL FOR
YOU'; 'THE KILLING OF GEORGIE (PARTS I & II)'.

1977   October   **Footloose And Fancy Free** (Riva RVLP5)
'HOT LEGS'; 'YOU'RE INSANE'; 'YOU'RE IN MY
HEART'; 'BORN LOOSE'; 'You Keep Me Hanging On';
(If Loving You is Wrong) I Don't Want to be Right';
'YOU GOT A NERVE'; 'I WAS ONLY JOKING'.

1978   November   **Blondes Have More Fun** (Riva RVLP8)
'DA YA THINK I'M SEXY?'; 'DIRTY WEEKEND'; 'AIN'T
LOVE A BITCH'; 'THE BEST DAYS OF MY LIFE'; 'IS
THAT THE THANKS I GET'; 'ATTRACTIVE FEMALE
WANTED'; 'BLONDES (HAVE MORE FUN)'; 'LAST
SUMMER'; 'STANDING IN THE SHADOWS OF LOVE';
'SCARRED AND SCARED'.

1980   November   **Foolish Behaviour** (Riva RVLP11)
'BETTER OFF DEAD'; 'PASSION'; 'FOOLISH
BEHAVIOUR'; 'SO SOON WE CHANGE'; 'OH GOD I
WISH I WAS HOME TONIGHT'; 'GI ME WINGS'; 'MY
GIRL'; 'SHE WON'T DANCE WITH ME'; 'SOMEBODY
SPECIAL'; 'SAY IT AIN'T TRUE'. [Cassette version
contains extra track: 'I Just Want to Make Love to You'
& extended version of 'PASSION']

1981   November   **Tonight I'm Yours** (Riva RVLP14)
'TONIGHT I'M YOURS (DON'T HURT ME)'; 'How
Long'; 'TORA TORA TORA (OUT WITH THE BOYS)';
'Tear It Up'; 'ONLY A BOY'; 'Just Like a Woman';
'JEALOUS'; 'SONNY'; 'YOUNG TURKS'; 'NEVER GIVE

UP ON A DREAM'.

1982 November   **Absolutely Live** (Riva RVLP17, 1982)/Double 'TONIGHT I'M YOURS (DON'T HURT ME)'; 'Sweet Little Rock 'n' Roller'; 'HOT LEGS'; 'TONIGHT'S THE NIGHT'; 'The Great Pretender'; 'PASSION'; 'SHE WON'T DANCE WITH ME'; 'Little Queenie'; 'YOU'RE IN MY HEART'; 'Rock My Plimsoul'; 'YOUNG TURKS', 'GUESS I'LL ALWAYS LOVE YOU'; 'GASOLINE ALLEY'; 'MAGGIE MAY'; 'Tear It Up'; 'DA YA THINK I'M SEXY?'; 'Sailing'; 'I Don't Want to Talk About It'; 'STAY WITH ME'.

1983 June   **Body Wishes** (Warner Bros. 92 38771) 'DANCIN' ALONE'; 'BABY JANE'; 'MOVE ME'; 'BODY WISHES'; 'SWEET SURRENDER'; 'WHAT AM I GONNA DO (I'M SO IN LOVE WITH YOU)'; 'GHETTO BLASTER'; 'READY NOW'; 'STRANGERS AGAIN'; 'SATISFIED'.

1984 June   **Camouflage** (Warner Bros. 92 50951) 'INFATUATION'; 'Alright Now'; 'Some Guys Have All the Luck'; 'Can We Still Be Friends'; 'BAD FOR YOU'; 'HEART IS ON THE LINE'; 'CAMOUFLAGE'; 'TROUBLE'.

1986 June   **Every Beat Of My Heart** (Warner Bros. WX 53) 'FROM HERE TO ETERNITY'; 'ANOTHER HEARTACHE'; 'A NIGHT LIKE THIS'; 'WHO'S GONNA TAKE ME HOME'; 'RED HOT IN BLACK'; 'Love Touch'; 'IN MY OWN CRAZY WAY'; 'EVERY BEAT OF MY HEART'; 'TEN DAYS OF RAIN'; 'In My Life'.

1988 May   **Out of Order** (Warner Bros. 925 684-2) 'LOST IN YOU'; 'THE WILD HORSE'; 'LETHAL DOSE OF LOVE'; 'FOREVER YOUNG'; 'MY HEART CAN'T TELL YOU NO'; 'DYNAMITE'; 'Nobody Wants You When You're Down and Out'; 'CRAZY ABOUT HER'; 'Try a Little Tenderness'; 'WHEN I WAS YOUR MAN'; 'ALMOST ILLEGAL'.

1991 March   **Vagabond Heart** (Warner Bros. 7599-26598-2) 'Rhythm of My Heart'; 'REBEL HEART'; 'Broken Arrow'; 'It Takes Two'; 'WHEN A MAN'S IN LOVE'; 'You Are Everything'; 'The Motown Song'; 'GO OUT DANCING'; 'NO HOLDING BACK'; 'Have I Told You Lately'; 'MOMENT OF GLORY'; 'Downtown Train'; 'IF ONLY'.

1993 May   **Unplugged And Seated** (Warner Bros. 9362-45289-2) 'HOT LEGS'; 'TONIGHT'S THE NIGHT'; 'Handbags and Gladrags'; 'Cut Across Shorty'; 'EVERY PICTURE TELLS A STORY'; 'MAGGIE MAY'; 'Reason to Believe'; 'People Get Ready'; 'Have I Told You Lately'; 'Tom Traubert's Blues (Waltzing Matilda)'; 'The First Cut is the Deepest'; 'MANDOLIN WIND'; 'HIGHGATE SHUFFLE'; 'STAY WITH ME'; 'Having a Party'.

Compilations released with Stewart's consent and co-operation

1973 August   **Sing It Again Rod** (Mercury 6499 153)
'Reason to Believe'; 'YOU WEAR IT WELL'; 'MANDOLIN WIND'; 'Country Comfort'; 'MAGGIE MAY'; 'Handbags and Gladrags'; 'Street Fighting Man'; 'Twistin' the Night Away'; 'LOST PARAGUAYOS'; '(I Know) I'm Losing You'; 'Pinball Wizard'; 'GASOLINE ALLEY'.

1979 November   **Rod Stewart Greatest Hits Vol. 1** (Riva ROD TV1)
'HOT LEGS'; 'MAGGIE MAY'; 'DA YA THINK I'M SEXY?'; 'YOU'RE IN MY HEART'; 'Sailing'; 'I Don't Want to Talk About It'; 'TONIGHT'S THE NIGHT'; 'THE KILLING OF GEORGIE (PARTS I & II)'; 'The First Cut is the Deepest'; 'I WAS ONLY JOKING'.

1989 November   **Best of Rod Stewart** (Warner Bros. 926 034-2)
'MAGGIE MAY'; 'BABY JANE'; 'DA YA THINK I'M SEXY?'; 'This Old Heart of Mine'; 'Sailing'; 'I Don't Want to Talk About It'; 'YOU'RE IN MY HEART'; 'YOUNG TURKS'; 'The First Cut is the Deepest'; 'TONIGHT'S THE NIGHT'; 'EVERY BEAT OF MY HEART'; 'Downtown Train'.

December   **Storyteller** (Warner Bros. 925 987-2)
[4-CD set]
'Good Morning Little Schoolgirl'; 'Can I Get a Witness?'; 'Shake'; 'SO MUCH TO SAY'; 'Little Miss Understood'; 'I've Been Drinking'; 'I Ain't Superstitious'; 'Shapes of Things'; 'In a Broken Dream'; 'Street Fighting Man'; 'Handbags and Gladrags'; 'GASOLINE ALLEY'; 'Cut Across Shorty'; 'Country Comforts'; 'It's All Over Now'; 'SWEET LADY MARY'; 'HAD ME A REAL GOOD TIME'; 'MAGGIE MAY'; 'MANDOLIN WIND'; '(I Know) I'm Losing You'; 'Reason to Believe'; 'EVERY PICTURE TELLS A STORY'; 'STAY WITH ME'; 'TRUE BLUE'; 'Angel'; 'YOU WEAR IT WELL'; 'I'd Rather Go Blind'; 'Twistin' the Night Away'; 'What'd Made Milwaukee Famous'; 'Oh No Not My Baby'; 'Pinball Wizard'; 'Sweet Little Rock 'n' Roller; 'Let Me Be Your Car'; 'YOU CAN MAKE ME DANCE, SING OR ANYTHING'; 'Sailing'; 'I Don't Want To Talk About It'; 'Stone Cold Sober'; 'To Love Somebody'; 'TONIGHT'S THE NIGHT'; 'The First Cut is the Deepest'; 'THE KILLING OF GEORGIE (PARTS I & II)'; 'Get Back'; 'HOT LEGS'; 'I WAS ONLY JOKING'; 'YOU'RE IN MY HEART'; 'DA YA THINK I'M SEXY?'; 'PASSION'; 'OH GOD, I WISH I WAS HOME TONIGHT'/'TONIGHT I'M YOURS'; 'YOUNG TURKS'; 'BABY JANE'; 'WHAT AM I GONNA DO (I'M SO IN

LOVE WITH YOU)'; 'PEOPLE GET READY'; 'Some Guys
Have All the Luck'; 'INFATUATION'; 'Love Touch';
'EVERY BEAT OF MY HEART'; 'LOST IN YOU'; 'My
Heart Can't Tell You No'; 'DYNAMITE'; 'CRAZY
ABOUT HER'; 'FOREVER YOUNG'; 'I Don't Want to
Talk About It'; 'This Old Heart of Mine'; 'Downtown
Train'.

1993 February   **Lead Vocalist** (Warner Bros. 9362-45281-2)
'I Ain't Superstitious'; 'Handbags and Gladrags'; 'CINDY
INCIDENTALLY'; 'STAY WITH ME'; 'TRUE BLUE';
'SWEET LADY MARY'/'HOT LEGS'; 'Stand Back'; 'Ruby
Tuesday'; 'Shotgun Wedding'; 'First I Look at the
Purse'; 'Tom Traubert's Blues'.

Album production work and guest appearances

1970 April   **Permanent Damage** (Straight STS 1059: GTO's)
'The Ghost Chained to the Past, Present and Future
(Shock Treatment)'.

1971   **It Ain't Easy** (Warner Bros. K 46088: John Baldry)
Rod produced side one. The album also features Baldry's
version of 'FLYING'.

1972 March   **Everything Stops For Tea** (Warner Bros. K 46160:
John Baldry)
Rod produced side one and also duets with Baldry on
'Mother Ain't Dead'.
Tommy (Ode SP 99001: Various)/Double
'Pinball Wizard'.

1973   **In A Broken Dream** (Youngblood SYB 3001: Python
Lee Jackson)
'In a Broken Dream'/'Cloud Nine'/'The Blues'.
The Story of British Blues (Blue
Horizon: Various)
'Stone Crazy' with Aynsley Dunbar's Retaliation.
Reading Festival (GM GML 1008:
Various)
'(I Know) I'm Losing You' [live].

1974   **Scotland Scotland** (Polydor 2383 282: Various)
'Angel' [duet with Denis Law].
I've Got My Own Album To Do (Warner Bros. K
56065: Ron Wood)
'Mystifies Me'/ 'Take a Look at the Guy'/'If You Gotta
Make a Fool of Somebody' [duets with R. Wood].

1976   **All This and World War II** (Riva RVLP2:
Various)/Double
'Get Back'.

1979   **The Music for UNICEF Concert** (Polydor 2335 214:
Various)

'DA YA THINK I'M SEXY?' [live].

1981 **1234** (CBS 85227: Ron Wood)
Rod produced the track 'Priceless'.

1982 **Night Shift** (Warner Bros. K 57024:
Various)
'That's What Friends Are For'.

1985 **Flash** (Epic EPC 26112: Jeff Beck)
'People Get Ready'.

1986 **The Princes Trust** (A&M AMA 3906: Various)
'Sailing' [live].

1987 **Innerspace** (Geffen GEF 460223: Various)
'Twistin' the Night Away'.

1991 **Two Rooms** (Mercury 845 749-1: Various)
'Your Song'.

1994 **Simple Mission** (Glass Tiger)
'My Town' [duet with Alan Frew].

The Three Musketeers (A&M 540-190-2: Original
movie soundtrack featuring various artists)
Rod sang 'All for Love' with Sting and Bryan Adams.

Resurrection (Continuum CD CTUM 8: Bobby
Womack album)
Rod sang with Womack on 'Don't Break Your Promise
(Too Soon)'.

Home Videos

1981 May **Rod Stewart Live at the L.A. Forum** (Warner
Home Video)
'HOT LEGS'; 'TONIGHT'S THE NIGHT'; 'DA YA THINK
I'M SEXY?'; 'I Just Wanna Make Love to You';
'BLONDES HAVE MORE FUN'; 'MAGGIE MAY'; ('If
Loving You is Wrong) I Don't Want to be Right'; 'Wild
Side of Life'; 'YOU'RE IN MY HEART'; 'Sweet Little
Rock 'n' Roller'; 'STAY WITH ME'; 'Twistin' the Night
Away'.

1982 December **Tonight He's Yours** (Embassy)
'GI ME WINGS'; 'Sweet Little Rock 'n' Roller'; 'Tear It
Up'; 'PASSION'; 'DANCE WITH ME – Little Queenie';
'YOU'RE IN MY HEART'; 'Rock My Plimsoul'; 'Get
Back'; 'HOT LEGS'; 'YOUNG TURKS'; '(If Loving You Is
Wrong) I Don't Want To Be Right'; 'TORA TORA TORA
(OUT WITH THE BOYS)'; 'GASOLINE ALLEY'; 'MAGGIE
MAY'; 'DA YA THINK I'M SEXY?'; 'I WAS ONLY
JOKING'; 'YOU WEAR IT WELL'; 'WILD SIDE OF LIFE'.

1988 July **Rod Stewart and The Faces Video
Biography 1969–1974** (Video Collection)
'THREE BUTTON HAND ME DOWN'; 'It's All Over
Now'; 'GASOLINE ALLEY'; 'MAGGIE MAY'; '(I Know)

I'm Losing You'; 'I Feel So Good'; 'Memphis Tennessee'; 'STAY WITH ME'; 'MISS JUDY'S FARM'; 'THAT'S ALL YOU NEED'; 'I'd Rather Go Blind'; 'TRUE BLUE'; 'YOU WEAR IT WELL'; 'Angel'; 'CINDY INCIDENTALLY'; 'POOL HALL RICHARD'; 'Sweet Little Rock 'n' Roller'; 'YOU CAN MAKE ME DANCE, SING OR ANYTHING'.

1991 November **Rod Stewart Videos 1984–1991** (Warner Music Vision)
'INFATUATION'; 'Some Guys Have All the Luck'; 'People Get Ready'; 'EVERY BEAT OF MY HEART'; 'LOST IN YOU'; 'FOREVER YOUNG'; 'My Heart Can't Tell You No'; 'Downtown Train'; 'This Old Heart of Mine'; 'It Takes Two'; 'Rhythm Of My Heart'; 'The Motown Song'; 'Broken Arrow'.

1992 November **Vagabond Heart Tour** (Warner Music Vision)
'INFATUATION'; 'Rhythm Of My Heart'; 'Sweet Little Rock 'n' Roller'; 'Some Guys Have all the Luck'; 'Downtown Train'; 'HOT LEGS'; 'PASSION'; 'FOREVER YOUNG'; 'Broken Arrow'; 'TONIGHT'S THE NIGHT'; 'EVERY PICTURE TELLS A STORY'; 'MAGGIE MAY'; 'Reason to Believe'; 'YOU WEAR IT WELL'; 'YOU'RE IN MY HEART'; 'The First Cut is the Deepest'; 'Sweet Soul Music'; 'Da Ya Think I'm Sexy?'; 'This Old Heart of Mine'; 'The Motown Song'; 'Twistin' the Night Away'.

Promotional Videos

1973 'Oh No Not My Baby'
1974 'FAREWELL'
'Bring It On Home to Me/You Send Me'
1975 'Sailing'
1976 'TONIGHT'S THE NIGHT'
'The First Cut is the Deepest'
1977 'YOU'RE IN MY HEART'
'HOT LEGS'
'I WAS ONLY JOKING'
'YOU'RE INSANE'
1978 'DA YA THINK I'M SEXY?'
'AIN'T LOVE A BITCH'
'BLONDES HAVE MORE FUN'
1980 'PASSION'
'DANCE WITH ME'
'OH GOD I WISH I WAS HOME TONIGHT'
1981 'TONIGHT I'M YOURS'
'YOUNG TURKS'
'How Long'
'Just Like a Woman'

1983 'BABY JANE'
      'WHAT AM I GONNA DO?'
1984 'INFATUATION'
      'Some Guys Have All the Luck'
      'Alright Now'
1986 'Love Touch'
      'EVERY BEAT OF MY HEART'
      'ANOTHER HEARTACHE'
1987 'Twistin' the Night Away'
1988 'LOST IN YOU'
      'FOREVER YOUNG'
      'My Heart Can't Tell You No'
1989 'CRAZY ABOUT HER'
      'This Old Heart of Mine'
      'Downtown Train'
1990 'It Takes Two'
1991 'Rhythm of My Heart'
      'The Motown Song'
      'Broken Arrow'
1992 'Tom Traubert's Blues'
1993 'Ruby Tuesday'
      'Shotgun Wedding'
      'Have I Told You Lately [Unplugged]'
      'Reason to Believe [Unplugged]'
      'People Get Ready [Unplugged]'
      'All For Love'

Important Overseas Releases – Singles

1971 'Maybe I'm Amazed' (studio version)/
      'Rear Wheel Skid'* (Warner Bros. 16078, France: Faces) Studio version
      of 'Maybe I'm Amazed' not released in the UK.
1976 'KILLING OF GEORGIE (PARTS I & II)'/'ROSIE'
      ('Warner Bros. WBS 8396, USA)
      'Rosie' not released in UK.
1978 'DA YA THINK I'M SEXY?' [remix]/'SCARRED AND SCARED' (Warner
      Bros. WBSD 8727, USA) 12"
      Re-mix of 'Da Ya Think I'm Sexy' not released in the UK.
1989 'CRAZY ABOUT HER'/'DYNAMITE' (Warner Bros. 7-27657, USA)
      A-side different mix to album version.
      'CRAZY ABOUT HER' [Just A Crazy Sure Mix]/
      'CRAZY ABOUT HER' [B! Crazy Dub]/
      'CRAZY ABOUT HER' [Kyle Wyld West Edit]/
      'CRAZY ABOUT HER' [Acca Dub]/'DYNAMITE' (Warner Bros.
      0-21268: USA) 12"
      4 different mixes of 'Crazy About Her', none were released in the UK.
      'CRAZY ABOUT HER' [Kyle Wyld West Edit]/
      'CRAZY ABOUT HER' [Just A Crazy Sure Mix]/

'CRAZY ABOUT HER' [instrumental] (Warner Bros. PRO: USA
Instrumental version unavailable elsewhere).

1991 'The Motown Song' [single remix]/
'The Motown Song' [Power Mix] (Warner Bros. PRO: USA).
Promotional CD, Power Mix unavailable elsewhere.

– Albums

1973 **Rock Generation Vol. 6** (BYG 529.706, France: Steam Packet)
'Back at the Chicken Shack'*; 'The In Crowd'*; 'Baby Take Me'; 'Can
I Get A Witness'; 'Baby Baby'*; 'Holy Smoke'*; 'Cry Me a River'*;
'Oh Baby Don't You Do It'; 'Lord Remember Me'. This album
contains demos recorded by Steam Packet in December 1965. It was
not given a UK release until 1977 when it was released as *The First
Supergroup* (Charley Records CR 300020)

1973 **Rod Stewart And The Faces** (Springboard SPB 4030, USA: Rod
Stewart/Small Faces)
'Just a Little Misunderstood'; 'Baby Come Home' (duet with P. P.
Arnold); remaining tracks by the Small Faces. A misleading title as this
album contains just two 60s Rod Stewart solo tracks and seven Small
Faces tracks. However, 'Just a Little Misunderstood' is an alternative
version of 'Little Miss Understood' and 'Baby Come Home' is a
previously unreleased duet with P. P. Arnold produced by Mick
Jagger. These two tracks were not given UK release until 1990 when
they appeared on the compilation *The Original Face* (Thunderbolt
THBL 085), although 'Baby Come Home' did feature on the
compilation album *In a Broken Dream* (CRC 3121 2) mistitled as
'Sparky Rides'.

1976 **A Shot Of Rhythm And Blues** (Private Stock PS 2021, USA)
'Shake'; 'Keep Your Hands Off Her'; 'Don't You Tell Nobody'; 'Just
Like I Treat You'; 'The Day Will Come'; 'I Just Got Some'; 'Bright
Lights Big City'; 'Ain't That Lovin' You Baby'; 'Moppers Blues';
'Why Does It Go On'. This album contains Rod's two Columbia
singles plus six demos recorded in August 1964. It was the subject of a
legal battle between Rod and Private Stock Records but eventually
Rod was unable to halt the release. The tracks were not released in the
UK until 1989 when remixed versions appeared on the compilation
CD *In A Broken Dream* (CRC 3121 2). The original versions were
eventually released in 1990 on *The Original Face* compilation album
(Thunderbolt THBL 085).

1977 **Rod Stewart And Steam Packet** (Springboard SPB 4063, USA)
'Bright Lights Big City'; 'Can I Get a Witness'; 'Lord Remember Me'.
Another misleading album containing one Rod Stewart solo track, two
Small Faces tracks and four Steam Packet tracks, two of which do not
feature Rod. However, the solo track by Rod is a live version of
'Bright Lights Big City' recorded circa 1964 which has never been
released in the UK.

– Home video

1986 **The Rod Stewart Concert Video** (Karl Lorimar, USA)
'INFATUATION'; 'BAD FOR YOU'; 'TONIGHT'S THE NIGHT'; 'I
Don't Want to Talk About It'; 'DANCE WITH ME'; 'HOT LEGS';
'YOU'RE IN MY HEART'; 'BABY JANE'; 'Sittin' on the Dock of the
Bay'; 'YOUNG TURKS'; 'PASSION'; 'DA YA THINK I'M SEXY?';
'MAGGIE MAY'; 'Some Guys Have All the Luck'; 'Stay with Me';
'We'll Meet Again'.

Songs Rod has performed live but has not recorded

1964 'Night Time is the Right Time'
    'Tiger in Your Tank'
    'Dimple in Your Jaw'
    'I Got My Mojo Working'
1966 'Hold On I'm Coming'
    'Knock on Wood'
    '6345789 – That's My Number'
    'Soulful Dress'
    'High Heel Sneakers'
1967 'Loving You Has Made My Life Sweeter Than Ever'
    'Telephone Blues'
    'Pretty Woman'
1968 'I've Got the Sweetest Little Angel'
    'The Sun is Shining'
1970 'The Evil'
    'Honky Tonk Women'
    'Love in Vain'
1971 'When Will I Be Loved'
1973 'The Stealer'
1979 'Me and Bobby McGee' (with Kris Kristofferson)
1980 'Oh Carol'
1984 'Hungry Heart'
    'Sittin' on the Dock of the Bay'
1985 'I Heard It Through the Grapevine (with Cindy Lauper)
1986 'My Girl'
1991 'In the Midnight Hour'
1993 'Chain of Fools' (with Aretha Franklin)
    'Baby Please Don't Go'
1994 'Maybe Baby'

Alphabetical list of songs written or co-written by Rod, recorded by other artists

1983 'Attractive (Fe) Male Wanted' (Lady Bee)
1986 'Baby Jane' (Black Lace)
1993 'Blondes (Have More Fun)' (Vince Neil)

1992 'Cindy Incidentally' (Del Amitri)
1979 'Da Ya Think I'm Sexy?' (Steve Dahl)
1979 'Da Ya Think I'm Sexy?' (Millie Jackson)
1980 'Da Ya Think I'm Sexy?' (Hybrid Kids)
1987 'Da Ya Think I'm Sexy?' (Sabrina)
1992 'Da Ya Think I'm Sexy?' (Junior Tucker)
1993 'Da Ya Think I'm Sexy?' (The Union Factory)
1993 'Da Ya Think I'm Sexy?' (The Revolting Cocks)
1987 'Every Picture Tells a Story' (Georgia Satellites)
1971 'Flying' (John Baldry)
1989 'Flying' (Jelly-Roll Morton's Red Hot Peppers)
1993 'Flying' (Bowlfish)
1982 'Gasoline Alley' (Elkie Brooks)
1981 'Gasoline Alley' (Phoebe Snow)
1975 'Gasoline Alley' (John Baldry)
      'Gasoline Alley' (Buffy St Marie)
1983 'Gasoline Alley' (Costa Linderholm)
1989 'Gasoline Alley' (Forgery)
1988 'Here to Eternity' (Billy Paul)
1985 'I Still Love You' (Foster & Allen)
1993 'I Still Love You' (Anne Pack)
1972 'Mandolin Wind' (The Everly Brothers)
1972 'Maggie May' (Arthur Conley)
1987 'Maggie May' (Bogdan Kominowski)
1989 'Maggie May' (Wet Wet Wet)
1990 'Maggie May' (Brian Armstrong)
1991 'Maggie May' (Tommy Darky)
1991 'Maggie May' (The Pogues)
1992 'Maggie May' (Blur)
1982 'Passion' (Millie Jackson)
1973 'Stay with Me (Rita)' (Arthur Conley)
1978 'Stay with Me' (Elkie Brooks)
1988 'Stay with Me' (The Gonads)
1991 'Stone Cold Sober' (Andy Taylor)
1979 'The Best Days of My Life' (Linda Lewis)
1981 'The Best Days of My Life' (David Soul)
1985 'The Best Days of My Life' (Art Sutter)
1978 'Tonight's the Night' (Charles Jackson)
1978 'Tonight's the Night' (Roy Head)
1990 'Tonight's the Night' (Terry Steele)
1978 'You're in My Heart' [instrumental] (Joe Farrell)
      (In addition, Tina Turner has featured 'Hot Legs', 'Foolish Behaviour
      [Kill His Wife]' and 'Tonight's the Night' on live videos and the
      Quireboys have featured 'Stay with Me' on live video.)

Terrestrial tv shows

1965 *An Easter with Rod*
      (Profile of a typical mod: Rediffusion)
1972 *Sounds For Saturday With The Faces*
      (Faces in concert: BBC2)
1975 *Rod Stewart and The Faces*
      (Live at Kilburn, London: LWT)
1976 *A Night on the Town*
      (TV Special: LWT)
1976 *Rod The Mod has Come of Age*
      (Documentary: BBC2)
1976 *Rod's Xmas Concert*
      (Live at Olympia, London: BBC2)
1979 *World Tour 1978/79* (Parts 1 & 2)
      (Live at Belle Vue, Manchester: BBC1)
1980 *The Russell Harty Show*
      (Special with Rod live from Dublin: BBC2)
1981 *Live At The Los Angeles Forum*
      (BBC1)
1982 *Tonight He's Yours – Live at the Los Angeles Forum*
      (LWT)
1987 *Rod Stewart in Concert*
      (Live at San Diego Sports Centre: CH4)
1988 *The Story of Rod Stewart*
      (Documentary: CH4)
1993 *MTV Unplugged*
      (Acoustic set: BBC2)

Fanzines

1983– *Foolish Behaviour.* Issues 1–4. Photocopied A5
1984   magazine run by the now defunct Rod Stewart & Faces Friends Club.
1981– *Smiler.* Issues 1–42, 1981–1994. Glossy high quality
1994   colour/B&W A5 quarterly. Available from The Official Rod Stewart
      Fan Club, PO Box 475, Morden, Surrey SM4 6AT, England.
1994   *Storyteller.* Issues 1–4, 1994. Photocopied A4
      German language magazine. Available from The Rod Stewart Fan
      Club Deutschland, Postfach 52 01 18, 44207 Dortmund, Germany.

Index